Citizenship Made Simple

Louise Quayle

Edited and prepared for publication by The Stonesong Press, Inc.

MADE SIMPLE BOOKS

A Made Simple Book
DOUBLEDAY   New York London Toronto Sydney Auckland

Edited and prepared for publication by The Stonesong Press
Managing Editor: Sheree Bykofsky
Editor: Sarah Gold
Design: Blackbirch Graphics, Inc.

A MADE SIMPLE BOOK
PUBLISHED BY DOUBLEDAY
a division of Bantam Doubleday Dell Publishing Group, Inc.
1540 Broadway, New York, New York 10036

MADE SIMPLE and DOUBLEDAY are trademarks of Doubleday,
a division of Bantam Doubleday Dell Publishing Group, Inc.

ISBN 0-385-26586-7
Copyright © 1991 by Doubleday, a division of Bantam Doubleday Dell Publishing Group, Inc.

All of the information in this book is current as of publication. However, immigration law periodically changes. This book is not intended as a complete legal guide to immigration and naturalization. Consult the Immigration and Naturalization Service or an immigration attorney about the particulars of your case.

The author wishes to thank Richard Burke, Esq.,who served as editorial consultant. With his twenty-five years as an immigration attorney, his thorough review of the manuscript added immeasurably to its quality and content.

Library of Congress Cataloging-in-Publication Data
Quayle, Louise.
   Citizenship made simple/ by Louise Quayle.
   1. Naturalization—United States—Popular Works. 2. Citizenship—
United States—Popular works.   I. Title.
KF4710.Z9Q39 1991
342.73'083–dc20
[347.30283]   90–36895
                                                      CIP

CONTENTS

Introduction

American politicians and the public have become increasingly concerned with immigration in recent years. In 1986, Congress passed legislation offering an amnesty program to thousands of illegal aliens in the United States. Today it is considering new legislation that will revise the current system, which allots immigrant visas to countries around the world based on employment and aliens' family relationships to citizens and permanent resident aliens. Now more than ever, America offers many people the world over economic opportunity and freedom from political persecution.

Still, the backlog of applications for permanent residency (Green Cards) from many countries (particularly from Central and South America) and outdated United States immigration law can make immigrating and becoming a citizen a daunting prospect. Whether you live in the United States or abroad, this book will help you make sense of the American immigration system. As with many government bureaucracies, the Immigration and Naturalization Service (INS) has become bogged down with paperwork; and immigration law rivals only tax law for its complexity. *Citizenship Made Simple* tells you which forms you should file and how. You'll find some of the more important forms reprinted here along with step-by-step guidelines for filling them out.

Unlike other guides to becoming naturalized, this book offers a short history of immigration law. If you have a better understanding of why immigration law became what it is, your frustration with the process can be greatly reduced. More importantly, this book helps you understand how the overall immigration and naturalization process works—whether you're applying from abroad or adjusting your status here.

Read through all of *Citizenship Made Simple* before you plan your strategy for becoming naturalized. You may find that more than one of the immigrant categories in Chapter Three applies to you. Try to choose the category that makes the strongest case for you, even if it means you have to wait a little longer. Throughout, you will find advice in selecting the appropriate forms to file. The appendices will help you choose a lawyer to represent you (if that is necessary); a list of addresses will guide you to the INS office nearest you. A glossary defines the important words you will need to know, and you'll also find an appendix listing additional forms you may need.

Once you are living in the United States as a permanent resident alien, refer to the last two chapters to prepare for becoming a citizen. Chapter Four's step-by-step guide to preparing your application—from filling out the forms to assembling the necessary supporting documents and photographs—will make this stressful time much easier. With the clear, concise explanation of the Constitution and the United States Government in Chapter Five, you should have no trouble preparing for the final naturalization interview and examination. A short history of the United States is included, too. Check over the review questions on government and history a few times, and the INS examiner should pass you with flying colors.

We have made every effort to include the most up-to-date information from the INS. With every form you file, however, be sure the rules have not changed since this book was published. The INS and current immigration law remain the final authorities on filing fees and procedures, and on the laws governing your particular case.

With a knowledge of the system and a familiarity with the forms required, you will be prepared for the process of achieving your goal of citizenship. You may encounter what seem to be unnecessary stumbling blocks as you deal with the INS. Through it all, remember that the United States welcomes its immigrants. Without them, America could not be what it is today.

CHAPTER ONE

Meet the Immigration and Naturalization Service

KEY TERMS

naturalization	nonimmigrant alien	family reunification
alien	deport	illegal alien
foreign born	public charge	excludability
foreign national	quota system	adjudicate
immigrant	Preference System	

Even to people whose first language is English, the Immigration and Naturalization Service (INS) and immigration law often seem complex, confusing, and sometimes unfriendly. As an agency of the United States Government, the INS has been accused of being an "unresponsive bureaucracy." By definition, a bureaucracy follows a fixed set of rules and is slowed down by endless paperwork and double-checking. The INS is one of the best examples of a bureaucracy. The guidelines and laws governing it are complicated, and it has a reputation for being slow and difficult to communicate with. When dealing with the INS, it helps to realize that its workers are underpaid and overworked, and the agency as a whole is undervalued. If the amount of time and paperwork required to achieve your immigration goals seem overwhelming to you, imagine how it feels to the immigration officer who has your paperwork load times one hundred, or more.

In addition to remembering that you are working with a large government agency, you can lower your level of frustration and impatience with the immigration process by learning to file the right papers at the right time with the right INS office. In the same way you would put a puzzle together, you should come up with a strategy for achieving your goal of becoming a citizen.

When piecing together a jigsaw puzzle, it's often wise to separate the edge pieces from the others and gather similarly colored pieces together. Likewise, as you read through this book, you can begin to identify those qualifications you possess that will build the strongest case for becoming naturalized. **Naturalization** is the legal process by which a person not born in the United States can become a citizen. You may find you can pursue naturalization through one or more routes. Every person's case is different, and you should select the strategy that offers the greatest chance for success. This may mean waiting a little longer, but the wait will be worth it.

While this book will help you determine which forms you should file, you probably will have many questions along the way. A lawyer who specializes in immigration law can help you. In the meantime, you can get started with this book. To those who are unfamiliar with them, the procedures governing immigration law may seem to make no sense at all. It is based on years of legislation passed by the United States Congress (the body of elected government officials who write the laws) and dates back nearly to the founding of America. We've included a little background on immigration law to help you understand how and why the immigration puzzle took shape. This short history is by no means complete, but it may help you understand how the immigration process works.

What Is Immigration?

Simply put, the INS refers to any person who was not born in the United States and enters the country as an **alien**. Aliens are sometimes referred to as **foreign born**, or **foreign nationals**. The INS refers to any foreign national who legally enters the United States with the proper documents and intends to live here as an **immigrant**. Those who enter the United States to stay here temporarily as students, visitors, tourists, or temporary workers are classified as **nonimmigrant aliens**. Over the years, the INS has devised many immigrant classifications to document the number and type of immigrants entering the United States. Let's look at why the United States government decided to pass laws governing immigration.

History of Immigration

Viewed the world over as the "Land of Opportunity," the United States bears the potential burden of millions of people emigrating to its shores for political refuge and economic prosperity. Globally, some 2 billion people are classified as poor, and observers estimate between 11 and 16 million people can be classified as refugees. The United States accepted 1.5 million immigrants between 1978 and 1980. America accepts twice as many immigrants as do all other countries combined. With that many people clamoring at its doors, immigration law serves a practical purpose. Like other countries, America has its own homeless, poor, and jobless inhabitants. Immigration law also protects the United States from potential immigrants or nonimmigrants who might threaten national security or "undesirables" such as convicted criminals and others whom the INS believes would not make a positive contribution to American society.

Originally, America's doors were open to any and all who wanted to settle here.

IMMIGRANT CLASSIFICATIONS

Alien: Any foreign-born person in the United States who is not a citizen.

Asylee: A foreign national who applies for and receives asylum while in the United States. Permission to remain in the United States is granted when foreign nationals demonstrate a "well-founded fear" of persecution, or that they would be in direct physical danger upon return to their country of origin.

Entrant: A classification created for Cubans and Haitians who arrived in the United States illegally in 1980.

Foreign born, foreign national: Any person who is not a United States citizen.

Green Card holder: A slang term for a permanent resident alien.

Immigrant: An alien who enters the United States with the proper documentation who intends to live here.

Legal alien: An alien who has permission to live in or visit the United States.

Nonimmigrant alien: A foreign-born person who may visit, tour, or study in the United States with a visa for a fixed period of time with a specific purpose.

Parolee: An alien who receives permission to live in the United States temporarily while his or her application for permanent residence is considered.

Permanent resident alien: A foreign national who can live and work in the United States permanently and eventually apply for citizenship.

Refugee: Like an asylee, except the alien applies from abroad for immigration to the United States because of persecution in his or her home country.

Student: An alien who has a visa stipulating that he or she may attend a school or university in the United States for a specific period of time.

Temporary worker: An alien who legally enters the United States to work for a limited period of time at a specific job.

Undocumented alien: Any alien in the United States whose visa has expired or who did not enter the country legally.

Visitor: A classification for tourists and those who have authorization to be in the United States for business purposes on a temporary basis.

Though some groups of Europeans may have reached North America's shores as early as a few hundred years B.C., the United States generally begins its history with settlements of Europeans during the seventeenth century. The Spanish explored the western portion of what would become America, while the British and French struggled for the land east of the Mississippi River. Overrunning tribes of Native Americans, pioneers from Britain, Spain, France, Portugal, and Germany took their places in what would become the great melting pot, the United States of America. After the French and Indian War between the French and British, Great Britain ruled thirteen colonies along the Eastern Seaboard. The original thirteen colonies rebelled against Britain because they had no representation in the British Government. They wanted to form a nation where all the people would have the right to live freely and govern themselves.

Once the new nation had won its freedom and formed its own government, it realized that it needed to protect its borders. In 1798, the new government passed its first immigration law. The law said the President of the United States could **deport**, or evict from the country through a civil proceeding, anyone who presented a danger to the security of the nation. Yet many believed the law contradicted one of the founding principles of the nation—that the United States was a free nation open to anyone who wanted to settle here. By 1800, the law was repealed.

As a young America continued to define itself, legislators realized that the country needed some mechanism to ensure that people settling here would support its government. In 1875, Congress passed the first immigration law governing those who could become naturalized. Its wording was revolutionary. For the first time in the history of the world, citizens of a country had to swear their allegiance to an idea—that of the Republic, as outlined in the Constitution—not to a ruler or king. This was an opportunity offered to rich and poor alike.

The first immigration law also introduced certain qualifications and restrictions for becoming a citizen, which have been revised by Congress periodically ever since. The 1875 law barred convicted criminals and prostitutes from immigrating or becoming citizens. Later immigration laws in the nineteenth century excluded those with mental defects, convicts, and paupers. By 1920, Congress also outlawed the immigration of the diseased, epileptics, idiots and the insane, polygamists, and people who had committed crimes of "moral turpitude" such as murder, rape, arson, and perjury. Though the laws have changed some in recent history, these restrictions resemble the ones in place today.

The United States accepted some of the world's poor, but not all. Many immigration laws resulted from the political and economic pressures of the time. An 1870 immigration act, for example, declared that children of foreign-born blacks born in this country were citizens, but the law did not extend to Chinese, Puerto Ricans, Native Americans, or Hawaiians. Another act in 1882, the Chinese Exclusion Act, banned immigration of the Chinese, in response to pressure from West Coast labor groups who believed cheap foreign labor would threaten the jobs of American citizens. Toward the beginning of the twentieth century, Congress also investigated which groups of immigrants were most "desirable." Immigrants from Italy, Greece, and Poland had become associated with urban slums because of the economic conditions of the times. Immigration restrictions on these groups were supported by what was then "scientific" evidence. Congress's Dillingham Commission reported in 1911 that some races—particularly those from southern and eastern Europe—were inferior. Immigration legislation limiting the number of immigrants from other areas of the world such as Asia would be justified with "evidence" that they did not assimilate as easily as other groups. By 1917, when the next major piece of immigration legislation passed, Congress had limited or denied immigration to the Japanese and all people from the area stretching from the Russian steppes and the Arabian Peninsula to Indonesia. During the early twentieth century Congress also passed laws limiting immigration based on a person's political affiliation. Anarchists and those who believed in the overthrow of the United States Government or laws with violence were banned in 1903.

Early immigration law also set precedents for restricting anyone who would become a **public charge.** The Immigration Act of 1917 barred entry to those who would likely become dependent on the state for economic or health assistance because they could not work or were sick. The 1917 Literacy Test Act also required that every immigrant be able to read and write. Though the requirement was not for English, the law did pave the way for the current English requirement for citizenship.

The Quota System

Legislation governing immigration until the early twentieth century limited certain groups of people from entering the country. The Johnson–Reed Act of 1924, sometimes called the Permanent National Origins Quota Act, imposed the first **quota system** in an attempt to regulate the flow of immigrants from different areas of the world. Under the quota system, visas were issued to countries based on a percentage of that nationality's overall contribution to the population of the United States. In other words, those groups representing a large percentage of the American population received the greatest number of visas. This system ensured the rise in population of favored groups, while continuing to limit immigrants from "undesirable" countries. The 1924 National Origins Quota Act allowed unlimited entry to those from the Western Hemisphere and to the foreign-born spouses and children of American citizens, but limited the number of immigrants from the Eastern Hemisphere to 150,000.

Shortly after the National Origins Quota Act passed, the Great Depression slowed the number of people who wanted to immigrate to the United States. While rising tensions in Nazi Germany led to huge numbers of German Jews entering the country—they comprised one-quarter of all immigrants during the 1930s—the threat of war and nativist attitudes severely limited the number of immigrants from Europe. The infamous refusal of the United States to grant entry to millions of Jewish children as the war began is just one example. Some Americans believed that German-Americans and Japanese-Americans were still loyal to their homelands. During World War II many Japanese-Americans were imprisoned by the government in the interest of national security.

Wartime heightened America's interest in securing its borders. In 1940, Congress passed the Alien Registration Act (the Smith Act), which said that aliens entering or living in the United States must register with the government and be fingerprinted. As the heat of battle waned at the close of World War II, the global political climate cooled along with it. After the war, American politicians became increasingly concerned with the influence of communism both around the world and within their own borders. In 1950, the Subversive Activities Control Act served to monitor the number of aliens believed to be involved in political causes antithetical to the United States Government.

UNITED STATES IMMIGRATION HISTORY

Period	Region	Reasons for Immigration	Total
1780–1830	Northern Europe: mostly England	Adventure and economic opportunity	152,000
1831–1890	Northern Europe: mostly England, Germany, and Ireland	Economic opportunity; political persecution in Germany; and potato blight in Ireland	15,284,000
1891–1930	Eastern and Southern Europe: Italy, Greece, Hungary, Poland, and Russia	Poverty in Southern Europe; Jews fleeing discrimination in Poland and Russia	22,326,000
1931–1950	Europe and rise in numbers from Latin America and Canada	Europeans fleeing World War II; Latin Americans and Canadians seeking economic opportunity	1,563,000
1951–1980	Asia and Latin America: Vietnam, Philippines, Mexico, Cuba, Guatemala, and Dominican Republic	Asians fleeing war; Latin Americans fleeing political persecution and seeking economic opportunity	10,330,000
1981–1987	Latin America and Asia: Mexico, Cuba, Haiti, Dominican Republic, Argentina, Colombia, India, Philippines, and Vietnam	Latin Americans fleeing political persecution and war; both Asians and Latin Americans seeking economic opportunity	4,068,000

Adapted from: Immigration and Naturalization Service, *United States History: 1600–1987* Washington, D.C. (U.S. Government Printing Office, 1987), p. 97; and *Statistical Abstracts of the United States,* 109th edition (U.S. Department of Commerce, 1989), pp. 9, 10.

In 1952, the Immigration and Nationality Act (referred to here as the INA and also known as the McCarran–Walter Act) revised the quota system and imposed stiff restrictions on Communists. The INA also established a percentage preference system: 50 percent of the visas reserved for workers with skills needed in the United States; second, third, and fourth preferences reserved for relatives of United States citizens and permanent resident aliens. While the preference system as outlined in the INA continued to discriminate against Eastern Europeans, certain ethnic groups, and limited access to America from developing Third World countries, it did provide a model for today's preference system.

The Preference System

Immigration law remained essentially unchanged until 1965 when the Hart–Celler Act, a series of amendments to the INA, became law. Congress and the President recognized the need for fairer immigration policies after they had to temporarily suspend the quota system as outlined by the INA on three separate occasions. The quota system was suspended in 1953 to admit refugees from Europe, in 1957 for Hungarian refugees, and in 1960 for refugees from Cuba.

At the foot of the Statue of Liberty, President Lyndon B. Johnson signed the Hart–Celler Act into law in October, 1965. Since the Chinese Exclusion Act of 1882 and the restrictive national origins quotas begun in the 1920s, America had not been, as the poem inscribed on the base of the Statue promised, a haven for all the world's poor and oppressed. The Hart–Celler Act dispensed with the national origins quota system and, in theory, offered an equal number of immigrant visas to countries all over the world with a new **Preference System**. It did, however, limit the total number of such visas issued to foreigners seeking permanent resident status in the United States.

The Preference System established by the Hart–Celler Act is based on **family reunification,** with a full 74 percent of the visas issued to relatives of citizens and permanent resident aliens. Four of the six categories in the Preference System pertain to relatives of citizens and permanent resident aliens. The other two categories cater to those with special professional, scientific, or artistic skill, workers who have skills lacking in the United States, and refugees. (Preference System categories are described in detail in Chapter Two.) Close relatives of U.S. citizens—spouses, parents, and minor children—receive the highest preference. No limits are set on the number who can enter the country. A full third (2.5 million) of all immigrants who came to America between 1965 and 1980 fell into this category.

The original Hart–Celler Act limited visas from the Western Hemisphere to 120,000 with no per-country limits and from the Eastern Hemisphere to a total of 170,000, with each country limited to 20,000 visas per year. While the number of visas issued to countries in the Eastern Hemisphere offered more opportunity to Asians, Africans, and Eastern Europeans, the act still favored immigrants from the Western Hemisphere.

In conjunction with more recent amendments to immigration law dealing with refugee status and the employment of illegal aliens, the Immigration and Nationality Act (INA) and the Hart–Celler Act form the basis of immigration law today. In 1976, Congress voted to set a 20,000-per-country limit in the Western Hemisphere with its own Preference System. Also, in response to the influx of thousands of illegal aliens from Latin America and to problems with admitting refugees (such as the Vietnamese Boat People) Congress passed the Refugee Act of 1980. This act placed refugees in a separate category, with the President and Congress setting the limits every year. The Refugee Act also defined refugees according to a United Nations definition, which includes persons from non-Communist countries. The Refugee Act set a worldwide limit of 270,000 visas issued to come to the United States.

With its emphasis on family reunification, the Hart–Celler Act led to increases in the number of immigrants from countries previously under-represented in the immigration profile. In 1960, 46 percent of all immigrants were from Asia, the Caribbean, and Latin America; in 1980, 80 percent of all immigrants were from these areas. Illegal immigration also became a concern as the growing economy of the American Southwest called for cheaper immigrant labor. At the same time, a 1964 act of Congress ended a program in which workers from Mexico could enter the United States temporarily to work on farms. The United States soon realized that thousands of aliens from Latin America were entering the country illegally. As some legislators in Congress phrased it, America needed to turn off the "job faucet," which seemed to be running nonstop from its neighbors to the south.

To deal with the problem, Congress passed the Immigration Reform and Control Act of 1986 (the Simpson–Rodino Bill). The law established an amnesty program in which illegal aliens could apply for legal temporary residence and permanent residence status if they could prove they had lived illegally in the United States since January 1, 1982. One important aspect of the bill made it illegal for employers to hire **illegal aliens.** Illegal, or undocumented, aliens live in the United States without a visa or with one that has expired. Until 1982, it was illegal for undocumented aliens to work, but employers who hired them did not fear prosecution from the government.

As with the immigration laws preceding it, the Hart–Celler amendments to the INA defined categories in which aliens can be denied entry. These are known as rules of **excludability**. These thirty-three categories are based on earlier immigration law and include those who abuse drugs and anyone who has stolen, cheated, or broken the law just once. Other grounds for excludability cover those whose political beliefs are objectionable to the United States and those whom the United States believes will act in ways that will be dangerous to national security.

The Preference System is far from perfect. Immigration from many countries, notably the Philippines and Mexico, can take months or even years because of the limits on the number of visas. To deal with the problem, Congress is considering a new "point system," in which applicants for immigrant visas would receive priority according to their age and job skills.

While recent attempts to amend immigration law may achieve Congress's short-term goal of addressing problems like illegal immigration, the cumulative effect of over 100 years of legislation makes immigration law complex and confusing. Critics say that only the tax laws compete with immigration law as the longest and most confusing pieces of legislation. The agency responsible for carrying out the law faces nearly insurmountable odds in administration and enforcement.

The INS

The Immigration and Naturalization Service (INS) bears the primary responsibility for processing all immigration documents. If the number of visa categories and restrictions don't make it difficult enough, the task of getting into America is made somewhat more confusing because three government agencies—the Department of State and its consulates abroad, the Department of Labor, and the Immigration and Naturalization Service—all play a role in immigration. Visitors to the United States must first apply for a visa through a consulate or embassy of the Department of State in a foreign country. Depending on the type of visa you apply for, your application may have to be cleared by the Department of Labor or Public Health.

The INS is part of the Department of Justice, a government agency that enforces federal law. Other agencies within the Department of Justice include the Federal Bureau of Investigation (FBI), the Office of the Attorney General, and the Drug Enforcement Administration (DEA). Despite the huge job the INS must handle, it often receives less money and attention than other offices within the Justice Department. The INS is referred to by some as the stepchild of the government bureaucracy.

Why Your Application Takes So Long

The INS performs two immigration functions: service and enforcement. Its service functions include processing visa applications and authorizing aliens to live, work, or visit in the United States. It also processes applications for changes in visa status, such as extensions of temporary stay, and screens and tests applicants for citizenship in English and in American civics. With all of these applications to keep track of, it's no wonder INS delays often are the rule rather than the exception.

The enforcement arm of the INS investigates aliens whom they believe are in America illegally and will detain and deport them. At the border, the enforcement arm of the INS can exclude any alien they believe will threaten United States security and those who do not conform to the terms of their visa. The INS also investigates cases in which an alien has applied for asylum. Applications for asylum are cleared through the State Department. To get asylum, you must prove a "well-founded" fear of persecution or that you would be in physical danger upon return to your country. The INS has thousands of asylum cases under investigation, and only a small percentage of them are approved each year.

Both the service and enforcement tasks of the INS are hampered by a small staff and lack of funds. The INS employs about 12,000 people in its thirty-eight offices nationwide. For example, one of the busiest immigration offices, New York, received 31,000 applications in one month. In addition to processing these applications, the office investigates immigration fraud, document counterfeiting, and smuggling. An office that processes 22 percent of all immigration applications nationwide employs a meager 7 percent of all INS workers. Though employee-application ratios may be better at other offices, this gives you some idea of the mountain of work INS officials face.

You can help avoid delays by making sure you have carefully filled out all forms and answered all questions completely. Bear in mind, however, that the INS believes some delays are necessary. To fulfill its duties, it must investigate and then **adjudicate** applications. In particular, the INS is sensitive to applications based on marriage to a United States citizen or permanent resident alien. The increasing incidence of marriage fraud—in which an alien marries a U.S. citizen solely to be naturalized—led Congress to rule that married aliens can become citizens only after two years of marriage. For the first two years, the alien has "conditional" permanent residence status. After two years, the conditional status will be removed if the INS finds that the marriage is genuine.

Delays are numerous and can be frustrating to applicants. In some cases, you may not be able to change jobs if your application is based on the job you have while your application is being investigated by the INS. You may not be able to travel because you'll have to file an additional application to ensure you'll be able to reenter the country. Public assistance or health care through state or federal governments is not legally available to you, and, if you do get it, it may make you ineligible for citizenship or some other immigration benefits. The government is sensitive to cases in which aliens take advantage of public assistance programs by misrepresenting their immigration status. Aliens who have received welfare, food stamps, or other forms of public assistance have violated the terms of their visas. According to immigration law, those likely to become a "public charge" are not eligible for citizenship.

A relatively new enforcement job for the INS involves investigating and prosecuting those who employ illegal aliens. Before the Simpson–Rodino Act was passed in 1986, it was illegal for undocumented aliens to work, but not to hire them. The smuggling of aliens into the country and counterfeit immigration documents such as Green Cards are also prosecuted by the INS.

Theoretically, the service and enforcement responsibilities of the INS complement each other. Political pressures from Congress and the current administration, and the burden of being an understaffed and underfunded agency make it difficult to achieve this balance. Nonetheless, this is the system you'll be dealing with as you go through the process of becoming naturalized. While it does have its obstacles, a little patience will carry you a long way in achieving your goal.

CHAPTER TWO

Getting into America

KEY TERMS

visa
temporary visa
immigrant visa
visa number
permanent resident alien

consular processing
adjustment of status
chargeability
priority date

advance parole
Arrival/Departure Record
overstay
voluntary departure

Whether you plan to visit relatives for a few weeks, tour the country for a month, or come to the United States to establish residency, you must first receive a **visa** from an American consulate or embassy abroad. Visas usually are stamped in your passport, but they may sometimes be issued on a separate sheet of paper. Issuing visas helps the government and the INS document who enters the country and protect the United States from undesirable visitors.

United States consulates abroad issue two kinds of visas—nonimmigrant and immigrant. Nonimmigrant visas, or **temporary visas**, allow a foreigner to visit the United States for a specific purpose and for a limited amount of time. **Immigrant visas** are issued to those who wish to come to the United States to live here permanently and become citizens. To receive an immigrant visa, you must first qualify for one of the categories in the Preference System, either as a relative of a United States citizen or permanent resident alien, or as a worker. The number of visas issued under the Preference System is limited. To qualify for permanent residence, you must wait until a **visa number** is available in your preference category from your country.

Those who do receive immigrant visas are called **permanent resident aliens**, or Green Card holders. To become naturalized, you must first become a permanent resident alien.

You may approach getting permanent residence status in one of two ways. By the first method, known as **consular processing**, you may apply through an American consulate abroad. All of the paperwork for your Green Card and permanent residence status is completed before you set foot in the United States. By the second method, known as **adjustment of status**, you may apply for permanent residence status after you have legally entered the United States on certain kinds of temporary visas. Most immigration lawyers agree that consular processing is the preferred route. Proving that you qualify for adjustment of status can be a difficult, time-consuming, and expensive process.

Some people find it useful to visit the United States before deciding whether or not they want to become permanent residents. For example, they may be able to make contact with an employer willing to hire them. Still, in most cases it will be easier to return to your country and pursue permanent residence through consular processing. To review all of your options, this chapter offers a general discussion of the kinds of temporary and immigrant visas issued by the United States. Most people who get their Green Card through adjustment of status will need an immigration lawyer's guidance. The general requirements for naturalization and your rights and responsibilities as an alien in the United States are also discussed in this chapter.

Temporary Visas

While Congress sets definite limits on the number of people who can become residents each year, there is no limit to the number of visas that can be issued for those who want to travel or study in the United States temporarily. There are many categories and subcategories of temporary visas: In all, there are fourteen separate classifications of nonimmigrant visas from foreign diplomats and government officials to students and temporary visitors for business or pleasure. The most common temporary visas are issued to tourists and students. Other temporary visas are specialized, such as those for business people and journalists. In many cases, the employers of aliens who come to America for business purposes will apply for a visa for them.

Temporary visas are described in the chart on pages 20–22. Though most will not apply to you, as you plan your visit to the United States, you may find it helpful to note the restrictions on the most common visas. Though adjusting your visa from temporary to permanent status can be difficult, the terms of some temporary visas make adjusting your status once you are in the United States easier than others.

Though the United States does not limit the number of temporary visas that can be issued, it is not always easy to receive one. The government assumes that anyone who wants to enter the country intends to stay here. It's up to the visa applicant to prove otherwise. When you apply for a visa, you must convince the American consulate that your trip to the United States really will be temporary. You may have to show proof of the job or family that you will return to.

Once you have received a temporary visa, the INS still may exclude you at the border (see pages 28–30 for rules of excludability). The fact that you have a temporary visa makes no difference to the INS: Border officials are trained to presume that any alien entering the United States will want to stay. The reasons for exclusion can be very arbitrary. The INS border official may find a letter from an employer, a resume, or some other item leading him or her to believe that you intend to stay in the United States permanently. In other cases, you may be excluded based on your political affiliations and activities.

Even prize-winning Canadian author Farley Mowat could not enter the country when he had a scheduled speaking tour to promote his book *Sea of Slaughter* in 1985. The INS believed he posed a threat to national security because of his outspoken criticism of American military activity in Canada. Other writers and activists who have been refused entry at the United States border include authors Carlos Fuentes and Gabriel García Márquez, and Italian playwright Dario Fo.

Though critics insist that the way the INS enforces the rules of excludability at the border is often arbitrary and discriminatory, they do have good reason for their diligence. They know that many people who visit the United States on temporary visas will in fact want to stay. Some people enter the country knowing they will try to get permanent residence status once here. Other visitors change their minds about staying after they arrive. With some kinds of visas, aliens may be able to change their nonimmigrant status once they are in the country to better position themselves for applying for permanent residence.

Depending on the kind of temporary visa they have, visitors can stay in the United States for months at a time. Most visitor visas (labeled "B-1/2") are issued for six months. Certain visas allow aliens to leave and reenter the country for as long as the visa is valid.

In some cases, you may adjust your status from temporary resident to permanent resident, so it's important to apply for the right kind of temporary visa. The time spent in the United States on a temporary visa, however, does not count toward the time required to establish permanent residency. Usually, you must be a permanent resident for five years before becoming a citizen. For example, if you lived in the United States on a temporary visa for a year and then applied to adjust your status, you would date the beginning of your permanent residency from the day you received approval from the INS. You cannot count the year you spent in the United States on a temporary visa toward permanent residency. In particular, exchange visitors under the two-year foreign residency requirement, crew members of ships or planes, and visitors in transit through the United States without a visa may not apply for permanent residence status. In many cases, you will have to apply to the consul abroad where you first received your visa to change your status (see Chapter Three).

With all of the forms you fill out, it's important to be as accurate as possible. The application you complete to receive your visa will become part of your file with the INS. An INS official will compare all your forms, looking for any inconsistencies. Some immigration lawyers advise their clients to fill out immigration forms completely, but not to say too much. While you may think that providing more information than asked for shows your honesty and integrity, the unasked for information may come back to haunt you later. Be truthful, be able to back up anything you say on a form, but don't confuse the issue with too much information.

While you may be able to enter the United States on a temporary visa and then apply for and receive permanent resident status, these requests are subject to numerous variables. You may have to receive certifi-

NONIMMIGRANT VISA CLASSIFICATIONS

Type   *Description*

Common Visas

Temporary Visitor Visas

B-1/2
business visitors and tourists

The most common visa issued to those who wish to visit the U.S. temporarily. Does not allow alien to work, but is issued to those employed abroad who wish to come to the U.S. for meetings, conferences, and those training for a foreign corporation. Experts in a field may also receive this visa. Length of stay depends on policy of American consul in country where issued, though most B-1/2 visas good for 6 months. Visa may be extended by applying to the INS.

This visa is so common that in a few countries such as the United Kingdom, Japan, and Germany, the U.S. Consul waives the formal visa stamp in the passport. The alien travels to the U.S. without any preliminary screening.

Students

F-1
academic student

Issued to those who will undertake a full course of study at a U.S. university or college. Usually expires after 1 year with the option to renew, or may be issued for full period of study. Must have Form I-20A from an INS-approved school. Easiest to get this visa through consul in native country. Cannot work with this visa, but may apply to do so. Applications to work approved only in unforeseen circumstances, such as the death of student's sponsor or a drastic drop in value of native country's currency.

Many permanent resident aliens in U.S. first entered with F-1 visas and later adjusted their status.

F-2
spouse and children of F-1 holder

Cannot work or apply for work permit.

Distinguished Merit and Ability, Temporary Workers, and Trainees

H-1
temporary worker of distinguished merit and ability

Includes athletes, engineers, entertainers of exceptional nature who do not intend to stay in U.S. Good for 3 years. Automatic authorization to work. Employer must file Form I-129B and be approved by INS before alien can enter with this status. Physicians ineligible for H-1 unless they work in research.

"Distinguished merit and ability" means person should work at level requiring at least a bachelor's degree or a license, such as a registered nurse or lawyer.

H-2A
temporary agricultural worker

Must have labor certification showing that work will not affect wages or working conditions of U.S. citizens. Employer files Form ETA-750 with Department of Labor. Usually valid for 1 year with maximum period being 3 years with extensions. Difficult to renew.

H-2B
temporary worker for service not available in U.S.

Employer files papers with the local Department of Labor for their approval.

H-3
trainee

No labor certification required. On invitation from U.S. individual, organization, or business to train in a particular field. Usually good for 2 years; cannot be renewed.

Exchange visitors
J-1
exchange visitor

Students, scholars, teachers, physicians, and leaders in a field who enter U.S. to teach, instruct, consult, or receive training. Exchange programs are designated by Secretary of State. Usually not granted for more than 1 year. Can work if stipulated by exchange program.

Terms of visa include a 2-year foreign residence requirement, which means you must leave U.S. for 2 years after visa expires. Cannot change status until 2 years have passed, with some exceptions. Waiver of 2-year requirement possible but difficult to obtain, even if you marry a U.S. citizen.

J-2
spouse and minor children

With permission of INS may work if necessary to support children and/or J-1 holder.

Fiancée or Fiancé
K-1
fiancée or fiancé of U.S. citizen

Must have met fiancé(e) within two years of filing time. When fiancé(e) arrives, must marry within 90 days. Can work in the 90-day period. Conditional permanent residence status for 2 years after marriage, then INS will grant permanent status. Cannot change status if marriage does not take place.

Vocational Students
M-1
vocational student

Like F student visa but more difficult to change schools or get extension. Difficult to obtain work authorization.

Specialized Visas

Diplomatic Visas
A-1; A-2; A-3
ambassador, public minister, consular officer and immediate family; other government officials and family; personal employees of A visa holders

Usually full diplomatic immunity for A-1; lesser immunity for A-2 and A-3. A-1 and A-2 visas good for length of assignment. A-3 issued for 1 year and may be renewed.

It is rare for the State Department to refuse entrance to the U.S. for these classifications.

Officials from governments not recognized by U.S. may travel on B, C, or G visas.

Transit Aliens

C-1; C-2; C-3
transit through U.S.

These visas issued to those people passing through U.S. airports and changing planes. Also for transit to U.N. or consulate.

D

Crew members of planes or ships

Treaty Traders and Treaty Investors

E-1; E-2
treaty trader and spouse and children; treaty investor and spouse and children

A sophisticated visa created for developing trade between the U.S. and foreign countries with which U.S. has a treaty. E visas good for 4 years; sometimes used as an alternative to permanent residence by supervisors, executives, and those with special skills or a corporation. Check with the U.S. consulate in your own country.

Employees of International Organizations

G-1; G-2; G-3; G-4; G-5
representatives of foreign government to international organization; representatives of governments not recognized by U.S.; employees of above representatives

Visas usually obtained by organization employing the applicant. All but the G-5 visa good for the duration of assignment. G-5 issued for 1 year and may be renewed.

Representative of Foreign Information Media

I
foreign press, radio, TV, film, and other foreign information media

Issued for 1 year with renewal available. Cannot change employer without approval from INS.

Intracompany Transferees

L-1
manager, executive, or person with specialized knowledge

Much supporting documentation required by INS. No labor certification required. Must be employed by foreign firm for 1 year and want to come to U.S. to work for affiliate of foreign company.

cation from the Department of Labor and wait for a visa number to become available. As a general rule, you'll have a better chance getting your application for permanent residence approved if you are a highly skilled professional whose services are in demand in America. With the exception of the parents, spouses, and children of United States citizens, in most cases you still have to apply for permanent residence through the consulate in your native country.

Immigrant Visas and the Preference System

Most aliens who come to the United States to reside permanently receive immigrant visas (or permanent residence visas) on the basis of the Preference System. Congress limits the total number of immigrant visas offered within this system to 270,000 per year, with a limit on the number of visas each country can receive. Some categories of permanent resident visas are not subject to these limitations. These include the spouses, parents, and minor children of United States citizens, and special immigrants including certain ministers of religion, some former employees of the United States government abroad, and sometimes those who once lost their United States citizenship. Those who qualify for refugee status and political asylum also are exempt from the numerical limitations.

The Preference System limits the number of visas issued for each country to 20,000 per year. Each colony (such as Hong Kong) receives 600 visas per year. Within the Preference System, the total number of visas is distributed among the six preference categories. First Preference—adult, unmarried sons and daughters of United States citizens—receive the highest percentage of visas, Third Preference slightly less, and so on. (See the Preference System chart on page 24). If all the available visas within one category are not used, the remainder drops to the next category. With this trickle-down effect, all 270,000 possible visas will be issued in a given year. In addition to the six preference categories, a seventh nonpreference group theoretically receives any remaining visas. Except for a lottery in 1987 and 1988, since 1978, no visas have been issued in this category because all visas were issued in the first six categories. Given the history of the seventh category, don't count on receiving a visa in this group.

The system places emphasis on reuniting families. Those not subject to numerical limitations are close family members. From looking at the Preference System chart, we see that four of the categories are reserved for family members. Originally the Preference System was designed to open America's doors to those previously limited by the percentage quota system. Yet the Preference System has created its own bias in admitting aliens from a particular country. As more aliens from a country immigrate and naturalize, they in turn create a better opportunity for their family members to immigrate.

As we'll see in Chapter Three, it's important for you to understand the requirements of each preference category. You may be eligible to enter the United States under one or more categories. Depending on what country you're from, you may have only a short wait of a few months or a longer one of a few years before a visa number becomes available. You'll need to know which cat-

PREFERENCE SYSTEM CATEGORIES

270,00 visas issued annually worldwide with a limit of 20,000 per country. Limit of 600 visas per colony.

Not Subject to Numerical Limitations
- spouses, parents, and minor children of U.S. citizens
- certain former employees of the U.S. government abroad
- certain persons who have lost their U.S. citizenship
- certain ministers of religion
- refugees and asylees

Subject to Numerical Limitations

Preference Category	Description	Visas Available Within Total Limitation
First	unmarried adult sons and daughters of U.S. citizens	20%; 4,000 per country
Second	spouses and unmarried sons and daughters of permanent resident aliens	26%; 5,200 per country
Third	professionals, scientists, artists of exceptional ability, and their spouses and children	10%; 2,000 per country
Fourth	married sons and daughters of U.S. citizens, and their spouses and children	10%; 2,000 per country
Fifth	brothers and sisters over the age of 21 of U.S. citizens, and their spouses and children	24%; 4,800 per country
Sixth	skilled and unskilled workers in demand in the U.S., and their spouses and children	10%; 2,000 per country
Seventh (Non-preference)	open to those not able to receive visas in other categories	inactive 1978–1986, but 30,000 visas available 1987–1988*

*Visas were available in 1987–1988 due to a special lottery offered to nationals of certain countries that Congress felt were "underrepresented" in immigration.

egories fill most quickly and have the longest backlog, and if you'll have an easier time getting in with a work or a family petition.

An immigration attorney or a consular officer can help you decide which of the preference categories will best suit your application for an immigrant visa. In general, it's wise to apply for every preference for which you think you may qualify. For example, if your brother is a United States citizen you may apply under the Fifth Preference category. If you then marry a permanent resident, you will not prejudice your case if you apply for permanent residence under the Second Preference category as well. Applying under the Second Preference will probably be quicker than applying under the Fifth Preference because more visas are issued in the second category.

Rules of Chargeability

Before you begin to identify which preference categories apply to you, an obvious question to ask yourself is from what country you will be applying. Immigration law limits the number of immigrant visas issued to each country. A few people may find that they can claim citizenship in a country in which they were not born. Though this rarely occurs, you may find it useful if your country has a long waiting list and you can claim citizenship in a country that has a shorter waiting list. In general, your nationality, or **chargeablity**, is attributed to your country of birth. There are four instances in which you may claim an exemption to charging your nationality to your country of birth. This is known as "cross-chargeability." If you fall into any of these categories, your application to enter the United States to

reside here permanently may not be limited by your country of birth's numerical limitations.

1. If you are married and your spouse is from a different country, you may be able to apply under your spouse's nationality.
2. Your child's nationality may be attributed to either you or your spouse's place of birth.
3. If you were born an American citizen and are not a citizen of any other country, you can attribute your nationality to the country where you last lived or were a citizen.
4. If you were born in a country where neither parent was born and in which they did not have residence, you may attribute nationality to either parent's place of birth.

Your Priority Date:
Getting a Visa Number

Those who apply for residence in the United States under the First, Second, Fourth, or Fifth Preferences generally have an easier time of it than those who apply under the preference categories based on employment. The Third and Sixth categories have long waiting lists for most countries. Third and sixth preference applicants also need certification from the Department of Labor, a long and involved process.

To receive an immigrant visa and get permanent residence status, a visa number must be available in your category. Many preference categories have long waiting lists. If you know you will be affected by a backlog, get on a waiting list for a visa number as soon as you can. Those who work with immigration law refer to this as "being in the pipeline." Being in the pipeline means you have received a **priority date**, based on the date your application for a visa was filed. In other words, your priority date is the day on which the INS first accepted your application for processing. If you need labor certification, your priority date is the day the Department of Labor first accepted your labor certification application for processing. Again, it must be stressed that your priority date stems from the day you *submit* the forms to the INS or the labor office, not from the day they are approved. The approval date may be many months after submission.

The Visa Office periodically reviews the number of backlog cases and estimates the demand for visas to determine the availability of visas from each country in each preference category. Based on this review, it issues a cutoff date for processing applications. If your priority date falls on or before the cutoff date, then a visa number is available in your preference category. If the number of backlog cases and estimated demand for visas is less than the number set by law, the category is said to be "current," meaning visas are immediately available.

The Visa Office can tell you when a visa number will be available in your category. To find out if a visa number is available in your preference category from your country, call the Visa Office at 202-647-0508. A recorded announcement will tell you the cutoff date in your preference category for your country of chargeability. If your priority date falls on or before the cutoff date provided by the Visa Office, a visa number is available in your category. If your priority date is later than the cutoff date, you have to wait a little longer. For example, if your priority date is August 6, 1991, and the Visa Office tells you the cutoff date is July 15, 1991, then a visa number is not yet available

to you. But the size of the backlog is re-evaluated periodically, and a new cutoff date is set. You might phone the Visa Office again after four to six weeks to see if a new, later, cutoff date has been announced.

So don't worry if your category isn't current when your relative or employer files your application for permanent residency or labor certification—they rarely are. The earlier you submit your petitions, the earlier your application will be processed.

We'll discuss the specifics of applying for permanent residence in Chapter Three. It's important to remember, however, that the process takes less time if you apply directly for permanent residence through a consulate abroad. Coming to the United States on a temporary visa and attempting to change your status is time-consuming. More importantly, in most cases you will have a difficult time convincing the INS to grant you permanent residence status without the skilled advice of a lawyer. Changing your status limits your ability to travel outside the United States. Although you are subject to the same kinds of limitations if you apply for permanent residence directly, the INS is less lenient if you travel when you are on an adjustment of status basis. If you do want to travel while applying for adjustment of status, you will have to request special permission, called **advance parole**, in order to return to the United States.

Entering the United States
At the Border:
The Arrival/Departure Record

All aliens, with the exception of Canadians, receive Form I-94, the **Arrival/Departure Record** at the border. This is a card

U.S. Department of Justice
Immigration and Naturalization Service

OMB 1115-0077

Admission Number

Welcome to the United States

319684164 01

I-94 Arrival/Departure Record - Instructions

This form must be completed by all persons except U.S. Citizens, returning resident aliens, aliens with immigrant visas, and Canadian Citizens visiting or in transit.

Type or print legibly with pen in ALL CAPITAL LETTERS. Use English. Do not write on the back of this form.

This form is in two parts. Please complete both the Arrival Record (Items 1 through 13) and the Departure Record (Items 14 through 17).

When all items are completed, present this form to the U.S. Immigration and Naturalization Service Inspector.

Item 7 - If you are entering the United States by land, enter **LAND** in this space. If you are entering the United States by ship, enter **SEA** in this space.

Form I-94 (04-15-86)Y

Admission Number

319684164 01

Immigration and
Naturalization Service

I-94
Arrival Record

1. Family Name

2. First (Given) Name

3. Birth Date (Day/Mo/Yr)

4. Country of Citizenship

5. Sex (Male or Female)

6. Passport Number

7. Airline and Flight Number

8. Country Where You Live

9. City Where You Boarded

10. City Where Visa Was Issued

11. Date Issued (Day/Mo/Yr)

12. Address While in the United States (Number and Street)

13. City and State

Departure Number

319684164 01

Immigration and
Naturalization Service

I-94
Departure Record

14. Family Name

15. First (Given) Name

16. Birth Date (Day/Mo/Yr)

17. Country of Citizenship

See Other Side

STAPLE HERE

This Side For Government Use Only

Primary Inspection

Applicant's
Name _____

Date
Referred _____ Time _____ Insp. # _____

Reason Referred

☐ 212A [ ] [ ]   ☐ PP ☐ Visa ☐ Parole ☐ SLB ☐ TWOV

☐ Other _____

Secondary Inspection

End Secondary
Time _____ Insp. # _____

Disposition _____

18. Occupation

19. Waivers

20. INS File
A -

21. INS FCO

22. Petition Number

23. Program Number

24. ☐ Bond

25. ☐ Prospective Student

26. Itinerary/Comments

27. TWOV Ticket Number

Warning - A nonimmigrant who accepts unauthorized employment is subject to deportation.

Important - Retain this permit in your possession; *you must surrender it when you leave the U.S.* Failure to do so may delay your entry into the U.S. in the future.

You are authorized to stay in the U.S. only until the date written on this form. To remain past this date, without permission from immigration authorities, is a violation of the law.

Surrender this permit when you leave the U.S.:
- By sea or air, to the transportation line;
- Across the Canadian border, to a Canadian Official;
- Across the Mexican border, to a U.S. Official.

Students planning to reenter the U.S. within 30 days to return to the same school, see "Arrival-Departure" on page 2 of Form I-20 **prior to surrendering this permit.**

Record of Changes

Port:

Date:

Carrier:

Flight #/Ship Name:

Departure Record

that the immigration officer attaches to your passport. It shows what kind of visa you have, when you entered the country, and when your visa expires. The expiration date on the Arrival/Departure Record, not the date stamped in the passport by the United States consulate, is the date you should follow. If you let your visa expire, the INS considers you an **overstay**, which means you are an illegal alien who has violated the terms of your visa. This makes it more difficult for you to change your status or reenter the country later if you do leave. Form I-94 is required for all other paperwork you do with INS. It is as important as your passport.

Rules of Excludability

Though many strategies exist for getting into and staying in the United States, all who want to enter the country or apply for citizenship are subject to the same rules. The Immigration and Naturalization Act (INA) lists thirty-three separate reasons why a person may be excluded from the United States. Unlike citizens of the United States, who may not be accused and convicted of a crime without a trial, aliens at the border have little recourse if they are refused entry.

Persons who may be excluded include those who are:

- mentally retarded, insane, psychopathic, sexual deviants, or those with mental defects;
- alcoholics or narcotic drug addicts;
- afflicted by a contagious disease or have limiting disabilities;
- paupers, beggars, vagrants, and some criminals;
- polygamists;
- likely to engage in immoral acts;
- stowaways;
- draft avoiders;
- illiterate;
- members of subversive groups and organizations such as the Communist Party, or anarchists, or those who are likely to engage in subversive acts;
- and those who have been previously deported or excluded, or do not have the proper visa or documents.

The rules for exclusion are sometimes vague, often redundant, and in some cases outdated, but the INS may still find ways to bar a person's entry. Homosexuals used to be excluded because they were considered sexual deviants with a psychopathic disorder. Those suspected of being homosexual would be examined by someone from the Public Health Service. Even though the Public Health Service abided by a 1979 decision by the American Psychiatric Association that homosexuality was not a disease, the INS can still refuse entry to homosexuals. The rule states that, if a third party attests to an alien's homosexuality, or if an alien answers "yes" when asked if he or she is a homosexual, the person may be refused.

The INS may also exclude someone because of his or her political affiliation and ideology. The INS can still exclude aliens under the McCarran–Walter Act of 1952, which says that someone can be refused entry simply on the *suspicion* that one has or will engage in political activities of which the United States does not approve. Critics of the system argue that excluding personalities such as Farley Mowat and other writers whose political views often differ from those of the United States Government endangers the right under the Constitution to the free exchange of ideas.

The rules concerning contagious diseases vary also. For example, the INS excludes foreigners who test positive for HIV antibodies or AIDS. While the INS does offer waivers for persons with AIDS, the policy is under debate. Congress is still working on legislation dealing with immigration for those who have AIDS. If you have any doubts, consult a lawyer.

The INS takes exclusion very seriously. If it happens to you, find a lawyer right away. Only someone with expertise in immigration law can help you sort through the charges being made against you. If an inspector at the border refuses to let you enter the country, you will be questioned by a second inspector. By law, the inspector must tell you that you can receive free legal services and request a hearing. Experience shows that it's up to the alien to insist on an exclusion hearing. Insist on a hearing if you have to; the inspector may decide to admit you to the country on parole and schedule a deferred inspection for you at the nearest immigration office. At this point if the issue is still not resolved, you may have your side heard by an immigration judge and be represented by counsel. The INS will provide you with instructions if you choose to appeal to the Board of Immigration Appeals.

If you think you might be excluded from the United States for any of these reasons, you should talk it over with an immigration lawyer. The lawyer may be able to file a waiver of ineligibility (Form I-601) that will allow you to enter the United States. Usually, the Attorney General of the United States makes the final ruling on applications like these. Obviously, it helps if you can claim some connection to United States citizens, such as close family members, but your waiver may be approved without it.

Whether you are a visitor, resident alien, or an overstay, once you get past the immigration inspection at the border, you are legally under the jurisdiction of the INS.

Though the First Amendment to the Constitution guarantees the freedom of speech, aliens in the United States may find this right somewhat restricted if they want to safely secure and maintain their citizenship. The exclusion rules explicitly state that an alien who is a member of the Communist Party or another "subversive" group may not remain in the country or become a citizen. If the INS thinks you are hostile to the United States Government because of your political affiliations or stated beliefs, chances are good that you will be asked to leave or be deported.

An "order to show cause" why you shouldn't be deported is a serious matter. INS regulations list numerous grounds for deporting aliens. In some cases, aliens have been deported when their "crime" was committed before the offense was actually considered an offense by the INS.

Other grounds for being deported include violating the terms of your visa. For example, if you work without a Green Card, become an **overstay** (the most common reason), or commit certain crimes while in the United States, the INS has reason to deport you. Sometimes the INS offers aliens who have violated immigration law the option of **voluntary departure** rather than being deported. This simply means that you agree to leave the country without a hearing. Voluntary departure allows an alien to apply for a visa again once he or she has left the United States, while someone who is deported (with rare exceptions) may not be issued a new visa. Often, however, aliens may not realize that they have the right to a hearing on their case. Consult a lawyer before waiving your deportation hearing.

Requirements for Naturalization

With all of the visa classifications and stipulations that we've examined so far, it may seem like becoming naturalized is an impossible task. If all of your visa documentation is in order, completing the process of becoming a citizen is not difficult. In the next chapter we'll discuss the specifics of what it takes to establish residency. You'll also see, step-by-step, which forms you should file and how to fill out the applications. The INS outlines six general requirements you must meet before applying to become a citizen. Before we discuss the specifics of the process in Chapter Three, you should understand the six criteria that make you eligible to become a U.S. citizen.

1. You Must Be at Least Eighteen Years Old

Of all the requirements, this one takes the least explanation. You'll see in Chapter Three that you should be able to provide a birth certificate proving your nationality and age. If you don't have a birth certificate, see Chapter Three for guidelines on other proofs of birth you can use.

2. Legal Admission and Permanent Residence

To apply for citizenship, in most cases you must have lived in the United States legally as a permanent resident—not a temporary visitor or student—for at least five years. If you became a permanent resident alien by marrying a United States citizen, you will be eligible to apply for citizenship after three years. You must show that you and your spouse were in fact married and living together for three years. Your application should be filed in the state where you lived for the last six months to fulfill the residency requirement.

While you may leave the country during the period required to establish residency, you should take care that the INS understands your intention to return to the United States and live here permanently. You must live in the United States for at least half of the five-year period (no less than thirty months) and, with certain exceptions, may be absent for no more than six months at a time.

If your permanent residence was obtained through marriage to a United States citizen, you may be eligible for citizenship after three years, provided you can show that you still live with your spouse and have resided at least thirty-six months in the United States.

Exemptions from the residency requirement include those who travel outside the country with their spouses who are citizens on business for the government or other American organizations; those who work abroad for some American organizations; members of the United States armed forces and their spouses and children; and workers for a religious group abroad that also exists in the United States.

You may get permission to live outside the United States for more than one year during the five-year residency period. If you have to travel outside the country for more than a year, you will have to apply for a Reentry Permit (Form I-131) at least thirty days before you plan to travel. The permit maintains your permanent residence status, but may not preserve the residence requirement for naturalization.

Instructions

Please read instructions carefully. Fee will not be refunded.

Please type or print plainly with a ball point pen.

I. Filing the Application
The application and supporting documents should be taken or mailed to:

The American Consulate at which the applicant is applying for a visa, if the application is not in the United States; or

The office of the Immigration and Naturalization Service having jurisdiction over the applicant's place of residence; if the applicant is in the United States, and is applying for status as a permanent resident.

II. Fee

No fee is required if this application is filed for an alien who:

Is afflicted with tuberculosis;

Is mentally retarded; or

Has a history of mental illness.

All other applications must be accompanied by a fee of forty-five dollars ($45). The fee cannot be refunded, regardless of the action taken on the application. **Do not mail cash.**

Payment must be made by a check or money order:

Drawn on a bank or other institution located in the United States;

Payable in United States currency; and

Payable in the exact amount ($45).

If the check is drawn on an account of a person other than the applicant, the name of the applicant must be entered on the face of the check.

Personal checks are accepted subject to collectibility. An uncollectible check will void the application and any documents issued pursuant to the application. A charge of $5.00 will be imposed if the check is not honored by the bank on which it is drawn.

Unless the applicant resides in the *Virgin Islands or Guam*, the check or money order must be made payable to the "Immigration and Naturalization Service".

If applicant resides in the Virgin Islands, make the check or money order payable to the "Commissioner of Finance of the Virgin Islands".

If applicant resides in Guam, make the check or money order payable to the "Treasurer, Guam".

III. Applicants with Tuberculosis

An applicant with active tuberculosis or suspected tuberculosis must complete Statement A on page two of this form. The applicant and his or her sponsor is also responsible for having:

Statement B completed by the physician or health facility which has agreed to provide treatment or observation, and

Statement D, if required, completed by the appropriate local or state health officer.

This form should then be returned to the applicant for presentation to the consular office, or to the appropriate office of the Immigration and Naturalization Service.

Submission of the application without the required fully executed statements will result in return of the application to the applicant without further action.

IV. Applicants with Mental Conditions

An alien who is mentally retarded or who has a history of mental illness shall attach a statement that arrangements have been made for the submission of a medical report, as follows, to the office where this form is filed:

The medical report shall contain:

A complete medical history of the alien, including details of any hospitalization or institutional care or treatment for any physical or mental condition;

Findings as to the current physical condition of the alien, including reports of chest X-rays and a serologic test if the alien is 15 years of age or older, and other pertinent diagnostic tests; and

Findings as to the current mental condition of the alien, with information as to prognosis and life expectancy and with a report of a psychiatric examination conducted by a psychiatrist who shall, in case of mental retardation, also provide an evaluation of the intelligence.

For an alien with a past history of mental illness, the medical report shall also contain available information on which the United States Public Health can base a finding as to whether the alien has been free of such mental illness for a period of time sufficient in the light of such history to demonstrate recovery.

The medical report will be referred to the United States Public Health Service for review and, if found acceptable, the alien will be required to submit such additional assurances as the United States Public Health Service may deem necessary in his or her particular case.

U.S. Department of Justice
Immigration and Naturalization Service

Application for Waiver of Grounds of Excludability

OMB No. 1115-0048

DO NOT WRITE IN THIS BLOCK

☐ 212 (a) (1)   ☐ 212 (a) (10)   Fee Stamp
☐ 212 (a) (3)   ☐ 212 (a) (12)
☐ 212 (a) (6)   ☐ 212 (a) (19)
☐ 212 (a) (9)   ☐ 212 (a) (23)

A. Information about applicant -

1. Family Name (Surname in CAPS)   (First)   (Middle)

2. Address (Number and Street)   (Apartment Number)

3. (Town or City)   (State/Country)   (ZIP/Postal Code)

4. Date of Birth *(Month/Day/Year)*   5. I&N File Number
A-

6. City of Birth   7. Country of Birth

8. Date of visa application   9. Visa applied for at:

10. Applicant was declared inadmissible to the United States for the following reasons: (List acts, convictions, or physical or mental conditions. If applicant has active or suspected tuberculosis, the reverse of this page must be fully completed.)

_____

_____

_____

_____

_____

11. Applicant was previously in the United States, as follows:
City & State   From (Date)   To (Date)   I&NS Status

_____

_____

_____

_____

_____

12. Social Security Number

B. Information about relative, through whom applicant claims eligibility for a waiver-

1. Family Name (Surname in CAPS)   (First)   (Middle)

2. Address (Number and Street)   (Apartment Number)

3. (Town or City)   (State/Country)   (Zip/Postal Code)

4. Relationship to applicant   5. I&NS Status

C. Information about applicant's other relatives in the U.S.
(List only U.S. citizens and permanent residents)

1. Family Name (Surname in CAPS)   (First)   (Middle)

2. Address (Number and Street)   (Apartment Number)

3. (Town or City)   (State/Country)   (Zip/Postal Code)

4. Relationship to applicant   5. I&NS Status

1. Family Name (Surname in CAPS)   (First)   (Middle)

2. Address (Number and Street)   (Apartment Number)

3. (Town or City)   (State/Country)   (Zip/Postal Code)

4. Relationship to applicant   5. I&NS Status

1. Family Name (Surname in CAPS)   (First)   (Middle)

2. Address (Number and Street)   (Apartment Number)

3. (Town or City)   (State/Country)   (Zip/Postal Code)

4. Relationship to applicant   5. I&NS Status

Signature *(of applicant or petitioning relative)*

Relationship to applicant   Date

Signature *(of person preparing application, if not the applicant or petitioning relative)* **I declare that this document was prepared by me at the request of the applicant, or petitioning relative, and is based on all information of which I have any knowledge.**

Signature

Address   Date

Initial receipt	Resubmitted	Relocated		Completed		
		Received	Sent	Approved	Denied	Returned

Form I-601 (Rev 5-4-89)Y
Page 1

To be completed for applicants with
active tuberculosis or suspected tuberculosis

A. Statement by Applicant

Upon admission to the United States I will:

1.Go directly to the physician or health facility named in Section B;

2. Present all X-rays used in the visa medical examination to substantiate diagnosis;

3. Submit to such examinations, treatment, isolation, and medical regimen as may be required; and

4. Remain under the prescribed treatment or observation whether on inpatient or outpatient basis, until discharged.

_____
Signature of Applicant

_____
Date

B. Statement by Physician or Health Facility

(May be executed by a private physician, health department, other public or private health facility, or military hospital.)

I agree to supply any treatment or observation necessary for the proper management of the alien's tuberculous condition.

I agree to submit Form CDC 75.18 "Report on Alien with Tuberculosis Waiver" to the health officer named in Section D:

1. Within 30 days of the alien's reporting for care, indicating presumptive diagnosis, test results, and plans for future care of the alien; or

2. 30 days after receiving Form CDC 75.18 if the alien has not reported.

Satisfactory financial arrangements have been made. (This statement does not relieve the alien from submitting evidence, as required by consul, to establish that the alien is not likely to become a public charge.)

I represent (enter an "X" in the appropriate box and give the complete name and address of the facility below.)

☐ 1. Local Health Department
☐ 2. Other Public or Private Facility
☐ 3. Private Practice
☐ 4. Military Hospital

_____
Name of Facility (please type or print)

_____
Address (Number & Street)   (Apartment Number)

_____
City, State & ZIP Code

_____
Signature of Physician   Date

C. Applicant's Sponsor in the U.S.

Arrange for medical care of the applicant and have the physician complete Section B.

If medical care will be provided by a physician who checked box 2 or 3, in Section B., have Section D. completed by the local or State Health Officer who has jurisdiction in the area where the applicant plans to reside in the U.S.

If medical care will be provided by a physician who checked box 4., in Section B., forward this form directly to the military facility at the address provided in Section B.

Address where the alien plans to reside in the U.S.

_____
Address (Number & Street)   (Apartment Number)

_____
City, State & ZIP Code

D. Endorsement of Local or State Health Officer

Endorsement signifies recognition of the physician or facility for the purpose of providing care for tuberculosis. If the facility or physician who signed in Section B is not in your health jurisdiction and is not familiar to you, you may wish to contact the health officer responsible for the jurisdiction of the facility or physician prior to endorsing.

_____
Endorsed by: *Signature of Health Officer*

_____
Date

Enter below the name and address of the Local Health Department to which the "Notice of Arrival of Alien with Tuberculosis Waiver" should be sent when the alien arrives in the U. S.

_____
Official Name of Department

_____
Address (Number & Street)   (Apartment Number)

_____
City, State & ZIP Code

Please read instructions with care.

If further assistance is needed, contact the office of the Immigration and Naturalization Service with jurisdiction over the intended place of U.S. residence of the applicant.

Form I-601 (Rev 5-4-89)Y

Page 2

3. Good Moral Character and Loyal to the United States

During the five-year period in which you establish residency, you must also show that you are of good moral character and loyal to the United States, and that you believe in its structure and laws and the principles of the Constitution. The government defines persons of good moral character as those who have not been:

- involved in narcotics, prostitution, or other criminal acts;
- a polygamist (someone who is married to more than one person at one given time);
- someone who derives their income from gambling;
- an alcoholic;
- jailed for more than six months;
- convicted of murder;
- found to have lied under oath in order to improve their standing under the immigration and naturalization laws.

If you have been ordered to leave the country because you have broken immigration laws, you will not be eligible to become naturalized.

In addition, a judge may deny your application if you refused to serve in the United States military (and did not obtain conscientious objector status) or deserted the armed forces. Your application may also be rejected if you applied and were accepted for an exemption from military service because you are an alien.

Your loyalty to the United States Government will be very important to the judge reviewing your application. You must not have been a member of the Communist Party, whether in another country or in the United States, less than ten years before the date of your application. If you can prove that you were forced to be a member of the Communist Party, that you had to be a member of the party to live in your country of origin, were under sixteen years of age, or are no longer affiliated with the party, the judge may decide in your favor. Membership in any organization that promotes a dictatorship in the United States or violence against the American government will hurt your chances for naturalization.

However, "good moral character" is a somewhat ambiguous term. Supreme Court rulings on the subject of good moral character state that a person must behave within the standards for the acceptable conduct of an average citizen of that community. Also, if you are worried that something in your history may raise questions about your loyalty to the principles of the Constitution, a 1943 Supreme Court ruling stipulates that an alien cannot be denied citizenship if he or she "advocated peaceful and constitutional change."

4. Understand English

To become a citizen, you should have a basic understanding of written and spoken English. The English requirement scares some people, but the test the examiner will give you is really very simple. The examiner will ask you questions about the naturalization application you completed and about United States government and history. Your answers will give the examiner a sense of your knowledge of spoken English. If you familiarize yourself with all the information on the forms you filled out, you should have no trouble convincing the examiner of your ability to speak English. You will also be asked to read and write some simple sentences in English. If you have doubts about your ability, you might want to enroll in a class. However, if you can read this book

U. S. Department of Justice
Immigration and Naturalization Service

**APPLICATION FOR ISSUANCE
OF PERMIT TO REENTER THE
UNITED STATES**

(PLEASE TEAR OFF THIS SHEET BEFORE
SUBMITTING APPLICATION)

INSTRUCTIONS
READ INSTRUCTIONS CAREFULLY. FEE WILL NOT BE REFUNDED.

Form I-151 or I-551 (Alien Registration Receipt Card) may be presented instead of a reentry permit at time of application for reentry into the United States, after an absence of not more than 1 year. That 1-year time limitation is not applicable to the spouse or child of a member of the Armed Forces of the United States or of a civilian employee of the United States Government stationed abroad pursuant to official orders, if the spouse or child presents Form I-151 or I-551, did not relinquish lawful permanent residence, and is preceding or accompanying the member or employee, or is following to join the member or employee in the United States within 4 months of the return of the member or employee. If you nevertheless prefer to receive a reentry permit, submit the attached application, Form I-131, in accordance with the instructions in the numbered paragraphs below.

EFFECT, UNDER IMMIGRATION LAWS, OF PERMIT TO RE-ENTER

A reentry permit shall have no effect under the immigration laws, except to show that the alien is returning from a temporary visit abroad; nor shall it be construed to be the exclusive means of establishing that the alien is so returning. The possession of an unexpired reentry permit relieves the alien to whom it is issued from the necessity of securing a visa from an American consul before returning to this country. It does not, however, relieve the person to whom the permit is issued from meeting all other requirements of the immigration laws. Persons who have been convicted of or admit having committed crimes involving moral turpitude either before or after entering the United States, other criminal, immoral, insane, mentally or physically defective aliens, those afflicted with a dangerous contagious disease, and others found to be inadmissable under the Immigration and Nationality Act are subject to exclusion if attempting to re-enter, notwithstanding they may be in possession of reentry permits.

EFFECT OF ABSENCE FROM UNITED STATES UPON NATURALIZATION ELIGIBILITY

A reentry permit does not relieve the person to whom issued from meeting the requirements of the naturalization laws. Notwithstanding the possession of a reentry permit, absence from the United States by an applicant for naturalization for a continuous period of 1 year or more during the period for which continuous residence in the United States is required for admission to citizenship will break the continuity of such residence, except where, prior thereto, the Attorney General has approved an absence in the employment of, or under contract with, the United States Government or an American institution of research recognized as such by the Attorney General, or in the employment of an American firm or corporation engaged in whole or in part in the development of foreign trade and commerce of the United States or a subsidiary thereof, more than 50 percent of whose stock is owned by an American firm or corporation, or in the employment of a public international organization of which the United States is a member by treaty or statute and by which the alien was not employed until after being lawfully admitted for permanent residence. In order to qualify for such approval the applicant must have been physically present and residing in the United States, after being lawfully admitted for permanent residence, for an uninterrupted period of at least one year. The granting of such approval does not exempt the applicant from the requirement that he/she be physically present in the United States for at least one-half of the period of residence required for naturalization except in the case of those persons who are employed by, or under contract with, the Government of the United States, those persons who are authorized to perform the ministerial or priestly functions of a religious denomination having a bona fide organization within the United States, and those persons who are engaged solely by a religious denomination or by an interdenominational mission organization having a bona fide organization within the United States as a missionary, brother, nun, or sister. Such approval should be applied for on Form N-470. "Application to Preserve Residence for Naturalization Purposes (under section 316(b) or 317, Immigration and Nationality Act)," available at any office of the Immigration and Naturalization Service. Aliens who are absent in connection with or for the purpose of performing the ministerial or priestly functions of a religious denomination having a bona fide organization in the United States, or who are engaged by such a denomination or an interdenominational mission organization having a bona fide organization within the United States, as a missionary, brother, nun, or sister are also eligible to make such application.

EFFECT OF CLAIM TO NONRESIDENT ALIEN STATUS FOR FEDERAL INCOME TAX PURPOSES

An alien who has actually established residence in the United States after having been admitted as an immigrant or after having adjusted status to that of an immigrant, and who is considering the filing of a nonresident alien tax return or the non-filing of a tax return on the ground that he/she is a nonresident alien, should consider carefully the consequences under the immigration and naturalization laws if he/she does so.

If an alien takes such action, he/she may be regarded as having abandoned residence in the United States and as having lost immigrant status under the immigration and naturalization laws. As a consequence he/she may be ineligible for a visa or other document for which lawful permanent resident aliens are eligible; he/she may be inadmissible to the United States if he/she seeks admission as a returning resident; and he/she may become ineligible for naturalization on the basis of his/her original entry or adjustment as an immigrant.

TREATY MERCHANTS

If you were lawfully admitted to the United States as a treaty merchant pursuant to section 3 (6) of the Immigration Act of 1924, between July 1, 1924 and July 5, 1932, both dates inclusive, and you intend to depart temporarily from the United States you should so inform the Immigration and Naturalization Service office having jurisdiction over your place of residence. You should then await the instructions of that office before submitting the application.

PENALTIES

Severe penalties are provided by law for knowingly and willfully falsifying or concealing a material fact or using any false document in the submission of this application or for knowingly forging, counterfeiting, altering, or otherwise misusing this permit.

(over)

1. Who May Apply - Any alien lawfully admitted to the United States for permanent residence who intends to depart temporarily from the United States, may apply under section 223 of the Immigration and Nationality Act for issuance of a permit to reenter the United States. A reentry permit will cover only one applicant. A reentry permit will not be issued to an alien who is in possession of a Refugee Travel Document previously issued unless such document is surrendered with this application.

2. Submission of Application - The application for issuance of a reentry permit must be submitted while you are in the United States, and should be submitted to the Immigration and Naturalization Service office having jurisdiction over your place of residence at least 30 days before the proposed date of your departure. A separate application must be submitted by each alien regardless of age. A parent, guardian or other person having a legitimate interest in a person under the age of 14, and a guardian of a mentally incompetent person may apply on behalf of such person. The first page of this application must be submitted to the Immigration and Naturalization Service in duplicate. The duplicate copy of the first page will be forwarded by this Service to the Social Security Administration for its information.

In answering item "COUNTRY OF CLAIMED NATIONALITY," fill in the country which you believe recognizes you as a national or citizen thereof. If you believe that no country recognizes you as a national or citizen, fill in "Stateless". The nationality you claim in your application will be shown on any permit to reenter issued to you; however, this does not indicate that the Immigration and Naturalization Service has determined that you are of the nationality claimed. If you desire any change to be made in your reentry permit after issuance with respect to nationality or any other information furnished in your application, a new application and fee, together with any relevant supporting evidence, will be required.

3. Alien Registration Receipt Card - You must attach to this application your Alien Registration Receipt Card (Form I-151, I-551, AR-3, or AR-103). If such card is not Form I-151 or I-551 and you are a lawful permanent resident of the United States, you may apply on Form I-90 without additional fee but with two additional photographs for the issuance of new Alien Registration Receipt Card on Form I-551. If your Alien Registration Receipt Card is lost or destroyed, you must execute and attach an application for such card on Form I-90 with fee in accordance with instructions on that form. Your Alien Registration Receipt Card or a replacement will be returned to you.

4. Other Documentary Evidence - If your name has been changed by marriage or by order of any court of competent jurisdiction, and you have never previously been issued a reentry permit or an Alien Registration Receipt Card (Form I-151 or I-551) in your changed name, you must attach to this application a certified copy of the public record of your marriage or of the decree of the court changing your name. If you live in a state where under such court decree further acts were required of you before the decree became final, you must also attach a certificate stating that you have complied with the conditions of the decree changing your name. Such documents must be submitted in the original. If you desire to have the original returned to you, you may also submit photostatic or typewritten copies. Photostatic copies unaccompanied by the original may be accepted if the copy bears a certification by an immigration or consular officer that the copy was compared with the original and found to be identical. Any document in a foreign language must be accompanied by a translation in English. The translators must certify that he/she is competent to translate and that the translation is accurate.

5. Photographs - Submit two color photographs of yourself taken within 30 days of the date of this application. These photos must have a white background, photos must be glossy, un-retouched, and not mounted; dimension of the facial image should be about 1 inch from chin to top of hair; subject should be shown in 3/4 frontal view showing right side of face with right ear visible; using pencil or felt pen, lightly print name (and alien Registration Receipt Number, if known) on back of each photograph. Failure to comply with the above instructions will delay the processing of your application.

6. Fee. - A fee of forty-five dollars ($45) must be paid for filing this application. It cannot be refunded regardless of the action taken on the application. DO NOT MAIL CASH. ALL FEES MUST BE SUBMITTED IN THE EXACT AMOUNT. Payment by check or money order must be drawn on a bank or other institution located in the United States and be payable in United States currency. If applicant resides in Guam, check or money order must be payable to the "Treasurer, Guam." If applicant resides in the Virgin Islands, check or money order must be payable to the "Commissioner of Finance of the Virgin Islands." All other applicants must make the check or money order payable to the "Immigration and Naturalization Service." When check is drawn on account of a person other than the applicant, the name of the applicant must be entered on the face of the check. If application is submitted from outside the United States, remittance may be made by bank international money order or foreign draft drawn on a financial institution in the United States and payable to the Immigration and Naturalization Service in United States currency. Personal checks are accepted subject to collectibility. An uncollectible check will render the application and any document issued pursuant thereto invalid. A charge of $5.00 will be imposed if a check in payment of a fee is not honored by the bank on which it is drawn.

7. Delivery of Permit - When reentry permit is issued, it will be mailed to the applicant at the address in the United States as shown on the application form, unless the applicant requests that it be mailed to a different address in the United States, or unless the applicant requests delivery abroad through a United States Embassy or Consular Post or through a U.S. Immigration and Naturalization Service Office outside the U.S. If an applicant for issuance of a reentry permit finds it absolutely necessary to depart from the U.S. before securing the permit, an Immigration and Naturalization Service officer should be consulted before leaving the United States.

8. Foreign Visas - The reentry permit contains pages on which consular officers of foreign countries may affix visas for entry into those countries. It is advisable for you to check with the consular representatives of foreign countries which you intend to visit concerning the visa requirements (if any) of those countries before traveling to them.

9. Authority - The authority to prescribe this form is contained in 8 U.S.C. 1203(a). Submission of the information requested on this form is voluntary. The solicited information will be used principally by the Service to determine whether the applicant will be eligible for issuance or extension of a permit to reenter the United States under the provisions of section 223 of the Immigration and Nationality Act, 8 U.S.C. 1203. It will be furnished also to the Social Security Administration. The information may also as a matter of routine use be disclosed to other federal, state, local, and foreign law enforcement and regulatory agencies, the Department of Defense including any component thereof (if the applicant has served, or is serving in the Armed Forces of the United States), the Department of State, Central Intelligence Agency, Interpol, and individuals and organizations, during the course of investigation to elicit further information required by this Service to carry out its functions. Failure to provide any or all of the solicited information may result in the denial of the application for issuance of a permit to reenter the United States; however, failure to provide the applicant's social security number will have no consequences, as the disclosure of such number is voluntary.

U.S. Department of Justice
Immigration and Naturalization Service

OMB No. 1115-0005
Approved expires 6/86

APPLICATION FOR ISSUANCE
OF PERMIT TO REENTER THE UNITED STATES
as provided in section 223 of the
Immigration and Nationality Act

Use typewriter or print in block letters with ball-point pen.

FEE STAMP

1. YOUR NAME	FAMILY NAME *(Capital Letters)* FIRST MIDDLE	
IN CARE OF	C/O	
MAILING ADDRESS IN U.S.	(No. and Street) (Apt. No.)	ALIEN REGISTRATION NUMBER
	(City) (State) (ZIP Code)	A-

2. DATE OF BIRTH *(Month, Day, Year)*	COUNTRY OF BIRTH	COUNTRY OF CLAIMED NATIONALITY	COLOR OF EYES	COLOR OF HAIR

HEIGHT _____ FEET _____ INCHES | VISIBLE MARKS AND SCARS

3. FILL IN THE ITEMS IN THIS BLOCK AS TO *first* ARRIVAL IN UNITED STATES FOR PERMANENT RESIDENCE OR ADJUSTMENT TO PERMANENT RESIDENT STATUS

NAME UNDER WHICH ADMITTED OR ADJUSTED	PORT OF ARRIVAL OR LOCATION OF IMMIGRATION OFFICE WHICH GRANTED ADJUSTMENT	DATE OF ARRIVAL OR DATE AS OF WHICH ADJUSTMENT OF STATUS WAS GRANTED

FILL IN REMAINING ITEMS IN THIS BLOCK ONLY IF YOU DID NOT ACQUIRE PERMANENT RESIDENCE THROUGH ADJUSTMENT.

MANNER OF FIRST ARRIVAL IN UNITED STATES FOR PERMANENT RESIDENCE *(Name of Vessel, Airline, etc.)*

FATHER'S NAME AT TIME OF YOUR ARRIVAL	MOTHER'S MAIDEN NAME

4. FILL IN THE ITEMS IN THIS BLOCK AS TO *LAST* ARRIVAL IN U.S. *(Exclude any re-entry after an absence of less than six months in Canada or Mexico.)*

NAME UNDER WHICH ADMITTED	PORT OF ARRIVAL	DATE OF ARRIVAL

NAME OF VESSEL, AIRLINE OR OTHER MEANS OF CONVEYANCE:

5. PORT OF *proposed* DEPARTURE FROM UNITED STATES	DATE OF *proposed* DEPARTURE	LENGTH OF INTENDED ABSENCE ABROAD
NAME OF TRANSPORTATION COMPANY	IF DEPARTURE IS TO BE BY VESSEL, GIVE NAME OF VESSEL	

6. FILL IN ITEM 6 ONLY IF YOU HAVE PREVIOUSLY OBTAINED A PERMIT TO REENTER

ISSUANCE DATE OF LAST PERMIT	LOCATION OF IMMIGRATION AND NATURALIZATION OFFICE ISSUING LAST PERMIT *(City and State)*	MY LAST PERMIT ☐ IS ATTACHED ☐ IS NOT ATTACHED
IF THE PERMIT IS NOT ATTACHED, STATE REASON:		IF PERMIT IS ATTACHED, STATE EXPIRATION DATE

7. PRESENT OCCUPATION:	NAME and ADDRESS OF EMPLOYER
SOCIAL SECURITY ACCOUNT NUMBER TELEPHONE NUMBER	

8. MAILING ADDRESS ABROAD *(Number and Street)*   *(City/Town)*   *(State/Province/District)*   *(Country)*

9. REASONS FOR GOING ABROAD *(Be concise and complete):*

	RECEIVED	TRANS. IN	RET'D-TRANS. OUT	COMPLETED
FORM 1-131 (REV. 4-1-84)Y **OVER**				

10. I ☐ have ☐ have not engaged in business or employment outside the United States since I became a permanent resident of the United States. (If you have engaged therein, briefly describe and show periods of such employment or business activity.)

11. Since I became a permanent resident of the United States I ☐ have ☐ have not claimed nonresident alien status for Federal income purposes, either by filing no income tax return at all or by filing a return as a nonresident. (If such status was claimed by filing an income tax return as a nonresident alien, state the years for which you filed such a return, your address shown in each such return, and the location (City and State) of the Internal Revenue Service office with which you filed each such return; if you failed to file an income tax return at all because you regarded yourself as a nonresident alien for Federal income tax purposes, state the years for which you did not file a return for that reason.)

12. I ☐ do ☐ do not intend to return to the United States after my temporary visit abroad.

13. I ☐ do ☐ do not intend to retain my status as a lawful permanent resident.

14. CHECK ONE: ☐ My Alien Registration Receipt Card is attached. ☐ Application Form I-90 for issuance of Alien Registration Receipt Card is attached.

15. The Permit to Reenter and my Alien Registration Receipt Card, if I submitted or applied for that card, should be forwarded to:

☐ My address as shown in block # 1, on reverse.

☐ U.S. Embassy or Consulate at _____

☐ U.S. Immigration and Naturalization Office at _____

☐ Other *(Specify)* _____

CERTIFICATION OF APPLICANT

16. The applicant must sign this block.
If application was completed by other than the applicant, that person must execute Item 17.

I certify, under penalty of perjury under the laws of the United States of America that the foregoing is true and correct.

Executed on *(date)* _____ , Signature _____

17. **SIGNATURE OF PERSON PREPARING FORM, IF OTHER THAN APPLICANT**

I declare that this document was prepared by me at the request of the applicant and is based on all information of which I have any knowledge.

(Signature)	(Address)	(Date)

APPLICANT — DO NOT WRITE BELOW THIS LINE

Action with regard to Alien Registration Receipt Card	Action with regard to application for issuance of Permit to Reenter
☐ I-151 or I-551 submitted by alien returned	☐ DENIED *(See denial notice for reason(s),*
☐ AR-103 or AR-3 submitted by alien returned	☐ GRANTED Permit valid to _____
☐ New I-551 issued on basis of I-90	☐ Single entry ☐ Multiple entries

DATE OF ACTION	SERIAL NO. OF PERMIT ISSUED:	DELIVERY OF PERMIT ☐ BY MAIL ☐ TO APPLICANT PERSONALLY	INITIALS OF EMPLOYEE EFFECTING DELIVERY
	OFFICE		DATE
OFFICE			

and answer the sample questions in Chapter Five, you should feel confident of your skills in English.

If you have a physical handicap making you unable to speak, read, or write, or if you are over fifty years old and have lived in the United States for more than twenty years, you may be exempted from the English requirement. (This is sometimes called the "50/20 waiver.") You may answer the questions about history and government in the language you understand and speak.

You should be able to sign your name in English. The 50/20 waiver applies here, too.

5. United States History and Government

During the examination, you will demonstrate your knowledge of some aspects of United States history and Government. This includes the principles of the Constitution and the Bill of Rights and important events in American history. Chapter Five describes the important concepts you should know, as well as sample questions that you may be asked. The government also offers two textbooks to help you prepare for this portion of the examination. Titled *U.S. Government Structure* and *United States History: 1600–1987*, the books are published at two reading levels. Use the code numbers M-291 and M-289 respectively to order the easiest reading level, Level 1, and the codes M-290 and M-288 for the Level 2 books. You can buy them from the Superintendent of Documents, United States Government Printing Office, Washington, D.C. 20402.

Be prepared, too, to describe the steps a person needs to take to become a naturalized citizen and the rights and responsibilities of citizens as they are outlined in this book and in the government pamphlet, "Citizenship Education and Naturalization Information" (M-287).

6. The Oath of Allegiance

When you have successfully completed the application and examination for naturalization, you must be prepared to take an oath of allegiance to the United States. By taking this oath, you renounce all ties to your country of origin and pledge your support to the United States. You promise to support and defend the Constitution and the laws of the United States. The oath reads:

I hereby declare, on oath, that I absolutely and entirely renounce and abjure all allegiance and fidelity to any foreign prince, potentate, state, or sovereignty of whom or which I have heretofore been a subject or citizen; that I will support and defend the Constitution and laws of the United States of America against all enemies, foreign and domestic; that I will bear true faith and allegiance to the same; that I will bear arms on behalf of the United States when required by law; that I will perform noncombatant service in the Armed Forces of the United States when required by the law; that I will perform work of national importance under civilian direction when required by the law; and that I take this obligation freely without any mental reservation or purpose of evasion; so help me God. In acknowledgment whereof I have hereunto affixed my signature.

Sometimes you can take the oath without saying, "I will bear arms on behalf of the United States when required by law; that I will perform noncombatant service in the Armed Forces of the United States when required by the law...." Check with your lawyer or the INS if you feel strongly about not taking this part of the oath.

If you think you will be able to fulfill all of the requirements for becoming a citizen, you first need to apply to become a permanent resident alien of the United States.

CHAPTER THREE

Becoming a Permanent Resident

KEY TERMS

Green Card
preconceived intent
preference alien
special immigrant

sham marriage
petitioner
beneficiary
good cause

labor certification
precertified
refugee
asylee

You need to establish permanent residency before you can become naturalized. As we saw in Chapter Two, aliens can enter the United States either with temporary or permanent residency (immigrant) visas. However, if you came to the United States on a temporary visa, you must now apply for an immigrant visa. Most people apply for an immigrant visa (which means they can live and work in the United States) through the consulate or embassy in their country of origin. When you apply for permanent resident status, you are applying for the Alien Registration Receipt Card, commonly known as the **Green Card.** This shows that you can work in the United States.

This chapter explains the requirements for each of the Preference System categories, and shows which forms to file and how to become a permanent resident alien. As you read, you can begin to plan your strategy. Can you file under more than one classification? What classification for which you best qualify will have available visa numbers from your country? Through it all, keep the ultimate goal—citizenship—in mind. Short cuts may cause you more trouble in the long run. Follow the strategy that best fits your background. While this may mean you'll have to wait a bit longer, the wait will be worth it if it means you achieve your goal.

Filling Out the Forms

At the end of the description of each Preference System classification in this chapter, you will find instructions for filling out the necessary forms. A few general guidelines that apply to all forms will save you time and headaches. The instructions for filling out forms in this book will explain what the INS wants to know in each case. Use them as a guideline. Check the form you receive from the INS to be sure you follow their directions carefully. While forms do not change often, it is a good idea to double-check the actual form you receive. For example, the filing fee may have changed since the publication of this book. (The fees are always nonrefundable.)

Some of the suggestions here may seem quite obvious. Even so, you can't be too careful when your success depends in part on filling out the forms accurately. For example, read the directions on each form from start to finish before you begin.

Type or print legibly in ink on all forms. More than one official will have to look over your file. You can make their job easier by completing the forms so they are easy to read. When supporting documents are required, be sure to make as many copies as the form calls for. *Always make and keep a copy of everything for yourself.* If the INS should lose any part of your file, you'll have the completed form on hand.

Any supporting documents you submit in a language other than English must be translated. You must submit original copies of important documents like birth and marriage certificates, and certificates of naturalization. If you are worried about losing these documents, copies may be certified by a consular officer or an attorney certified to practice in the United States.

The INS may also accept a copy certified by an INS-certified representative. Submit certified copies or originals of any documents (with the translation) with the form. If you submit copies, be sure to bring the original documents with you to the interview.

Follow all instructions carefully and answer only the question that is asked. Sometimes unnecessary additional information will draw attention to your application and slow down the process. Answer all questions on the form. If a question does not apply to you, write "N/A" in the space provided. If you run out of space, write the rest of your answer on a separate sheet of paper and attach it to the form. Clearly label the attached sheet with your name, the date, the form number, and the item number. Be sure to sign any attached sheets.

The instructions on each form will tell you how much it costs to file and where you should file. Unless the directions specifically tell you to file at a regional processing center or consulate abroad, file the form at the INS office that has jurisdiction where you live. To be safe, call the INS before sending them the form to find out where you should file. It's best to deliver the form yourself, but if you must mail it, send it certified mail with a return receipt requested, so you have a record that the INS received it. For most forms you file, you should have lived in the area (or jurisdiction) of that particular INS office for at least six months.

Your filing fee will not be returned to you if your application is denied. Do not send cash. Make checks or money orders payable to the Immigration and Naturalization Service for the exact amount due. If you live in Guam, make the check to the Treasurer, Guam. In the United States Virgin Islands, make checks to the Commissioner of Finance of the Virgin Islands.

All the forms you will need to fill out in the process of getting permanent residency status and becoming naturalized can be obtained free from the INS.

Review your answers on the forms before any interview. You should be familiar with every answer.

Some of the procedures outlined in this chapter for applying for permanent residence status can be quite complicated. If you get help from an immigration lawyer or someone else qualified in immigration, he or she should file Notice of Appearance of Attorney or Representative (Form G-28). Anyone who officially helps you fill out the forms should sign the form with you and file Form G-28.

The Green Card: Your Rights and Responsibilities as a Permanent Resident Alien

When you apply for alien registration or permanent residency, you are applying for a Green Card. About the size of a credit card, a Green Card or Alien Registration Receipt Card, allows an alien to work in the United States and live here permanently. Whether or not you will work in the United States, you must have a Green Card to establish permanent residency. If you pursue an immigrant visa through consular processing (from abroad), your relative or employer in the United States must also have filed a visa petition on your behalf. If you are a visitor in the United States who wants to change their visa (adjustment of status), you will have to file Form I-485, Application for Permanent Residence Status. Aliens al-

ready in the United States also should ask their relatives or employers to file a visa petition on their behalf. These forms are described within each of the sections of this chapter. The sections are arranged by Preference System categories.

The Green Card bears the alien's photograph, fingerprint, and signature. Green Cards issued since 1989 also show the card's expiration date (new cards expire after ten years). Cards issued before 1989 have no expiration date. When the United States first fingerprinted and registered aliens during World War II, the card was in fact green. Over the years, its color has been changed many times. The newest version is off-pink and is designed to deter forgeries of the coveted document.

Whether you're abroad or in the United States, once your application for permanent residency is approved you will receive a temporary stamp in your passport showing you can work in the United States. Later, the INS will send you a permanent Green Card, Form I-551.

Once you become a permanent resident alien, you have most of the rights and all of the same protection guaranteed to United States citizens by the Constitution. Like United States citizens, you must obey the law and you will receive equal protection under the law, as well as the protection of the Fifth and Sixth Amendments in criminal trials. However, because you are not officially a citizen, your rights in large measure are decided by Congress and the court system.

While the card offers many benefits of American citizenship, it carries some responsibilities with it. One responsibility is taxation. If you work in the United States, you will have to file a tax return with the

Internal Revenue Service (IRS) and pay taxes. By law, everyone in the United States must pay taxes based on their income. If you are a permanent resident and earn money in another country, you must pay taxes on that income just as other Americans do.

Detailed tax considerations are beyond the scope of this book, but you should be aware that the IRS considers any alien taxable as an American resident if that person lives in America for more than 180 days per year. As with most tax guidelines, there are many exceptions to this rule. Nonetheless, if you intend to become a United States citizen, check with the IRS or a tax lawyer about when and how much tax you should pay. *You may be required to file tax forms with the IRS from the day you apply for permanent residence.*

As a permanent resident, you may also have to register with the Selective Service. When you register with this agency, you sign up to be drafted to serve in the military. Generally, any male permanent resident alien born during or after 1963 and over the age of eighteen should register. Check with the Selective Service if you think you should register.

Finally, as a Green Card holder, you may not vote, hold elective office, or serve on a jury. And unlike United States citizens, you do not receive any diplomatic protection outside America's borders.

Once you have your Green Card, the law requires that you carry it with you at all times. As the permanent residency requirements stipulate, your card may be taken away from you if you leave the United States for more than one year. You must show that you intend to live in the United States. If you travel across the border many times once you have your permanent residence status, the INS may suspect you do not plan to live here permanently. Your Green Card also may be taken away if the INS suspects you of fraud. This is why you should be careful about your answers on all forms and know the answers to the questions inside out.

Find a lawyer immediately if the INS questions the validity of your card.

Consular Processing or Adjustment of Status?

As we discussed in Chapter Two, there are two routes to obtaining an immigrant visa. If you apply for permanent residence status through the American embassy or consulate in your country of origin, the method is known as consular processing. If you entered the United States on a temporary visa and then applied for permanent residence, the method is known as adjustment of status.

You will fill out a different set of forms depending on which route you take. Those applying through a consulate abroad will file Form 230, and those adjusting their status in the United States will file Form I-485.

In general, consular processing is easier and less expensive than adjustment of status. If you are already in the United States, unless you are the parent, child, or spouse of a United States citizen, you must return to your country of origin to file your petition through an American embassy or consulate. One drawback to consular processing is that, if your application is denied, you do not have the opportunities to appeal the decision that you might have if you seek adjustment of status.

Consular Processing:
What to File from Abroad

An American embassy or consulate designated to issue immigrant visas will give you an application to apply for a permanent residence visa. Remember that once you apply, a visa number must be available before your application will be processed. Then, when the consulate approves your preliminary visa petition and receives any necessary certification from the Department of Labor, the State Department will send documents sometimes known as "Packet Three." These documents include:

- Form OF-169, which describes the forms and supporting documents you should gather for your application;
- Form OF-179, which provides biographical information about you; and
- in some cases Form 222, Preliminary Questionnaire to Determine Immigrant Status.

When you have gathered all of the information required on Form OF-169, sign it and return it to the consulate along with Form OF-179. Do not send the supporting documents you have collected. You should bring these with you to the consulate when you go in for an interview.

After the consulate receives the completed forms OF-169 and OF-179, they will mail you a date for an interview, a list of local doctors to obtain a medical exam, and Form 230, Application for Immigrant Visa and Alien Registration.

The United States requires that you be examined by a government-approved doctor—your family doctor may not qualify. Be sure to schedule your medical appointment well in advance of your interview at the consulate.

When the day of your interview arrives, you should bring your completed Form 230 and the documents you gathered when you completed Form OF-169. These include:

- passport;
- birth certificate;
- police certificates for all members of your family over the age of fourteen, showing your good conduct in every locality where you lived for more than six months over the age of sixteen;
- court and prison records and military records, if applicable;
- photographs;
- marriage certificate;
- results from your medical exam in a sealed envelope from your doctor;
- letter from a prospective employer, if applicable, showing that a job is waiting for you; or
- an affidavit of support, showing that you will not become a public charge.

All members of your family included on your petition should come to the interview.

Usually, your permanent residence visa—in the form of an envelope to present to the immigration officer at the border—will be given to you just after the interview. You and your family must enter the United States no more than four months after receiving the visa. When you do enter the country, the INS will stamp a temporary Green Card in your passport. Two to four months later, you should get your Green Card in the mail. If you do not receive your card, ask a lawyer to check into it, or visit the INS yourself. Green Cards often arrive late, and mistakes in mailing them are not unheard of.

THE FOREIGN SERVICE
OF THE
UNITED STATES OF AMERICA

APPLICANT'S PRIORITY DATE
FOREIGN STATE CHARGEABILITY
Preference Category

Dear Visa Applicant:

1. This letter concerns your interest in immigrating to the United States. The box checked below indicates the basis on which you may proceed with your immigrant visa application.

☐ This office has received an approved petition according you status as an immediate relative of an American citizen.

☐ This office has received an approved petition according you _____ preference status.

☐ This office has received an approved certification from the Department of Labor.

☐ It has been determined that you are exempt from the labor certification requirement.

II. You should now prepare for your appointment to file a formal immigrant visa application by taking the three steps listed in paragraph III. If you have any questions, please communicate with this office.

III. The steps you should take to prepare for your appointment to file your formal immigrant visa application are:

A. FIRST, complete and return immediately to this office the enclosed Optional Form 179 (Formerly DSP-70), Biographic Data for Visa Purposes.

B. SECOND, obtain the following documents. DO NOT SEND THEM TO THIS OFFICE. As you obtain each document, check the box before each item:

☐ 1. Passports.—A passport must be valid for at least six months and it must be endorsed by the issuing authority for travel to the United States. Each child 16 years of age or older, who is included in the parents' passport but whose photograph does not appear in such passport must obtain his own separate passport.

☐ 2. Birth Certificates.—Two certified copies of the birth record of each person named in the application are required, unless birth certificate is being submitted at this time in connection with a separate visa application. This includes all unmarried children under age 21 (if deceased, so state giving year of death) even though they may not wish to immigrate at this time. The certificate must state the date and place of birth and the names of both parents. It must also be indicated on the certificate that it is an extract from the official records. Photostatic copies are acceptable provided the original is offered for inspection by the consular officer.

☐ Unobtainable Birth Certificate.—In rare cases, it may be impossible to obtain a birth certificate because records have been destroyed, or the government will not issue one. In such a case, a baptismal certificate, in duplicate, may be submitted for consideration provided it contains the date and place of the applicant's birth and information concerning parentage and provided the baptism took place shortly after birth. Should a baptismal certificate be unobtainable, a close relative, preferably the applicant's mother, should

50169–105
OPTIONAL FORM 169
DEPT. OF STATE

(Rev. 9–81)

NSN 7540–00–130–8143
Previous Edition Not Usable

prepare a notarized statement in duplicate, stating the place and date of the applicant's birth, the names of both parents and maiden name of the mother. The statement must be executed before an official authorized to administer oaths or affirmations.

☐ 3. Police Certificates.—Each visa applicant aged 16 years or over is required to submit a police certificate, in duplicate. Such certificates must be obtained from the police authorities of each locality, with the exception of places in the United States, where the applicant has resided for six months or more since attaining the age of 16 years. A police certificate must also be obtained from the police authorities of any place where the applicant has been arrested for any reason, regardless of how long he lived there. Such certificates must cover the entire period of the applicant's residence in the area. A certificate issued by local police authorities must be of recent date when presented to the consular officer. The term "police certificate" as used in this paragraph means a certification by the appropriate police authorities stating what their records show concerning the applicant, including any and all arrests, the reasons therefor, and the disposition of each case of which there is a record. NOTE: Based on the applicant's completed OF-179, this office will provide assistance in obtaining certain police certificates, such as those to cover residences in the U.S. or U.K. If specific questions arise, please consult this office.

☐ 4. Court and Prison Records.—Persons who have been convicted of a crime must obtain two certified copies of each court record and of any prison record, regardless of the fact that they may have subsequently benefited from an amnesty, pardon or other act of clemency.

☐ 5. Military Records.—Two certified copies of any military record, if applicable, are required.

☐ 6. Photographs.—Three (3) color photographs with white background on glossy paper, untouched and not mounted. The photograph must be a three-quarter frontal portrait with the right side of the face and right ear visible. The dimension of the facial image must measure at least one inch (25 mm) from chin to top of hair. No head covering or dark glasses should be worn. Color Polaroid photos are acceptable. Photos are required of all applicants, regardless of age.

☐ 7. Evidence of Support.—Any evidence which will show that you and the members of your family, who will accompany you, are not likely to become public charges while in the United States. The enclosed information sheet, Optional Form 167 (Formerly DSL 815), list evidence which may be presented to meet this requirement of the law.

☐ 8. Marriage Certificates.—Married persons are required to present two certified copies of their marriage certificate. Proof of the termination of any previous marriage must also be submitted, in duplicate (e.g., death certificate of spouse; decree of divorce or annulment).

☐ 9. Translations.—All documents not in the official language of the country in which application for a visa is being made, or in English, must be accompanied by certified translations into English. Translations must be in duplicate and certified by a competent translator and sworn to by him before a Notary Public.

C. THIRD, as soon as you have obtained all of the documents listed above which are applicable in your case, carefully read the statement at the bottom of this page, sign it and return this form.

SPECIAL INSTRUCTIONS:

Sincerely,

Vice Consul of the United States of America

Enclosures:

1. Optional Form 179, Biographic Data for Visa Purposes (Formerly DSP-70)
2. Optional Form 167, Evidence Which May Be Presented to Meet Public Charge Provision of the Law (Formerly DSL-845)

APPLICANT'S STATEMENT

I have in my possession and am prepared to present all of the documents listed in items 1 through 9 which apply to my case, as indicated by the check marks I have placed in the appropriate boxes. I fully realize that no advance assurance can be given that a visa will actually be issued to me and I also understand that I should NOT give up my job, dispose of property, nor make any final travel arrangements until a visa is actually issued to me. At such time as it is possible for me to receive an appointment to make formal visa application, I intend to apply. (Check appropriate box)

☐ *1. Alone*   ☐ *2. Together with my spouse*   *3. Together with my spouse and the following minor children: (print first names of each child who will accompany you).*

_____
(Signature)

PLEASE DO NOT SEND ANY DOCUMENTS TO THIS OFFICE UNTIL YOU ARE SPECIFICALLY REQUESTED TO DO SO BY THIS OFFICE.

POST SYMBOL:	BIOGRAPHIC DATA FOR VISA PURPOSES	Form Approved Budget Bureau No. 47-R151.2

INSTRUCTIONS

Complete this form for your entire family (yourself, spouse and unmarried children under 21 years of age).

1. NAME (Family name) (First name) (Middle names)

OTHER NAMES, ALIASES (If married woman, maiden name and surname of any previous spouses)

NAME IN NATIVE LETTERS OR CHARACTERS IF DIFFERENT FROM ABOVE

2. PLACE OF BIRTH (City) (State or province) (Country)   DATE OF BIRTH (Month) (Day) (Year)

SEX ☐ Male ☐ Female   PRESENT NATIONALITY   PAST NATIONALITY

3. NAME OF FATHER   **4. MAIDEN NAME OF MOTHER**

5. FATHER'S BIRTHPLACE (City) (State or province) (Country)   **6. MOTHER'S BIRTHPLACE (City)** (State or province) (Country)

7. NAME OF SPOUSE (Maiden or family name) (First name) (Middle names)

8. SPOUSE'S BIRTHPLACE (City) (State or province) (Country)   **9. SPOUSE'S BIRTHDATE (Month)** (Day) (Year)   **10. WILL SPOUSE IMMIGRATE WITH YOU?** ☐ Yes ☐ No

11. NAME OF SPOUSE'S FATHER   **12. NAME OF SPOUSE'S MOTHER**

13. BIRTHPLACE OF SPOUSE'S FATHER (City) (State or province) (Country)   **14. BIRTHPLACE OF SPOUSE'S MOTHER (City) (State or province)** (Country)

15. LIST UNMARRIED CHILDREN UNDER 21 YEARS, NOT U.S. CITIZENS WHO WILL ACCOMPANY YOU

NAME OF CHILD	PLACE OF BIRTH (City, state or province, country)	BIRTHDATE

16. IF YOU OR YOUR SPOUSE ARE NOW, OR HAVE BEEN, IN THE UNITED STATES, STATE:

	WHERE WAS VISA OBTAINED	WHEN WAS VISA GRANTED (Month, Year)
☐ APPLICANT		
☐ SPOUSE		

CHECK TYPE OF VISA USED FOR SUCH ENTRY:

☐ Immigrant   ☐ Government or international organization official or employee   ☐ Exchange Visitor
☐ Other nonimmigrant   Specify

17. IF YOU OR YOUR SPOUSE PREVIOUSLY LIVED IN THE UNITED STATES, STATE:

DATE ADMITTED	DATE DEPARTED	REASON FOR DISCONTINUING RESIDENCE

50179-101   (Over)   OPTIONAL FORM 179
(FORMERLY DSP-70)
MAY 1975
DEPT. OF STATE

18. LIST BELOW IN DATE ORDER ALL PLACES WHERE YOU, YOUR SPOUSE AND UNMARRIED CHILDREN NAMED ON THE OTHER SIDE HAVE LIVED SINCE REACHING THE AGE OF 16. (It is not necessary to list the places where you have lived less than six months).

FIRST NAME OF FAMILY MEMBER	CITY OR TOWN, PROVINCE, COUNTRY	OCCUPATION	FROM (Month, Year)	TO (Month, Year)

19. MEMBERSHIP OR AFFILIATION IN ORGANIZATIONS IN EACH COUNTRY NAMED IN ITEM 18: CULTURAL, SOCIAL, LABOR OR POLITICAL

ORGANIZATION	FROM	TO

I certify that all information given is complete and correct.

DATE	SIGNATURE AND PRESENT ADDRESS

NOTE: If space above is insufficient to answer any questions properly, the additional information may be printed below or on a separate sheet of paper and attached to this form.

Form Approved
OMB No. 47–R156.3

PRELIMINARY QUESTIONNAIRE TO DETERMINE IMMIGRANT STATUS

TO:

　　THE UNITED STATES CONSUL AT

DO NOT WRITE IN THIS SPACE

Approved _____　Status _____

Priority date _____

　　　　　　　　　　　　　　　　　Consular Officer

INSTRUCTIONS—If a careful reading of Letter OF–168 indicates that you should file this form, please complete it and return it to this office. This form should be typed or printed in legible block letters. When this form is returned to you, please retain it as it must be attached to any future correspondence addressed to this office concerning your desire to immigrate to the United States. **IMPORTANT:** If you are married and (1) your spouse will immigrate with you, (2) your spouse has educational or professional qualifications, and (3) your spouse intends to work in the United States, give the information required by items 17 through 23 for your spouse on a separate sheet of paper. If your spouse does not intend to work, this information need not be given.

1. NAME　　*(Last name)*　　　　　*(First name)*　　　　　*(Middle names)*

2. OTHER NAMES, ALIASES *(If married woman, give maiden name and surnames of any previous spouses)*

3. HOME ADDRESS AND TELEPHONE NUMBER *(House number, street, city, state or province, and country)*

4. PLACE OF BIRTH *(City, state or province, country)*

5. DATE OF BIRTH *(Month, Day, Year)*

6. MARITAL STATUS　　☐ Single　　☐ Married　　☐ Widowed　　☐ Divorced

6a. NAME OF SPOUSE *(If presently married)* *(Maiden or family name)*　　*(First name)*　　*(Middle names)*

7. SPOUSE'S BIRTHPLACE *(City, state or province, and country)*

8. SPOUSE'S BIRTHDATE *(Month, Day, Year)*

9. WILL SPOUSE IMMIGRATE WITH YOU?　☐ Yes　☐ No

10. IS YOUR SPOUSE A UNITED STATES CITIZEN?　☐ Yes　☐ No

11. IS YOUR SPOUSE A LEGALLY ADMITTED PERMANENT RESIDENT OF THE UNITED STATES?　☐ Yes　☐ No

12. WAS YOUR OR YOUR SPOUSE'S FATHER OR MOTHER BORN OR NATURALIZED IN THE USA?　☐ Yes　☐ No

13. IS YOUR FATHER OR MOTHER A PERMANENT RESIDENT OF THE UNITED STATES?　☐ Yes　☐ No

14. DO YOU OR YOUR SPOUSE HAVE A BROTHER OR SISTER WHO IS A UNITED STATES CITIZEN?　☐ Yes　Age_____　☐ No

15. DO YOU AND/OR YOUR SPOUSE HAVE A SON OR DAUGHTER WHO WAS BORN OR NATURALIZED IN THE U.S.?　☐ Yes　Age_____　☐ No

16. DO YOU AND/OR YOUR SPOUSE HAVE A SON OR DAUGHTER WHO IS A PERMANENT RESIDENT OF THE UNITED STATES?　☐ Yes　☐ No

16a. IF YOU OR YOUR SPOUSE ARE NOW, OR HAVE BEEN, IN THE UNITED STATES, STATE:

	WHERE WAS VISA OBTAINED?	WHEN WAS VISA GRANTED? *(Month, Year)*
☐ APPLICANT		
☐ SPOUSE		

CHECK TYPE OF VISA USED FOR SUCH ENTRY:

☐ Immigrant　　☐ Government or international organization official or employee　　☐ Exchange Visitor

☐ Other nonimmigrant　　Specify

16b. IF YOU OR YOUR SPOUSE PREVIOUSLY LIVED IN THE UNITED STATES, STATE:

DATE ADMITTED	DATE DEPARTED	REASON FOR DISCONTINUING RESIDENCE

17. PLEASE DESCRIBE THE TYPE OF UNIVERSITY OR COLLEGE DEGREE YOU POSSESS, IF ANY, OR YOUR HIGHEST LEVEL OF ACADEMIC OR VOCATIONAL TRAINING

18. WHAT IS YOUR PRESENT PROFESSION OR OCCUPATION?

19. PLEASE DESCRIBE SPECIFICALLY THE TYPE OF WORK YOU DO IN YOUR PROFESSION OR OCCUPATION

20. ARE YOU SELF-EMPLOYED?	**21.** GIVE NAME AND ADDRESS OF PRESENT EMPLOYER, IF ANY
☐ Yes ☐ No	

22. WHAT IS YOUR PURPOSE IN GOING TO THE UNITED STATES?

23. IF YOU INTEND TO BE GAINFULLY EMPLOYED IN THE UNITED STATES, WHAT IS YOUR INTENDED PROFESSION OR OCCUPATION?

24. IF YOU DO NOT INTEND TO BE GAINFULLY EMPLOYED IN THE UNITED STATES, EXPLAIN BELOW HOW YOUR LIVING EXPENSES WILL BE MET:

THIS SPACE FOR OFFICE USE ONLY

FORM APPROVED
O.M.B. No. 1405-0015

OPTIONAL FORM 230 (English) (Rev. 6-82)
DEPT. OF STATE
50230—105

APPLICATION FOR IMMIGRANT VISA AND ALIEN REGISTRATION

INSTRUCTIONS: This form must be filled out in ~~DUPLICATE~~ by typewriter, or if by hand in legible block letters. All questions must be answered, if applicable. Questions which are not applicable should be so marked. *If there is insufficient room on the form, answer on separate sheets, in duplicate, using the same numbers as appear on the form.* Attach the sheets to the forms. DO NOT SIGN this form until instructed to do so by the consular officer. The fee for filing this application for an immigrant visa is $25.00. The fee should be paid in United States dollars or local currency equivalent or by bank draft, when you appear before the consular officer.

WARNING: Any false statement or concealment of a material fact may result in your permanent exclusion from the United States. Even though you should be admitted to the United States, a fraudulent entry could be grounds for your prosecution and/or deportation.

1. Family name	First name	Middle name

2. Other names used or by which known *(If married woman, give maiden name)*

3. Full name in native alphabet *(If Roman letters not used)*

4. Date of birth *(Day)* *(Month)* *(Year)*	5. Age	6. Place of birth *(City or town)* *(Province)* *(Country)*

7. Nationality	8. Sex ☐ Male ☐ Female	9. Marital status ☐ Single *(never married)* ☐ Married ☐ Widowed ☐ Divorced ☐ Separated Including my present marriage, I have been married .... times.

10. Occupation	11. Present address

12. Name, address, date and place of birth of wife/husband *(Give maiden name of wife)*

Date and place of marriage

13. Names, addresses, dates and places of birth of all children

SAMPLE ONLY

14. Person(s) named in **12** and **13** who will accompany or follow me to the United States	15. Final address in the United States
16. Person you intend to join *(Give name, address, and relationship, if any)*	17. Name and address of sponsoring person or organization *(If different from 16)*

18. Personal description (a) Color of hair (c) Height .... feet .... inches	19. Marks of identification
(b) Color of eyes (d) Complexion	20. Purpose in going to the United States

21. Length of intended stay *(If permanently, so state)*	22. Intended port of entry	23. Do you have a ticket to final destination?

THIS FORM MAY BE OBTAINED GRATIS AT CONSULAR OFFICES OF THE UNITED STATES OF AMERICA

NSN 7540-00-149-0919

Previous edition not usable

OPTIONAL FORM 230 (English) (Rev. 6-82)
Page 2

24. Personal financial resources
    (a) Cash ....
    (c) Real estate (value) ....
    (b) Bank deposits ....
    (d) Other (describe) ....

25. Father's name, address, date and place of birth *(If deceased, so state giving year of death)*

26. Mother's maiden name, address, date and place of birth *(If deceased, so state giving year of death)*

27. Name, address, and relationship of next of kin in home country *(If neither parent is living)*

28. List all places of residence for 6 months or more since your 16th birthday

City or town	Province	Country	Dates (From-To)	Calling or occupation

29. List all organizations you are now or have been a member of or affiliated with since your 16th birthday *(Include professional, vocational, social, and political organizations)*

Name and address	Dates (From-To)	Type of membership and office held, if any

30. List all languages, including your own, that you can speak, read, and write

Language	Speak	Read	Write

31. Inclusive dates of previous residence in or visits to the United States *(Give type of visa or status) (If never, so state)*

32. Have you ever been treated in a hospital, institution, or elsewhere for a mental disorder, drug addiction, or alcoholism? *(If answer is Yes, explain)*   Yes ☐ No ☐

33. Have you ever been arrested, convicted, or confined in a prison, or have you ever been placed in a poorhouse or other charitable institution? *(If answer is Yes, explain)*   Yes ☐ No ☐

34. Have you ever been the beneficiary of a pardon, amnesty, rehabilitation decree, other act of clemency, or similar action? *(If answer is Yes, explain)*   Yes ☐ No ☐

35. Have you ever applied for a visa to enter the United States? *(If answer is Yes, state where and when, whether you applied for a nonimmigrant or an immigrant visa, and whether the visa was issued or refused)*   Yes ☐ No ☐

36. Have you been refused admission to the United States during the last 12 months? *(If answer is Yes, explain)*   Yes ☐ No ☐

37. Have you ever registered with a draft board under United States Selective Service Laws? *(If answer is Yes, explain)*   Yes ☐ No ☐

38. Have you ever applied for relief from training and service in the United States Armed Forces or departed from or remained outside the United States to avoid or evade military service? *(If answer is Yes, explain)*   Yes ☐ No ☐

39. Do you intend to enter the United States from Canada, Mexico, or an island adjacent to the United States within 2 years after arrival in Canada, Mexico, or such adjacent island? *(If answer is Yes, give the name of the transportation company by which you entered or intend to enter Canada, Mexico, or such island)*   Yes ☐ No ☐

OPTIONAL FORM 230 (English) (Rev. 6-82)   Page 3

40. United States laws governing the issuance of visas require each applicant to state whether or not he or she is a member of any class of individuals excluded from admission into the United States. The excludable classes are described below. You should read carefully the following paragraphs; your understanding of their content and the answers you give the questions that follow will assist the consular officer to reach a decision on your eligibility to receive a visa.

EXCEPT AS OTHERWISE PROVIDED BY LAW, ALIENS WITHIN ANY OF THE
FOLLOWING CLASSES ARE INELIGIBLE TO RECEIVE AN IMMIGRANT VISA:

(a) Aliens who are mentally retarded, insane, or who have suffered one or more attacks of insanity; aliens afflicted with psychopathic personality, sexual deviation, a mental defect, narcotic drug addiction, chronic alcoholism, or any dangerous contagious disease; aliens who have a physical defect, disease, or disability affecting their ability to earn a living; aliens who are paupers, professional beggars, or vagrants; aliens convicted of a crime involving moral turpitude or who admit committing the essential elements of such a crime, or who have been sentenced to confinement for at least 5 years in the aggregate for conviction of two or more crimes; aliens who are polygamists, or who practice or advocate polygamy; aliens who are prostitutes, or who have engaged in, benefited financially from, procured, or imported persons for the purpose of prostitution, or who seek entry to the United States to engage in prostitution or other commercialized vice, or any immoral sexual act; aliens who seek entry to perform skilled or unskilled labor and who have not been certified by the Secretary of Labor; and aliens likely to become a public charge in the United States.

Do any of the foregoing classes apply to you?   Yes ☐   No ☐   *(If answer is Yes, explain)*

(b) Aliens who seek re-entry within 1 year of their exclusion from the United States, or who, within the past 5 years, have been arrested and deported from the United States, or removed at Government expense in lieu of deportation, or removed as an alien in distress or as an alien enemy; aliens who procure or attempt to procure a visa or other documentation by fraud or willful misrepresentation; aliens who are not eligible to acquire United States citizenship, or who have departed from or remained outside the United States to avoid United States military service in time of war or national emergency; aliens who have been convicted for violating or for conspiring to violate certain laws or regulations relating to narcotic drugs or marihuana, or who are known or believed to be, or to have been, an illicit trafficker in narcotic drugs or marihuana; aliens seeking entry from foreign contiguous territory or adjacent islands within 2 years of their arrival therein on a non-signatory carrier; aliens who are unable to read and understand some language or dialect; aliens who, knowingly and for gain, have encouraged or assisted any other alien to enter, or attempt to enter, the United States in violation of law; aliens who are former exchange visitors who have not fulfilled the 2-year foreign residence requirement; and aliens who are graduates of foreign medical schools destined to the United States to perform medical services are ineligible for a visa unless they have passed parts I and II of the NBME Exam or an equivalent exam as determined by the Department of Health and Human Services.

Do any of the foregoing classes apply to you?   Yes ☐   No ☐   *(If answer is Yes, explain)*

(c) Aliens who are, or at any time have been, anarchists, or members of or affiliated with any Communist or other totalitarian party, including any subdivision or affiliate thereof; aliens who advocate or teach, or who have advocated or taught, either by personal utterance, or by means of any written or printed matter, or through affiliation with an organization, (1) opposition to organized government, (2) the overthrow of government by force and violence, (3) the assaulting or killing of government officials because of their official character, (4) the unlawful destruction of property, (5) sabotage, or (6) the doctrines of world communism, or the establishment of a totalitarian dictatorship in the United States; aliens who seek to enter the United States to engage in prejudicial activities or unlawful activities of a subversive nature.

Do any of the foregoing classes apply to you?   Yes ☐   No ☐   *(If answer is Yes, explain)*

(d) Aliens who during the period beginning on March 23, 1933, and ending on May 8, 1945, under the control, direct or indirect, of the Nazi Government of Germany or of the government of any area occupied by, or allied with, the Nazi Government of Germany, ordered, incited, assisted, or otherwise participated in the persecution of any person because of race, religion, national origin, or political opinion.

Does the foregoing class apply to you?   Yes ☐   No ☐   *(If answer is Yes, explain)*

41. Were you assisted in completing this application? *(If answer is Yes, give name and address of person assisting you*   Yes ☐   No ☐
indicating whether relative, friend, travel agent, attorney, or other)

Name   *Address*   *Relationship*

OPTIONAL FORM 230 (English) (Rev. 6-82)

Page 4

42. The following documents are submitted in support of this application:

- ☐ Passport
- ☐ Birth certificate
- ☐ Police certificate(s)
- ☐ Marriage certificate
- ☐ Death certificate
- ☐ Divorce decree
- ☐ Military record

- ☐ Evidence of own assets
- ☐ Affidavit of support
- ☐ Offer of employment
- ☐ Medical record(s)
- ☐ Photographs
- ☐ Other (describe)
- ☐ Birth certificate of spouse

☐ Birth certificates of unmarried children under age 21 who will not be immigrating at this time *(List those for whom birth certificates are not available or whose birth certificates are being submitted at this time in connection with a visa application.)*

DO NOT WRITE BELOW THE FOLLOWING LINE
The consular officer will assist you in answering parts 43 and 44

---

43. I claim to be exempt from ineligibility to receive a visa and exclusion under item.............. in part 40 for the following reasons:

212(a)(14)
- ☐ Not applicable
- ☐ Attached

Beneficiary of Waiver under
- ☐ 212(a)(28)(I)(i)
- ☐ 212(a)(28)(I)(ii)
- ☐ 212(b)(1)
- ☐ 212(b)(2)

- ☐ 212(e)
- ☐ 212(g)
- ☐ 212(h)
- ☐ 212(i)

44. I claim to be a

- ☐ .... preference immigrant subject to the numerical limitation for ....
  (Foreign state or dependent area)
- ☐ Special immigrant not subject to limitation
- ☐ Immediate relative of a United States citizen

My claim is based on the following facts:

- ☐ I am (my .... is) the beneficiary of a .... petition.
- ☐ I am a returning resident alien.
- ☐ I derive foreign state chargeability under Section 202(b) through my ....
- ☐ Other (specify)

I understand that I am required to surrender my visa to the United States Immigration Officer at the place where I apply to enter the United States, and that the possession of a visa does not entitle me to enter the United States if at that time I am found to be inadmissible under the immigration laws.

I understand that any willfully false or misleading statement or willful concealment of a material fact made by me herein may subject me to permanent exclusion from the United States and, if I am admitted to the United States, may subject me to criminal prosecution and/or deportation.

I, the undersigned applicant for a United States immigrant visa, do solemnly swear (or affirm) that all statements which appear in this application have been made by me, including the answers to parts 32 through 41 inclusive, and are true and complete to the best of my knowledge and belief. I do further swear (or affirm) that, if admitted into the United States, I will not engage in activities which would be prejudicial to the public interest, or endanger the welfare, safety, or security of the United States; in activities which would be prohibited by the laws of the United States relating to espionage, sabotage, public disorder, or in other activities subversive to the national security; in any activity a purpose of which is the opposition to, or the control, or overthrow of, the Government of the United States, by force, violence, or other unconstitutional means.

I understand all the foregoing statements, having asked for and obtained an explanation on every point which was not clear to me.

(Signature of Applicant)

The relationships claimed in items 12 and 13 verified by documentation submitted to consular officer except as noted:

Subscribed and sworn to before me this ....day of........................... , 19.......... at...........................

(Consular Officer)

TARIFF ITEM NO. 20

Adjustment of Status: What to File in the United States

Those who seek permanent residence through adjustment of status must file the appropriate forms once they have legally entered the United States. With few exceptions, if you have worked illegally in the United States or entered the country illegally, you cannot file for permanent resident status. Also, some kinds of temporary visas may make you ineligible to apply for permanent residence (see Nonimmigrant Visa Classifications in Chapter Two). Remember, a visa number in your preference category must be current when you file the forms for adjustment of status. In most cases, visa numbers will not be available.

Even so, adjustment of status gives you the advantage of being in the United States while you wait for your Green Card. Yet the process is lengthy and full of stumbling blocks. For example, if you apply for adjustment of status too soon after you arrive in the United States on a temporary visa, the INS may accuse you of **preconceived intent**, which means you made false, or fraudulent, statements about your plans for visiting the United States when you crossed the border. Making fraudulent statements to the INS may get you deported. Those who seek to adjust their status by marrying a United States citizen solely to gain citizenship with no intention to enter into a real marriage relationship also risk being deported and forfeiting any possibility of returning to America.

However, if your temporary visa allows you to apply for permanent resident status, you should file:

- Form I-485, Application for Permanent Resident Status;
- Form G-325A, Biographic Information;
- fingerprint chart;
- two passport-size photographs;
- passport and Form I-94, Arrival/Departure Record;
- letter from an employer, if your application is based on employment, showing that a job is waiting for you; and
- results from your medical exam, which the INS will review during your interview.

All members of your family included on the application should have these documents. However, children under the age of fourteen do not have to submit the Biographic Information sheet or fingerprints. While all family members should have a medical exam, those under fourteen and pregnant women will not have to be X-rayed.

Different offices have different rules for submitting applications. All accept applications in person. If your application is accepted, an interview will be scheduled sixty to seventy days later. Some immigration offices will grant you permission to work when you file, while other immigration offices will review your application first and advise you on work permission later. At the formal immigration interview, an officer will review your case. If you qualify, your permanent residence status will be indicated by a temporary stamp in your passport or on a separate piece of paper. Depending on the office, your Green Card will be mailed to you anywhere from two to six months after receiving the stamp. Again, if you do not receive your Green Card within the period stated on the temporary stamp, call the INS. In some cases, you will have to file a tracer with the sending office located in Texas.

FILLING OUT THE APPLICATION FOR PERMANENT RESIDENCE (FORM I-485)

The first two pages of this form outline the requirements for filing it. Read these pages carefully. They will tell you if you are eligible to apply and the supporting documents you will need.

If your application is based on family relationship to a United States citizen, that citizen should file Form I-130 for you. If your application is based on employment, your future employer in the United States should file Form I-140 for you.

Each family member who wishes to become a permanent resident with you also must file Form I-485. The principal member of the family is known as the **preference alien**. If this person qualifies, all other members of the family can derive their status from him or her.

A. Reason for this application

Do not fill out the area above this section. Check the boxes in Section A that apply to you. If you already received notice that an immigrant visa number is available, be sure to attach a copy of the notice you received.

B. Information about you

1–10 These questions should present no problems for you. In rare cases, your country of birth (*question 3*) may differ from your country of citizenship (*question 9*). Review the description of "chargeability" on page 25 if you have any questions.

7 If you have authorization to work, you should have a social security number.

8 Find the number beginning with "A" on your approval notice for the petition of alien relative or alien employee. This number may also appear on your Arrival/Departure Record (Form I-94). If you do not have one, write "none."

11–19 Check your Arrival/Departure Record to be sure you supply the correct information here. Your answers tell the INS about your immigration history.

11 If the date you write here is recent, the INS may suspect you of preconceived intent. This means they believe you made false statements about your intention for being in the United States when you entered the country.

14 Check "yes" if you entered the country legally, spoke with an immigration officer, and received an Arrival/Departure Record.

18–19 Use the number of the visa you most recently used when you entered the country. You will find the visa number and consulate stamped in your passport.

20–21 The INS asks about your marriages to show that your current spouse qualifies as a "derivative" immigrant. You will need to supply marriage certificates for your current marriage as well as documents showing your current spouse's previous marriages have legally ended.

20 If you have been married before, be sure to provide proof that the marriage is no longer valid.

21 Proof is required for the previous spouse(s) of your spouse, too. If your spouse also files Form I-485, he or she should provide proof, such as a divorce decree, that any previous marriages are legally over.

22 List the names of your spouse and all children regardless of whether they plan to

U.S. Department of Justice
Immigration and Naturalization Service (INS)

Application for Permanent Residence

OMB # 1115-0053

DO NOT WRITE IN THIS BLOCK		
Case ID#	Action Stamp	Fee Stamp
A#		
G-28 or Volag#		

Section of Law		Eligibility Under Sec. 245
☐ Sec. 209(b), INA		☐ Approved Visa Petition
☐ Sec. 214(d), INA		☐ Dependent of Principal Alien
☐ Sec. 13, Act of 9/11/57		☐ Special Immigrant
☐ Sec. 245, INA		☐ Other _____
☐ Sec. 249, INA	Country Chargeable _____	Preference _____

A. Reason for this application

I am applying for lawful permanent residence for the following reason: (check the box that applies)

1. ☐ **An immigrant visa number is immediately available to me because**

    ☐ **A visa petition has already been approved for me** (approval notice is attached)

    ☐ **A visa petition is being filed with this application**

2. ☐ **I entered as the fiance(e) of a U.S. citizen and married within 90 days** (approval notice and marriage certificate are attached)

3. ☐ **I am an asylee eligible for adjustment**

4. ☐ **Other:** _____

B. Information about you

1. **Name** (Family name in CAPS)   (First)   (Middle)

2. **Address** (Number and Street)   (Apartment Number)

    (Town or City)   (State/Country)   (ZIP/Postal Code)

3. **Place of Birth** (Town or City)   (State/Country)

4. **Date of Birth** (Mo/Day/Yr)   5. **Sex** ☐ Male ☐ Female   6. **Marital Status** ☐ Married ☐ Widowed ☐ Single ☐ Divorced

7. **Social Security Number**   8. **Alien Registration Number** (if any)

9. **Country of Citizenship**

10. **Have you ever applied for permanent resident status in the U.S.?**
    ☐ Yes ☐ No
    (If Yes, give the date and place of filing and final disposition)

11. **On what date did you last enter the U.S.?**

12. **Where did you last enter the U.S.?** (City and State)

13. **What means of travel did you use?** (Plane, car, etc.)

14. **Were you inspected by a U.S. immigration officer?**
    ☐ Yes ☐ No

15. **In what status did you last enter the U.S.?**
    (Visitor, student, exchange alien, crewman, temporary worker, without inspection, etc.)

16. **Give your name EXACTLY as it appears on your Arrival/Departure Record (Form I-94).**

17. **Arrival/Departure Record (I-94) Number**   18. **Visa Number**

19. **At what Consulate was your nonimmigrant visa issued?**   **Date** (Mo/Day/Yr)

20. **Have you ever been married before?** ☐ Yes ☐ No
    If Yes,   (Names of prior husbands/wives)   (Country of citizenship)   (Date marriage ended)

21. **Has your husband/wife ever been married before?** ☐ Yes ☐ No
    If Yes,   (Names of prior husbands/wives)   (Country of citizenship)   (Date marriage ended)

INITIAL RECEIPT	RESUBMITTED	RELOCATED		COMPLETED		
		Rec'd	Sent	Approved	Denied	Returned

FORM I-485 (REV. 2-27-87)N

immigrate. Also list relatives who are United States citizens. Your spouse and children over the age of eighteen should file separately for permanent residence.

23   Listing the organizations you belong to tells the INS about your background and character. The INS also reviews this information to be sure you have not violated any of the excludability rules. The INS wants you to list all organizations you belong to, from automobile clubs to political groups. List any professional and social organizations you belong to here or in another country as well as political parties or groups, and labor unions. If you served in the military, include that information here, too.

You should also list organizations to which your children belong.

Being a member of a professional organization can enhance your claim to qualify on the basis of a job offer. Your membership in other groups shows the INS that you will make a positive contribution to American society.

24   If you answer "yes" to any of these questions, consult an immigration lawyer who can help you determine your eligibility to apply for permanent residence. You should list all crimes here and abroad for which you have been convicted. List any traffic violations you may have, too. Unless you have not paid for them, traffic tickets will not affect your application. For other crimes for which you have been indicted or convicted, you may be eligible for a waiver.

Some crimes, especially those dealing with drugs, will create problems, but are not necessarily fatal to the application. Consult a lawyer if you think you will have any trouble.

25   Technically, aliens should not receive welfare, food stamps, or other forms of public assistance. If you have received any public assistance fraudulently, your application will be denied and you risk being deported.

26   These questions relate directly to the rules of excludability. Your answers assure the INS that you are a person of good moral character and that you are not a danger to national security. If you must answer "yes" to any of them, an immigration lawyer can help you determine if any of the items can or will be waived by the INS.

27   You must file the Biographic Information sheet, Form G-325A, with this form if you are over 14 and under 70 years of age. Your Biographic Information should agree with the answers on Form I-485. When you complete the Biographic Information form and sign it, check this box. Be sure to attach it. (Directions for filling out the Biographic Information form appear in Chapter Four of this book.)

Signature   When you have provided the correct answers to all the questions on the form, read the section titled "Your Certification" and sign and date the form in the space provided. Also write in your telephone number. Your signature tells the INS that you have truthfully answered all the questions on the form. It also gives the INS permission to examine any records relevant to your application.

If you missed the bold-face type, lying on any portion of the application—or on any INS form—means that you are guilty of *perjury,* a crime punishable by law with a fine of up to $10,000, imprisonment, or deportation.

Do not sign your name twice. You will be asked to sign the form again after you have been interviewed.

22. List your present husband/wife, all of your sons and daughters, all of your brothers and sisters (If you have none, write ''N/A'')

Name	Relationship	Place of Birth	Date of Birth	Country of Residence	Applying With You?
					☐ Yes ☐ No
					☐ Yes ☐ No
					☐ Yes ☐ No
					☐ Yes ☐ No
					☐ Yes ☐ No
					☐ Yes ☐ No
					☐ Yes ☐ No
					☐ Yes ☐ No
					☐ Yes ☐ No
					☐ Yes ☐ No

23. List your present and past membership in or affiliation with every organization, association, fund, foundation, party, club, society or similar group in the United States or in any other country or place, and your foreign military service (If this does not apply, write ''N/A'')

A _____ 19 _____ to 19 _____
B _____ 19 _____ to 19 _____
C _____ 19 _____ to 19 _____
D _____ 19 _____ to 19 _____
E _____ 19 _____ to 19 _____
F _____ 19 _____ to 19 _____
G _____ 19 _____ to 19 _____

24. Have you ever, in or outside the United States:

a) knowingly committed any crime for which you have not been arrested? ☐ Yes ☐ No

b) been arrested, cited, charged, indicted, convicted, fined, or imprisoned for breaking or violating any law or ordinance, including traffic regulations? ☐ Yes ☐ No

c) been the beneficiary of a pardon, amnesty, rehabilitation decree, other act of clemency or similar action? ☐ Yes ☐ No

If you answered Yes to (a), (b), or (c) give the following information about each incident:

Date	Place (City) (State/Country)	Nature of offense	Outcome of case, if any
1)			
2)			
3)			
4)			
5)			

25. Have you ever received public assistance from any source, including the U.S. Government or any state, county, city or municipality?

☐ Yes ☐ No   (If Yes, explain, including the name(s) and Social Security number(s) you used.)

26. Do any of the following relate to you? (Answer Yes or No to each)

A. Have you been treated for a mental disorder, drug addiction, or alcoholism?	☐ Yes ☐ No
B. Have you engaged in, or do you intend to engage in, any commercialized sexual activity?	☐ Yes ☐ No
C. Are you or have you at any time been an anarchist, or a member of or affiliated with any Communist or other totalitarian party, including any subdivision or affiliate?	☐ Yes ☐ No

D. Have you advocated or taught, by personal utterance, by written or printed matter, or through affiliation with an organization:

1) opposition to organized government	☐ Yes ☐ No
2) the overthrow of government by force or violence	☐ Yes ☐ No
3) the assaulting or killing of government officials because of their official character	☐ Yes ☐ No
4) the unlawful destruction of property	☐ Yes ☐ No
5) sabotage	☐ Yes ☐ No
6) the doctrines of world communism, or the establishment of a totalitarian dictatorship in the United States?	☐ Yes ☐ No
E. Have you engaged or do you intend to engage in prejudicial activities or unlawful activities of a subversive nature?	☐ Yes ☐ No

F. During the period beginning March 23, 1933, and ending May 8, 1945, did you order, incite, assist, or otherwise participate in persecuting any person because of race, religion, national origin, or political opinion, under the direction of, or in association with any of the following:

1) the Nazi government in Germany	☐ Yes ☐ No
2) any government in any area occupied by the military forces of the Nazi government in Germany	☐ Yes ☐ No
3) any government established with the assistance or cooperation of the Nazi government of Germany	☐ Yes ☐ No
4) any government that was an ally of the Nazi government of Germany	☐ Yes ☐ No
G. Have you been convicted of a violation of any law or regulation relating to narcotic drugs or marijuana, or have you been an illicit trafficker in narcotic drugs or marijuana?	☐ Yes ☐ No

H. Have you been involved in assisting any other aliens to enter the United States in violation of the law? ☐ Yes ☐ No

I. Have you applied for exemption or discharge from training or service in the Armed Forces of the United States on the ground of alienage and have you been relieved or discharged from that training or service? ☐ Yes ☐ No

J. Are you mentally retarded, insane, or have you suffered one or more attacks of insanity? ☐ Yes ☐ No

K. Are you afflicted with psychopathic personality, sexual deviation, mental defect, narcotic drug addiction, chronic alcoholism, or any dangerous contagious disease? ☐ Yes ☐ No

L. Do you have a physical defect, disease, or disability affecting your ability to earn a living? ☐ Yes ☐ No

M. Are you a pauper, professional beggar, or vagrant? ☐ Yes ☐ No

N. Are you likely to become a public charge? ☐ Yes ☐ No

O. Are you a polygamist or do you advocate polygamy? ☐ Yes ☐ No

P. Have you been excluded from the United States within the past year, or have you at any time been deported from the United States, or have you at any time been removed from the United States at government expense? ☐ Yes ☐ No

Q. Have you procured or have you attempted to procure a visa by fraud or misrepresentation? ☐ Yes ☐ No

R. Are you a former exchange visitor who is subject to, but has not complied with, the two-year foreign residence requirement? ☐ Yes ☐ No

S. Are you a medical graduate coming principally to work as a member of the medical profession, without passing Parts I and II of the National Board of Medical Examiners Examination (or an equivalent examination)? ☐ Yes ☐ No

T. Have you left the United States to avoid military service in time of war or national emergency? ☐ Yes ☐ No

U. Have you committed or have you been convicted of a crime involving moral turpitude? ☐ Yes ☐ No

If you answered Yes to any question above, explain fully (Attach a continuation sheet if necessary):

_____

_____

_____

_____

27. ☐ **Completed Form G-325A (Biographic Information) is signed, dated and attached as part of this application.** Print or type so that all copies are legible. ☐ **Completed form G-325A (Biographic Information) is not attached because applicant is under 14 or over 79 years of age.**

Penalties: You may, by law, be fined up to $10,000, imprisoned up to five years, or both, for knowingly and willfully falsifying or concealing a material fact or using any false document in submitting this application.

Your Certification

I certify, under penalty of perjury under the laws of the United States of America, that the above information is true and correct. Furthermore, I authorize the release of any information from my records which the Immigration and Naturalization Service needs to determine eligibility for the benefit that I am seeking.

Signature _____ Date _____ Phone Number _____

Signature of Person Preparing Form if Other than Above

I declare that I prepared this document at the request of the person above and that it is based on all information of which I have any knowledge.

_____

(Print Name)   (Address)   (Signature)   (Date)

G-28 ID Number _____

Volag Number _____

Stop Here

*(Applicant is **not** to sign the application below until he or she appears before an officer of the Immigration and Naturalization Service for examination)*

I, _____ swear (affirm) that I know the contents of this application that I am signing including the attached documents, that they are true to the best of my knowledge, and that corrections numbered ( ) to ( ) were made by me or at my request, and that I signed this application with my full, true name:

_____

(Complete and true signature of applicant)

Signed and sworn to before me by the above-named applicant at _____ on _____

(Month)   (Day)   (Year)

_____

(Signature and title of officer)

Special Immigrant Applications

Who Qualifies?

The spouses, unmarried minor children, and parents of United States citizens are classified in the **special immigrant** category and are not subject to the numerical limitations of the Preference System. Other special immigrants include: 1) returning resident aliens; 2) some former United States citizens; 3) certain ministers of religion; and 4) certain former United States government employees.

The immediate relatives of United States citizens who qualify for special immigrant visas include:

1. Spouses.   You must show the marriage is real and not merely one of form only for immigration purposes. The frequency of **sham marriages**, or paper marriages, has made the INS suspicious of many couples. If the age difference between the two is great or you haven't known each other for very long, the INS will be particularly wary of your application.

2. Unmarried children.   Legitimate, unmarried children of United States citizens under the age of twenty-one also qualify for special immigrant status.

3. Parents.   The parents of a United States citizen who is over twenty-one years of age may receive a special immigrant visa.

Children Who May Qualify

In some cases an illegitimate child may qualify for special immigrant status. The Immigration Reform and Control Act of 1986 allows both a mother and father to file a petition for an illegitimate child. The father must prove that a father–child relationship exists or existed by showing that he supports the child or by demonstrating that their behavior indicates a father–child relationship.

An illegitimate child may be legitimated if the parents can prove they were married when the child was born or if they marry before the child is eighteen years old.

A stepchild may also qualify as an immediate relative. Whether the child is legitimate or illegitimate, he or she must be under eighteen when the parent and stepparent marry. In this case, the natural father of an illegitimate child cannot petition, but the stepmother may file the petition.

United States citizens may also petition for adopted children and orphans. The adoption process must have been completed before the child turned sixteen. The child should have lived with the parent for two years either before or after the adoption. An adopted child also must have been in the legal custody of the adopting parent for two years. Any United States citizen may petition for adopted children even if the spouse is not a United States citizen. United States citizens who wish to petition for an orphan can file with a spouse (who may not be a citizen), or alone if he or she is at least twenty-five years of age.

Petitioners should include an authorization from an adoption agency in the state where the child will live showing that it conducted a study of the home and recommends the adoption. Neither adopted children nor orphans who become United States citizens may petition for the immigration of their natural parents.

Others Who May Qualify

In rare cases, some aliens who are not close relatives of United States citizens also may qualify for a special immigrant visa. These include:

1. Returning resident aliens. Any alien who had permanent resident status and left the United States for a temporary visit must show that he or she never intended to give up permanent resident status. Ideally, a returning resident alien will have applied for and received a reentry permit by filing the Application for Issuance of Extension of Permit to Reenter the United States, Form I-131, at least thirty days before having left the country. If you were outside the United States for more than a year, you should be able to show that your stay was unavoidable or beyond your control. Usually this is done at an American consulate.

2. Certain former United States citizens. This category of special immigrant was created for those:
- women who married an alien and lost their citizenship before September 22, 1922;
- women who lost their citizenship because they married an alien who could not become a citizen after September 22, 1922;
- women who lost their citizenship because their spouses lost their citizenship; and
- people who lost their citizenship during World War II because they served in the armed forces of countries not allied with the United States.

3. Certain ministers of religion. Ministers of a religious denomination abroad that also exists in the United States may qualify for special immigrant status. They must have been practicing their religious ministry for two years in their country immediately before filing their petition for immigration, and intend to serve a religious organization in the United States. The spouses and minor children of ministers also can be admitted in this category.

4. Certain former United States government employees. An alien who has worked for the United States government for at least fifteen years may qualify. A senior official of the government office where you worked recommends you for special immigrant status. Spouses and minor children may be admitted in this category.

What to File

As with all immigrants, regardless of the type of visa you seek, applicants must be eligible to enter the United States. Your relationship to a United States citizen or special immigrant status gives your application a higher priority, but not if you have been convicted of a crime or are disqualified under any of the other eligibility requirements.

To apply for permanent residence, those special immigrants who are in the United States must file form I-485, Application for Permanent Residence.

The applicant's immediate relative in the United States who is a citizen should file:
- Form I-130, Petition for Alien Relative for each alien relative. (See the section in this chapter titled "Petition for Alien Relatives" for instructions on this form.)

The immediate relatives—spouses, unmarried children under twenty-one, and parents—of United States citizens receive a higher priority than other Preference System visa applicants. However, they still must prove their relationship to a citizen. Depending on your relationship to the citizen, you should provide supporting documents such as birth or marriage certificates. You also should show proof that you will not become a public charge by submitting an affidavit of support or a letter from a prospective employer.

Petition for Alien Relatives: First, Second, Fourth, and Fifth Preference Aliens

Form I-130, Petition for Alien Relative, is used to file for permanent residence status for the Preference System categories that apply to relatives of United States citizens and permanent resident aliens. The relative in the United States should file the I-130 on behalf of the alien. The person who files the form is called the **petitioner**. The alien for whom the petitioner files the form is called the **beneficiary**.

Since the Preference System places emphasis on family reunification, generally you will have an easier time immigrating to America within one of these preference categories. From most countries it is a fairly simple task to prove your relationship with a birth or marriage certificate. At the same time, high demand for this type of visa limits the number of available visa numbers. In particular, applicants from China, India, Korea, Mexico, Hong Kong, and the Philippines probably will have to wait longer than those from other countries. However, the other two Preference System classifications, which apply to workers, have even longer waiting lists. Petitioning for perma-

nent residence status through one of the family-oriented Preference categories usually offers a better success rate, though you should check on the backlog in each category from your country.

Who Qualifies?

If you are the relative of a United States citizen, the citizen should file this form for you if you are his or her:
- spouse, unmarried son or daughter, or parent (Special Immigrant);
- unmarried son and daughter over twenty-one (First Preference);
- married sons and daughters of any age (Fourth Preference);
- brother or sister who is at least twenty-one years old (Fifth Preference).

The relatives of permanent resident aliens living in the United States should ask their relative to file this form if they are their:
- husband or wife and unmarried son or daughter of any age (Second Preference).

What to File

If you seek permanent residence status through adjustment of status, you need to file Form I-485, Application for Permanent Residence, and Form G-325A, Biographic Information. These should be filed after a relative has filed the I-130, Petition for Alien Relative, and the INS has approved it.

The petitioner can file Form I-130 either abroad at a United States consulate or embassy, or at an INS office in the United States. At a consulate abroad, both the petitioner and beneficiary should be present when filing the form to ensure accuracy. If the beneficiary lives in the United States, he or she may apply for adjustment of status at the same time.

Remember, a visa number must be available within your preference category before your application will be processed. If abroad, check with the American consulate. In the United States, call the Visa Office at 202-647-0508 to find out if your category is current (see also page 25). The State Department updates visa information every month.

The Petition for Alien Relative (Form I-130) asks the petitioner for information both about him or herself and about the alien for whom the petition is filed. When filling out the petition, be sure all information matches the answers provided on Form I-485 or 230 by the alien. Any inconsistencies will slow the application process, and the INS may suspect you of fraud.

The INS requires proof of the petitioner's citizenship or permanent residence status and of the petitioner's relationship to the beneficiary. Petitioners who are United States citizens should provide one of the following documents to prove their relationship to the alien:

- an American birth certificate;
- Certificate of Naturalization;
- Report of Birth Abroad of a United States Citizen (Form FS-240) and your Certificate of Citizenship if you were born outside the United States but are a citizen; or
- a valid United States passport issued to you for at least five years.

If the petitioner was born in the United States and does not have the required documents, the second page of Form I-130 lists alternatives such as church records, school records, census records, or affidavits from people the petitioner knows. The INS considers these documents "secondary evidence," and may reject them if they feel that other forms of proof are available.

Petitioners who are permanent resident aliens should be able to show the INS:

- Form I-151, or Form I-551, the Alien Registration Receipt Card.

Unless a copy of the petitioner's Certificate of Naturalization, Certificate of Citizenship, or Alien Registration Card is attested or certified by an INS or consular officer, or an attorney certified to practice in the United States, the *original* document should be submitted. Sometimes the INS will accept a copy certified by an INS-certified representative. *It is a federal offense to copy a naturalization certificate.*

When you collect supporting documents to prove your relationship to the alien for the I-130, follow these guidelines for each of the Preference System categories:

Unmarried son and daughter over twenty-one (First Preference) or child under twenty-one (Nonpreference). If you are the child's mother, provide a birth certificate. Fathers and stepparents should submit a marriage certificate and proof that any previous marriages are legally over. In the case of an adopted child, file proof that the adoption has occurred. The adoption must have been final before the child turned sixteen and you must have lived with the child for at least two years.

Husband or wife and unmarried sons and daughters of any age of a permanent resident alien in the United States (Second Preference). As stated earlier, the petitioner needs to submit his or her Alien Registration Receipt Card to prove residence status. For a spouse, you'll need a valid marriage certificate. Be sure to include documents showing that any previous marriages are legally over. For sons and daughters, submit birth certificates showing your rela-

U.S. Department of Justice (INS)   **Petition for Alien Relative**   OMB No. 1115-0054

DO NOT WRITE IN THIS BLOCK — FOR EXAMINING OFFICE ONLY

Case ID#

A#

G-28 or Volag #

Section of Law:
- ☐ 201 (b) spouse   ☐ 203 (a)(1)
- ☐ 201 (b) child   ☐ 203 (a)(2)
- ☐ 201 (b) parent   ☐ 203 (a)(4)
- ☐ 203 (a)(5)

AM CON:

REMARKS:

Action Stamp

Fee Stamp

Petition was filed on _____ (priority date)
- ☐ Personal Interview   ☐ Previously Forwarded
- ☐ Pet .☐ Ben. "A" File Reviewed   ☐ Stateside Criteria
- ☐ Field Investigations   ☐ I-485 Simultaneously
- ☐ 204 (a)(2)(A) Resolved   ☐ 204 (h) Resolved

A. Relationship

1. The alien relative is my:
☐ Husband/Wife   ☐ Parent   ☐ Brother/Sister   ☐ Child

2. Are you related by adoption?
☐ Yes   ☐ No

3. Did you gain permanent residence through adoption?
☐ Yes   ☐ No

B. Information about you

1. Name (Family name in CAPS)   (First)   (Middle)

2. Address (Number and Street)   (Apartment Number)

(Town or City)   (State/Country)   (ZIP/Postal Code)

3. Place of Birth (Town or City)   (State/Country)

4. Date of Birth (Mo/Day/Year)

5. Sex
☐ Male   ☐ Female

6. Marital Status
☐ Married   ☐ Single
☐ Widowed   ☐ Divorced

7. Other Names Used (including maiden name)

8. Date and Place of Present Marriage (if married)

9. Social Security number

10. Alien Registration Number (if any)

11. Names of Prior Husbands/Wives

12. Date(s) Marriage(s) Ended

13. If you are a U.S. citizen, complete the following:
My citizenship was acquired through (check one)
- ☐ Birth in the U.S.
- ☐ Naturalization
  Give number of certificate, date and place it was issued

- ☐ Parents
  Have you obtained a certificate of citizenship in your own name?
  ☐ Yes   ☐ No
  If "Yes," give number of certificate, date and place it was issued

14a. If you are a lawful permanent resident alien, complete the following:
Date and place of admission for, or adjustment to, lawful permanent residence, and class of admission:

14b. Did you gain permanent resident status through marriage to a United States citizen or lawful permanent resident?   ☐ Yes   ☐ No

C. Information about your alien relative

1. Name (Family name in CAPS)   (First)   (Middle)

2. Address (Number and Street)   (Apartment Number)

(Town or City)   (State/Country)   (ZIP/Postal Code)

3. Place of Birth (Town or City)   (State/Country)

4. Date of Birth (Mo/Day/Year)

5. Sex
☐ Male   ☐ Female

6. Marital Status
☐ Married   ☐ Single
☐ Widowed   ☐ Divorced

7. Other Names Used (including maiden name)

8. Date and Place of Present Marriage (if married)

9. Social Security number

10. Alien Registration Number (if any)

11. Names of Prior Husbands/Wives

12. Date(s) Marriage(s) Ended

13. Has your relative ever been in the U.S.?
☐ Yes   ☐ No

14. If your relative is currently in the U.S., complete the following:
He or she last arrived as a (visitor, student, stowaway, without inspection, etc.)

Arrival/Departure Record (I-94) Number   Date arrived (Month/Day/Year)

Date authorized stay expired, or will expire as shown on Form I-94 or I-95

15. Name and address of present employer (if any)

Date this employment began (Month/Day/Year)

16. Has your relative ever been under immigration proceedings?
☐ Yes   ☐ No   Where _____   When _____
☐ Exclusion   ☐ Deportation   ☐ Rescission   ☐ Judicial Proceedings

SAMPLE ONLY

INITIAL RECEIPT	RESUBMITTED	RELOCATED		COMPLETED		
		Rec'd	Sent	Approved	Denied	Returned

Form I-130 (Rev. 02-28-87) N

C. (Continued) Information about your alien relative

16. List husband/wife and all children of your relative (if your relative is your husband/wife, list only his or her children).

Name	Relationship	Date of Birth	Country of Birth

17. Address in the United States where your relative intends to reside

(Number and Street)   (Town or City)   (State)

18. Your relative's address abroad

(Number and Street)   (Town or City)   (Province)   (Country)

19. If your relative's native alphabet is other than Roman letters, write his/her name and address abroad in the native alphabet:

(Name)   (Number and Street)   (Town or City)   (Province)   (Country)

20. If filing for your husband/wife, give last address at which you both lived together: From   To

(Name)   (Apt. No.)   (Town or City)   (State or Province)   (Country)   (Month)   (Year)   (Month)   (Year)

21. Check the appropriate box below and give the information required for the box you checked:

☐ Your relative will apply for a visa abroad at the American Consulate in _____

(City)   (Country)

☐ Your relative is in the United States and will apply for adjustment of status to that of a lawful permanent resident in the office of the Immigration and Naturalization Service at _____ . If your relative is not eligible for adjustment of status, he or she will

(City)   (State)

apply for a visa abroad at the American Consulate in _____

(City)   (Country)

(Designation of a consulate outside the country of your relative's last residence does not guarantee acceptance for processing by that consulate. Acceptance is at the discretion of the designated consulate.)

D. Other Information

1. If separate petitions are also being submitted for other relatives, give names of each and relationship.

2. Have you ever filed a petition for this or any other alien before?   ☐ Yes   ☐ No
If "Yes," give name, place and date of filing, and result.

Warning: The INS investigates claimed relationships and verifies the validity of documents. The INS seeks criminal prosecutions when family relationships are falsified to obtain visas.

Penalties: You may, by law be imprisoned for not more than five years, or fined $250,000, or both, for entering into a marriage contract for the purpose of evading any provision of the immigration laws and you may be fined up to $10,000 or imprisoned up to five years or both, for knowingly and willfully falsifying or concealing a material fact or using any false document in submitting this petition.

Your Certification

I certify, under penalty of perjury under the laws of the United States of America, that the foregoing is true and correct. Furthermore, I authorize the release of any information from my records which the Immigration and Naturalization Service needs to determine eligibility for the benefit that I am seeking.

Signature _____ Date _____ Phone Number_____

Signature of Person Preparing Form if Other than Above

I declare that I prepared this document at the request of the person above and that it is based on all information of which I have any knowledge.

(Print Name)   (Address)   (Signature)   (Date)

Volag Number _____   G-28 ID Number_____

NOTICE TO PERSONS FILING FOR SPOUSES IF MARRIED LESS THAN TWO YEARS

Pursuant to section 216 of the Immigration and Nationality Act, your alien spouse may be granted conditional permanent resident status in the United States as of the date he or she is admitted or adjusted to conditional status by an officer of the Immigration and Naturalization Service. Both you and your conditional permanent resident spouse are required to file a petition, Form I-751, Joint Petition to Remove Conditional Basis of Alien's Permanent Resident Status, during the ninety day period immediately before the second anniversary of the date your alien spouse was granted conditional permanent residence.

Otherwise, the rights, privileges, responsibilities and duties which apply to all other permanent residents apply equally to a conditional permanent resident. A conditional permanent resident is not limited to the right to apply for naturalization, to file petitions in behalf of qualifying relatives, or to reside permanently in the United States as an immigrant in accordance with the immigration laws.

> **Failure to file Form I-751, Joint Petition to Remove the Conditional Basis of Alien's Permanent Resident Status, will result in termination of permanent residence status and initiation of deportation proceedings.**

NOTE: You must complete items 1 through 6 to assure that petition approval is recorded. Do not write in the section below item 6.

1. Name of relative (Family name in CAPS)   (First)   (Middle)

2. Other names used by relative (Including maiden name)

3. Country of relative's birth   4. Date of relative's birth (Month/Day/Year)

5. Your name (Last name in CAPS)   (First)   (Middle)   6. Your phone number

Action Stamp

SECTION
☐ 201 (b)(spouse)
☐ 201 (b)(child)
☐ 201 (b)(parent)
☐ 203 (a)(1)
☐ 203 (a)(2)
☐ 203 (a)(4)
☐ 203 (a)(5)

DATE PETITION FILED

☐ STATESIDE
CRITERIA GRANTED

SENT TO CONSUL AT:

CHECKLIST

Have you answered each question?
Have you signed the petition?
Have you enclosed:

☐ The filing fee for each petition?
☐ Proof of your citizenship or lawful permanent residence?
☐ All required supporting documents for each petition?

If you are filing for your husband or wife have you included:

☐ Your picture?
☐ His or her picture?
☐ Your G-325A?
☐ His or her G-325A?

Relative Petition Card
Form I-130A (Rev. 02-28-87) N

tionship as the mother or father as outlined for the First Preference category above.

The married sons and daughters of any age of a United States citizen (Fourth Preference). Like the other categories, be able to provide birth and marriage certificates proving your relationship to your children.

Brothers and sisters of a United States citizen who is at least twenty-one years old (Fifth Preference). You'll need both your own and the alien's birth certificate if you are siblings from the same mother. If you have different mothers but the same father, submit your parents' marriage certificate as well as that of your alien brother or sister.

File this form and the filing fee with the INS office nearest where you live or at a consulate abroad.

Marrying a United States Citizen

Years ago, marrying a United States citizen virtually meant automatic citizenship for a foreigner. In recent years, however, the INS has discovered that an alarming number of marriages take place only because an alien wants to become a United States citizen. These are known as sham marriages, paper marriages, or marriages of convenience, because the people who get married are only pretending to be married for immigration purposes. As a result, the INS pays particular attention to applications for permanent residence based on marriage to a citizen.

Who Qualifies?

Congress passed the Immigration Marriage Amendments in 1986, which makes obtaining permanent residence through marriage more difficult. The law says that, if an alien marries a citizen, he or she will receive conditional permanent residence status for two years. According to the law, the conditional residence status begins after the couple is interviewed by the INS, not when the couple is married. At least ninety days before the two-year period is over, you must apply for permanent residence status. Do not wait until after two years have passed. Your two years of conditional permanent residence can be counted as part of the three years of permanent residence required for applying for naturalization based on a marriage to a United States citizen.

Unfortunately, this system makes it more difficult for those who really want to get married. Everyone who seeks citizenship through marriage comes under the same scrutiny. The INS is so sensitive to sham marriages, it may suspect a real marriage of fraud. That's why it's important to carefully follow the rules set by Congress and the INS to achieve permanent residence status through marriage.

While the INS does offer a special K visa to the fiancé or fiancée of an American citizen who wants to enter the country, in most cases the marriage takes place after an alien has entered the country on another kind of visa. (As discussed in Chapter Two, the K visa stipulates that the marriage must take place within ninety days of the alien entering the country. Still, the alien must file Form I-485 for permanent residence status.)

What to File

To apply for permanent residence status after receiving a conditional permanent resident card, you and your spouse must submit Form I-751, Joint Petition to Remove the Conditional Basis of Alien's Permanent Resident Status, within ninety days of the end of your two-year conditional status.

You may not file the petition more than ninety days before or at any time after the two-year period ends. If you miss the filing deadline, you lose your permanent residence status and may be deported. (However, if you can prove that you missed the deadline for reasons beyond your control, the INS may decide to consider your petition.)

Form I-751 should be sent with the filing fee to an INS regional processing center. These centers are listed in Appendix Four of this book.

Ninety days after filing the I-751, the INS may ask you to come in for an interview. (If the INS decides to investigate your marriage, it must make a decision within ninety days after the investigation is concluded.) During the interview, the examiner will ask you questions about your petition. He or she also will ask questions about where you live, your spouse's habits, and other things that a married couple would know about each other. INS officials may also decide to make a surprise visit to your home and interview your co-workers and neighbors. During its investigation, it also may interview anyone who supplied an affidavit on your behalf.

The INS calls for specific documents on Form I-751 designed to show that your marriage is valid. Though only two of the five documents called for are required, keep them in mind during the two years of your conditional permanent residence status. Your application is more likely to be approved if you keep careful records of:

- leases or mortgages showing that you jointly rent or own your home;
- your finances, such as a joint checking account or assets and property owned by both of you;
- birth certificates of any children born to both of you;
- any other documents showing that you lived together during the two-year conditional period, including utility bills, canceled mail, etc.

Sometimes couples may have trouble proving that they lived together. If this is the case, you should have at least two people who knew both of you during the two-year conditional residence period submit affidavits testifying to your marriage.

Sometimes couples who marry have trouble proving their relationship. Maybe they weren't able to live together for the entire period of the two-year conditional status. The INS's wariness of applications for permanent residence on the basis of marriage can sometimes lead to mistakes in these cases. If you anticipate any trouble with your joint petition, you should consult a lawyer for help with your case.

If You Divorce or Separate

The INS recognizes that some real marriages end for various reasons before the two-year conditional period is over. If you are separated or divorced from your spouse before the two-year period ends, you may still apply to have your conditional status changed. This is a difficult procedure, and a lawyer is highly recommended.

Ask your lawyer to file Form I-752, Application for Waiver of Requirement to File Joint Petition for Removal of Conditions.

You still must file before the two-year conditional period ends and may not file afterward. As with the I-751, if you do not file your application, you will lose your conditional permanent residence status.

In addition to proving that the marriage was valid and true, you must show the INS why you should have your conditional status removed. The INS requires that you prove the marriage ended for valid reasons, or for **good cause**. The divorce court already decided that the marriage should end. The INS does not need you to prove it again. Rather, you need to convince the INS that you should be excused from the normal requirements for leaving the country.

In some cases, you may be able to prove extreme hardship, which means that you would experience hardships greater than other aliens who are deported. You must show the INS that hardship arose after you became a conditional permanent resident.

Show the INS the same documents to prove the validity of the marriage that you would have for Form I-751, such as leases, mortgages, financial records, and affidavits. You should also file a copy of your divorce decree or annulment.

As with other INS forms, the fee for filing Form I-752 is not refundable.

Immigration on the Basis of Work: Third and Sixth Preference Aliens

The Third and Sixth Preference categories are reserved for those aliens who have a job offer in the United States. A much lower number of visas is available for these preferences than for those for family rela-
tions. Consequently, it can take two years or more before a visa number becomes available in a labor preference category. As we've seen, applying for permanent residence status can be a complicated process. This is especially true for the Third and Sixth Preference categories. You will need **labor certification** from the Department of Labor, which shows you will not displace an American worker.

Who Qualifies?

The Preference System categories split labor into two groups: professionals, and workers with skills in short supply.

The Third Preference category includes professionals—doctors, lawyers, teachers, architects, engineers and business executives—as well as those who have exceptional ability in their field. You may qualify if you have an unusual talent in a specialized area of the arts or sciences, which has been well-documented in trade or professional magazines and journals, television, and other media. Applying under this category usually is quicker, but not everyone can qualify for it.

The Sixth Preference category includes those who work in specific skilled and unskilled jobs like live-in servants, live-in aids to care for the disabled or sick, or specialty cooks. The work may not be temporary or seasonal. In addition, applicants in this category must show, through an application for labor certification with a local department of labor, that there is a shortage of United States citizens who are willing or able to do this kind of work.

Obtaining labor certification is a time-consuming and complicated process. Finding a lawyer to help you probably will increase your chances of success.

U.S. Department of Justice
Immigration and Naturalization Service

Joint Petition to Remove the Conditional
Basis of Alien's Permanent Resident Status

Instructions - Form I-751
Please read the instructions carefully.
If you do not follow the instructions, we may have to return your petition, which may delay final action.

1. Who must file?
A lawful permanent resident who obtained such status through marriage to a citizen of the United States or through marriage to another lawful permanent resident, and who was admitted or adjusted as a conditional resident must file this petition jointly with the spouse through whom the status was obtained (the "Petitioning Spouse").

2. Must a dependent child file this petition?
A dependent child who entered the United States as a conditional permanent resident within 90 days of the entry of his or her conditional resident parent may be included on the same petition filed by the child's parents (see block C-6). If the child entered more than 90 days before or after the parent, or if no petition is being filed by the parents (for example, if the conditional resident parent is now deceased), the child should file an Application for Waiver of Requirement to File Joint Petition to Remove Conditional Basis of Status (Form I-752).

3. What if you are no longer married to the spouse through whom your status was obtained?
A conditional resident who is unable to file this petition jointly with the spouse through whom status was obtained may be eligible for a waiver of the filing requirement (see Form I-752).

4. When must the petition be filed?
The petition must be filed during the ninety day period immediately preceding the second anniversary of the date on which conditional permanent residence was obtained (i.e., two years from the date on which you first entered with your immigrant visa, or two years from the date on which your status was adjusted from nonimmigrant to permanent resident).

5. What if you fail to file the petition during this time period?
If the petition is not filed, you will automatically lose your permanent resident status as of the second anniversary of the date such status was granted. You will then become deportable from the United States. If your failure to file this petition was through no fault of your own, you may file it after the required time period with a written explanation of the tardiness requesting that the INS excuse the late filing. The INS may only excuse your tardiness if you establish that the reasons for the late filing were beyond your control.

6. What documents do you need?
A. You must give INS certain documents with this form to show that your marriage was not entered into for the purpose of circumventing the immigration laws of the United States. These documents should include at least two of the following:
  1) a lease or mortgage contract showing joint occupancy and/or ownership of your communal residence,
  2) financial records showing joint ownership of assets and/or joint responsibility for liabilities,
  3) birth certificate(s) of child(ren) born to the marriage,
  4) affidavits from at least two people who have known both of you since conditional permanent residence was granted (such persons may be required to testify before an immigration officer as to the information contained in the affidavit), or
  5) other documentation establishing that a bona-fide marital relationship exists.
B. For each document needed, give INS the original and one copy. Originals will be returned to you. If you do not wish to give INS the original documents, you may give INS a properly certified copy. INS still may require originals. The copy must be certified by:
  1) an INS or U.S. consular officer, or
  2) an attorney admitted to practice law in the United States, or
  3) an INS accredited representative.
C. Documents in a foreign language must be accompanied by a complete English translation. The translator must certify that the translation is accurate and that he or she is competent to translate.

7. Will you have to appear for an interview?
After reviewing the information contained on the petition and the accompanying supporting documents, INS may require both petitioners to appear at your local INS office for an interview before an immigration officer. If your petition is supported by affidavits, the affiants may also be interviewed.

8. Will you be able to travel outside the United States while the joint petition is pending?
The Alien Registration Receipt Card (Form I-551) issued to a conditional permanent resident is not valid beyond the second anniversary of the date on which he or she obtained residence, and may not be used for return to the United States after that second anniversary date. If you must travel outside the United States after your card has expired and before the petition is approved, you should first contact your local office of this Service to request advance authorization to travel. If the joint petition is approved you will receive instructions on how to obtain a new Alien Registration Receipt Card.

9. How should you prepare this form?
A. Type or print legibly in ink.
B. If you need extra space to complete any item, attach a continuation sheet, indicate the item number, and date and sign each sheet.
C. Answer all questions fully and accurately. If any item does not apply please write "none".

10. Where should you file this form?
Mail this form to the INS Regional Service Center having jurisdiction over your place of residence. The address of the appropriate center is listed on the reverse of this instructions sheet.

11. What is the fee?
You must pay $35.00 to file this form. The fee will not be refunded, whether the petition is approved or not. *Do not mail cash.* All checks or money orders, whether U.S. or foreign, must be payable in U.S. currency at a financial institution in the United States. When a check is drawn on the account of a person other than yourself, write your name on the face of the check. If the check is not honored, INS will charge you $5.00.

Pay by check or money order in the exact amount. Make the check or money order payable to "Immigration and Naturalization Service". However,
A. if you live in Guam; Make the check or money order payable to "Treasurer, Guam", or
B. if you live in the U.S. Virgin Islands: Make the check or money order payable to "Commissioner of Finance of the Virgin Islands.

12. What are the penalties for committing marriage fraud or submitting false information?
Title 8, United States Code, Section 1325 states that any individual who knowingly enters into a marriage contract for the purpose of evading any provision of the immigration laws shall be imprisoned for not more than five years, or fined not more than $250,000 or both.

Title 18, United States Code, Section 1001 states that whoever willfully and knowingly falsifies a material fact, makes a false statement, or makes use of a false document will be fined up to $10,000 or imprisoned up to five years, or both.

13. What is our authority for collecting this information?
We request the information on this form to carry out the immigration laws contained in Title 8, United States Code, Section 1186. We need this information to determine whether a person is eligible for immigration benefits. The information you provide may also be disclosed to other federal, state, local, and foreign law enforcement and regulatory agencies during the course of the investigation required by this Service. You do not have to give this information. However, if you refuse to give some or all of it, your petition may be denied.

INS recommends that you retain photocopies of all submissions for your records.
It is not possible to cover all the conditions for eligibility or give instructions for every situation.
If you have carefully read all the instructions and still have questions, please contact your nearest INS office.

Jurisdiction and Addresses of Regional Processing Centers			
If you reside in : Connecticut Delaware *District of Columbia* Maine Maryland Massachusetts New Hampshire New Jersey New York Pennsylvania *Puerto Rico* Rhode Island Vermont *Virgin Islands* Virginia West Virginia	**Mail completed application, with fee, to:** Immigration & Naturalization Service Regional Service Center P.O. Box 1270 St. Albans, Vermont 05478-1270	**If you reside in:** Alabama Arkansas Florida Georgia Kentucky Louisiana Mississippi New Mexico North Carolina Oklahoma South Carolina Tennessee Texas	**Mail completed application, with fee, to:** Immigration & Naturalization Service Regional Service Center P.O. Box 568808 Dallas, Texas 75356-8806
If you reside in : Alaska Colorado Idaho Illinois Indiana Iowa Kansas Michigan Minnesota Missouri Montana Nebraska North Dakota Ohio Oregon South Dakota Utah Washington Wisconsin Wyoming	**Mail completed application, with fee, to:** Immigration & Naturalization Service Regional Service Center Federal Building and U.S. Courthouse Room 393 - 100 Centennial Mall North Lincoln, Nebraska 68508	**If you reside in:** Arizona California *Guam* Hawaii Nevada	**Mail completed application, with fee, to:** Immigration & Naturalization Service Regional Service Center, Room I-752 P.O. Box 73016 San Ysidro, California 92073

If you are stationed outside the United States on government business (either civilian or military), mail the petition to the center having jurisdiction over your home of record in the United States. Include a copy of your orders assigning you overseas.

U. S. Department of Justice
Immigration and Naturalization Service

Joint Petition to Remove the Conditional
Basis of Alien's Permanent Resident Status

OMB # 1115-0145

Do not write in this block		
Case ID #	ACTION STAMP	FEE STAMP
A #		
G-28 or VOLAG #		
Remarks		

	Receipt	Resubmitted	Relocated		Completed		
			Rec'd	Sent	Ret	App	Den

A. Information About Conditional Permanent Resident

1. Name (Family name in CAPS)   (First)   (Middle)

2. Other names used (including maiden name)

3. INS A #   4. Telephone #

5. Address (Number and Street)

   (Town or City)   (State/Country)   (ZIP/Postal Code)

6. Have you resided at any other address since becoming a permanent resident? (If yes, attach a list of all addresses and dates).

   ☐ Yes   ☐ No

7. Date of Birth

8. Place of Birth   9. Country of Citizenship

10. Social Security #

11. Current Employer (Name)

12. Employer's Address (Number and Street)

    (Town or City)   (State/Country)   (ZIP/Postal Code)

13. Employer's Telephone #

14. Job Title

15. Supervisor's Name

16. Supervisor's Telephone #

17. Have you been employed anywhere else since becoming a conditional permanent resident? (If yes, attach a list including all information requested in items 9 through 14 for each.)

    ☐ Yes   ☐ No

B. Information About Petitioning Spouse

1. Name (Family name in CAPS)   (First)   (Middle)

2. Other names used (including maiden name)

3. INS A #   4. Telephone #

4. Address (Number and Street)

   (Town or City)   (State/Country)   (ZIP/Postal Code)

5. Have you resided at any other address since your spouse became a permanent resident? (If yes, attach a list of all addresses and dates).

   ☐ Yes   ☐ No

6. Date of Birth

7. Place of Birth   9. Country of Citizenship

10. Social Security #

11. Current Employer (Name)

12. Employer's Address (Number and Street)

    (Town or City)   (State/Country)   (ZIP/Postal Code)

13. Employer's Telephone #

14. Job Title

15. Supervisor's Name

16. Supervisor's Telephone #

17. Have you been employed anywhere else since your spouse became a conditional permanent resident? (If yes, attach a list including all information requested in items 9 through 14 for each.)

    ☐ Yes   ☐ No

Form I-751 (4/15/88)

C. Information Common to Both Conditional Permanent Resident and Petitioning Spouse

1. Date of Marriage

2. Place of Marriage

3. Is this the same marriage through which conditional resident status was obtained? ☐ Yes ☐ No

4. Has the marriage through which conditional residence was obtained ever been annulled or judicially terminated? (If yes, attach a statement of explanation and a copy of the relevant decree.) ☐ Yes ☐ No

5. Was a fee paid to anyone other than an attorney in connection with the filing of the petition through which status was obtained, or in connection with this petition? (If yes, attach a statement of explanation.) ☐ Yes ☐ No

6. Children (Indicate in "Parent(s)" column "H" if child of husband, "W" if child of wife, or "B" if child of both.) Attach an additional sheet if there are more than six children.

Name	Date of Birth	Place of Birth	INS File Number	Parent(s) H/W/B	Address of Child

Warning:
The INS investigates information claimed on petitions and verifies the authenticity of documents. The INS seek criminal prosecutions when information or documents are falsified to obtain benefits.

Documentation:
All supporting documentation must be submitted in accordance with parts A., B., and C., Item number 6, in the instructions of this form.

Penalties:
You may, by law, be fined up to $250,000 or imprisoned up to five years, or both, for entering into a marriage contract for the purpose of evading any provision of the immigration laws. Furthermore, you may be fined up to $10,000 or imprisoned up to five years, or both, for knowingly and willfully falsifying or concealing a material fact or using any false document in submitting this petition.

D. Certification of Information and Authorization for Release of Information.

Your certification *(must be signed in ink by both conditional permanent resident and petitioning spouse)*:
We certify, under penalty of perjury under the laws of the United States of America, that the foregoing is true and correct, and that the marriage described above was entered into in accordance with the laws of the place where the marriage took place and not for the purpose of procuring the conditional permanent resident's entry as an immigrant. Furthermore, we authorize the release of any information from either or both of our records which the Immigration and Naturalization Service needs to determine eligibility for the benefit being sought.

Signature of Conditional Permanent Resident   *Date*   *Signature of Petitioning Spouse*   *Date*

Signature of Person Preparing Form, if Other than Above:
I declare that I prepared this document at the request of the persons above and that it is based on all information of which I have any knowledge.

Signature of Preparer   *Date*   Print Name and Address

Form I-751 (04/15/88)

☆U.S. GPO: 1989—241-708

U.S. Department of Justice
Immigration and Naturalization Service

Application for Waiver of Requirement to
File Joint Petition for Removal of Conditions

Instructions - Form I-752
Please read the instructions carefully.
If you do not follow the instructions, we may have to return your petition, which may delay final action.

1. **Who must file?**
   This application may be filed by an alien who was admitted as a conditional permanent resident and who is unable to file a Joint Petition to Remove the Conditional Basis of Alien's Permanent Resident Status (Form I-751). A conditional permanent resident is any alien who obtained permanent resident status as the spouse or child of a citizen or lawful permanent resident of the United States on or after November 10, 1986 based upon a marriage which was less than two years old at the time. There are two grounds for which INS may, in its discretion, approve a waiver of the requirement to file Form I-751:
   A. Extreme Hardship -- This waiver requires that you establish that your deportation from the United States would result in hardships which are far greater than those normally encountered by an alien who is deported. In adjudicating the application, INS may only consider those factors which arose *after* you acquired conditional permanent residence.
   B. Good Faith and Good Cause -- This waiver requires that you establish (1) that you entered into the marriage with the intent of forming a permanent marital relationship and not for the purpose of circumventing immigration laws and (2) that you sought termination of the marriage for good reasons.

2. **What does INS mean by "in its discretion"?**
   One of the purposes of the Immigration and Nationality Act is to promote the unity of bona fide families by allowing the immigration of alien members of such families. Section 216 of the Act places conditions upon the permanent residence status of most aliens who obtain permanent residence through marriage to a citizen or to another alien who is already a permanent resident. It also provides that the conditions may be removed after two years if the marriage was not entered into in order to circumvent the immigration laws of the United States and if the marriage has not been terminated. Otherwise, the permanent residence of the alien is terminated and the alien must leave the United States. However, the law also provides that under certain circumstances, INS may waive these requirements and allow the alien to remain in the United States. In considering the application for a waiver, INS does not determine whether the termination of the marriage was appropriate (that issue has already been decided by the courts), but rather whether the alien should be excused from the normal requirement to leave the country. INS is not limited to considering only the evidence which you submit and may also consider:
   A. Evidence contained within its files,
   B. Evidence derived through INS investigation, or
   C. Evidence received from other sources.

   If the decision on your application is based (in whole or in part) on evidence of which you are not already aware, INS will permit you to review and rebut such evidence prior to the decision.

3. **When must a dependent child file this applicaton?**
   If a dependent child who entered the United States as a conditional permanent resident cannot be included in the Form I-751 filed on behalf of his or her conditional resident parent because either:
   A. The child became a resident more than 90 days before or after the parent did, or
   B. The parent did not become a conditional resident or is now deceased,
   The child may apply for a waiver of the requirement to file the joint petition.

   If the conditional resident parent has already filed Form I-751, the relevant information should be indicated on an attachment to the application. If the conditional resident parent is filing this application for himself or herself, any dependent children may be included in the same application (see block D4 of the application).

4. **When must the application be filed?**
   The application must be filed prior to the second anniversary of the date on which conditional permanent residence was obtained (i.e., two years from the date on which you first entered with your immigrant visa, or two years from the date on which your status was adjusted from nonimmigrant to permanent resident.

5. **What if you fail to file the application during this time period?**
   If the application is not filed, you will automatically lose your permanent resident status as of the second anniversary of the date such status was granted and become deportable from the United States. If your failure to file this application was through no fault of your own, you may file it after the required time period with a written explanation of the tardiness requesting that INS excuse the late filing. INS may only excuse your tardiness if you establish that the reasons for the late filing were beyond your control.

6. **What documents do you need to submit for an "extreme hardship" waiver?**
   You must submit evidence that your deportation from the United States will result in hardship which is significantly greater than that encountered by other aliens deported from this country. The evidence must relate to factors which arose after you became a conditional permanent resident, but the law does not otherwise limit the types of evidence which you may submit. It is the responsibility of INS to evaluate all of the evidence (both favorable and unfavorable) in adjudicating the application.

7. **What documents do you need to submit for a "good faith" waiver?**
   A. You must give INS certain documents with this form to show that your marriage was not entered into for the purpose of circumventing the immigration laws of the United States. These documents should include at least two of the following:
      1) a lease or mortagage contract showing joint occupancy and/or ownership of your communal residence,
      2) financial records showing joint ownership of assets and/or joint responsibility for liabilities,
      3) birth certificate(s) of child(ren) born to the marriage,
      4) affidavits from at least two people who have known both parties since conditional permanent residence was granted (such persons may be required to testify before an immigration officer as to the information contained in the affidavit), or
      5) other documentation establishing that a bona fide marital relationship existed.
   B. You must submit a copy of the annulment or divorce decree showing that you were the moving party (i.e., the petitioner) in the proceedings. You must also submit clear and convincing evidence that you sought the termination of the marriage for "good cause".
   C. You must submit any other evidence which you wish INS to consider in weighing the discretionary factors (see instruction number 2).

8. **What are the rules for submission of documents?**
   A. For each document needed, give INS the original and one copy. *Originals will be returned to you.* If you do not wish to give INS the original documents, you may give INS a properly certified copy (INS may still require originals). The copy must be certified by:
      1) an INS or U.S. consular officer, or
      2) an attorney admitted to practice law in the United States, or
      3) an INS accredited representative.
   B. Documents in a foreign language must be accompanied by a complete English translation. The translator must certify that the translation is accurate and that he or she is competent to translate.

INS recommends that you retain photocopies of all submissions for your records.
It is not possible to cover all the conditions for eligibility or give instructions for every situation.
If you have carefully read all the instructions and still have questions, please contact you nearest INS office.

9. **Will you have to appear for an interview?**

   After reviewing the information contained on the application and the accompanying supporting documents, INS may require you to appear at your local INS office for an interview before an immigration officer. If your application is supported by affidavits, the affiants may also be interviewed.

10. **Will you be able to travel outside the United States while the joint petition is pending?**

    The Alien Registration Receipt Card (Form I-551) issued to a conditional permanent resident is not valid beyond the second anniversary of the date on which he or she obtained residence, and may not be used for return to the United States after that second anniversary date. If you must travel outside the United States after your card has expired and before the application is approved, you should first contact your local office of this Service to request advance authorization to travel. If the application is approved you will receive instructions on how to obtain a new Alien Registration Receipt Card.

11. **How should you prepare this form?**
    A. Type or print legibly in ink.
    B. If you need extra space to complete any item, attach a continuation sheet, indicate the item number, and date and sign each sheet.
    C. Answer all questions fully and accurately. If any item does not apply please write "none".

12. **Where should you file this form?**

    Mail this form to the INS Regional Service Center having jurisdiction over your place of residence. The address of the appropriate center is listed below.

13. **What is the fee?**

    You must pay $65.00 to file this form. The fee will not be refunded, whether the application is approved or not. *Do not mail cash.* All checks or money orders, whether U.S. or foreign, must be payable in U.S. currency at a financial institution in the United States. When a check is drawn on the account of a person other than yourself, write your name on the face of the check. If the check is not honored, INS will charge you $5.00.

    Pay by check or money order in the exact amount. Make the check or money order payable to "Immigration and Naturalization Service". However,
    A. if you live in Guam; Make the check or money order payable to "Treasurer, Guam", or
    B. if you live in the U.S. Virgin Islands: Make the check or money order payable to "Commissioner of Finance of the Virgin Islands.

14. **What are the penalties for committing marriage fraud or submitting false information?**

    Title 8, United States Code, Section 1325 states that any individual who knowingly enters into a marriage contract for the purpose of evading any provision of the immigration laws shall be imprisoned for not more than five years, or fined not more than $250,000 or both.

    Title 18, United States Code, Section 1001 states that whoever willfully and knowingly falsifies a material fact, makes a false statement, or makes use of a false document will be fined up to $10,000 or imprisoned up to five years, or both.

15. **What is our authority for collecting this information?**

    We request the information on this form to carry out the immigration laws contained in Title 8, United States Code, Section 1186. We need this information to determine whether a person is eligible for immigration benefits. The information you provide may also be disclosed to other federal, state, local, and foreign law enforcement and regulatory agencies during the course of the investigation required by this Service. You do not have to give this information. However, if you refuse to give some or all of it, your application may be denied.

Jurisdiction and Addresses of Regional Processing Centers

If you reside in:	Mail completed application, with fee, to:	If you reside in:	Mail completed application, with fee, to:
Connecticut Delaware *District of Columbia* Maine Maryland Massachusetts New Hampshire New Jersey New York Pennsylvania *Puerto Rico* Rhode Island Vermont *Virgin Islands* Virginia West Virginia	Immigration & Naturalization Service Regional Service Center P.O. Box 1270 St. Albans, Vermont 05478-1270	Alabama Arkansas Florida Georgia Kentucky Louisiana Mississippi New Mexico North Carolina Oklahoma South Carolina Tennessee Texas	Immigration & Naturalization Service Regional Service Center P.O. Box 568808 Dallas, Texas 75356-8806
Alaska Colorado Idaho Illinois Indiana Iowa Kansas Michigan Minnesota Missouri Montana Nebraska North Dakota Ohio Oregon South Dakota Utah Washington Wisconsin Wyoming	Immigration & Naturalization Service Regional Service Center Federal Building and U.S. Courthouse Room 393 - 100 Centennial Mall North Lincoln, Nebraska 68508	Arizona California *Guam* Hawaii Nevada	Immigration & Naturalization Service Regional Service Center, Room I-752 P.O. Box 73016 San Ysidro, California 92073

If you are stationed outside the United States on government business (either civilian or military), mail the application to the center having jurisdiction over your home of record in the United States. Include a copy of your orders assigning you overseas.

U. S. Department of Justice
Immigration and Naturalization Service

Application for Waiver of Requirement to
File Joint Petition for Removal of Conditions

OMB # 1115-0146

Do not write in this block

Case ID #	ACTION STAMP	FEE STAMP					
A #							
G-28 or VOLAG #							
Remarks					Relocated		Completed
		Receipt	Resubmitted	Rec'd	Sent	Ret	App	Den

A. Basis of Application for Waiver

I am applying for a waiver of the requirement to file a joint petition for removal of the conditional basis of my residence on the basis of (check one:

☐ A. The termination of my status and deportation from the United States would result in an extreme hardship.

☐ B. I entered into the marriage through which I obtained conditional permanent residence in good faith, but terminated the marriage through divorce or annulment for good cause.

☐ C. I am a child who entered as a conditional permanent resident and I am unable to be included in a Joint Petition to Remove the Conditional Basis of Alien's Permanent Residence (Form I-751) filed by my parent(s). (If Form I-751 was already filed by the applicant's parent(s), attach a copy of that petition or an explanation listing the parents' names and INS file numbers and the date of filing of the petition.)

(Note: Regardless of the reason on which your application is based, you must attach a statement of explanation and any documentation which you wish to be considered in support of your application. Please refer to the instructions.)

B. Information About Conditional Permanent Resident	**C. Information About (Former) Petitioning Spouse/ Parent**
1. Name (Family name in CAPS) (First) (Middle)	1. Name (Family name in CAPS) (First) (Middle)
2. Other names used (including maiden name)	2. Other names used (including maiden name)
3. INS A# 4. Social Security #	3. INS A# 4. Social Security #
5. Telephone # 6. Country of Citizenship	5. Telephone # 6. Country of Citizenship
7. Address (Number and Street)	6. Address (Number and Street)
(Town or City) (State/Country) (ZIP/Postal Code)	(Town or City) (State/Country) (ZIP/Postal Code)
8. Have you resided at any other address since becoming a permanent resident? (If yes, attach a list of all addresses and dates). ☐ Yes ☐ No	8. Has this person resided at any other address the applicant became a permanent resident? (If yes, attach a list of all addresses and dates). ☐ Yes ☐ No
9. Date of Birth 10. Place of Birth	9. Date of Birth 10. Place of Birth
11. Current Employer (Name)	11. Current Employer (Name)
12. Employer's Address (Number and Street)	12. Employer's Address (Number and Street)
(Town or City) (State/Country) (ZIP/Postal Code)	(Town or City) (State/Country) (ZIP/Postal Code)
13. Employer's Telephone # 14. Job Title	13. Employer's Telephone # 14. Job Title
15. Supervisor's Name	15. Supervisor's Name
16. Supervisor's Telephone #	16. Supervisor's Telephone #
17. Have you been employed anywhere else since becoming a conditional permanent resident? (If yes, attach a list including all information requested in items 9 through 14 for each.) ☐ Yes ☐ No	17. Has this person been employed anywhere else since the applicant became a conditional permanent resident? (If yes, attach a list including all information requested in items 9 through 14 for each.) ☐ Yes ☐ No

Form I-752 (4/15/88)

D. Information Pertaining to the Marriage Through Which You Obtained Conditional Permanent Resident

1. Date of Marriage   2. Place of Marriage

3. Was a fee paid to anyone other than an attorney in connection with
the filing of the petition through which status was obtained, or in
connection with this application? (If yes, attach a statement of
explanation.)   ☐ Yes   ☐ No

4. Children of applicant. Attach an additional sheet if there are more than six children.

Name	Date of Birth	Place of Birth	INS File Number	Address of Child

Warning:

The INS investigates information claimed on petitions and verifies the authenticity of documents. The INS seek criminal prosecutions when information or documents are falsified to obtain benefits.

Documentation:

All supporting documentation must be submitted in accordance with parts A., B., and C., Item number 6, in the instructions of this form.

Penalties:

You may, by law, be fined up to $250,000 or imprisoned up to five years, or both, for entering into a marriage contract for the purpose of evading any provision of the immigration laws. Furthermore, you may be fined up to $10,000 or imprisoned up to five years, or both, for knowingly and willfully falsifying or concealing a material fact or using any false document in submitting this application.

E. Certification of Information and Authorization for Release of Information.

Your certification (*must be signed in ink*):

I certify, under penalty of perjury under the laws of the United States of America, that the foregoing is true and correct. Furthermore, I authorize the release of any information from my records which the Immigration and Naturalization Service needs to determine eligibility for the benefit being sought.

_____   _____
Signature of Conditional Permanent Resident   *Date*

Signature of Person Preparing Form, if Other than Above:
I declare that I prepared this documents at the request of the persons above and that it is based on all information on which I have any knowledge.

_____   _____   _____
Signature of Preparer   *Date*   *Print Name and Address*

Form I-752 (4/15/88)

U.S. GPO:1990-262-210/08846

To define your job qualifications for the Third or Sixth Preference categories consult the United States Department of Labor. They list job descriptions and their titles and processing codes in three publications. The Department of Labor's *Dictionary of Occupational Titles* (DOT) describes and lists the codes for jobs in the United States. Once you have found the job title, consult the *Occupational Outlook Handbook* (OOH) for general descriptions of the jobs at various stages of experience and expertise. Will you need to show an university degree? Does the job title in your country match the title and description in OOH? *Specific Vocational Preparation* (SVP) shows how much training is required for vocational positions.

As a rule of thumb, aim high when determining your labor code in the DOT, OOH, or SVP. Thumb measurements aren't always precise, so beware of exceptions. If you aim too high, you may price yourself out of the United States labor market. What are the job opportunities for you in the United States? Your success with the Department of Labor will depend on the number of positions in the United States labor market for which there aren't enough citizens to fill the job. Also, in many areas, fewer higher wage positions are made available to immigrants and people of color, especially women.

Not all labor preference applications for permanent residence need approval from the Department of Labor. Two other job lists published by the Department of Labor—Schedule A and Schedule B—will help you determine if you need labor certification. Schedule A lists occupations for which the United States is in short supply (such as nurses and physical therapists), and in which aliens would not displace American workers. If you can prove you have a Schedule A job, you will have little trouble receiving permanent residency. The jobs listed in Schedule A are **precertified,** and do not need labor certification.

Most aliens who receive immigrant visas, however, do not qualify for Schedule A. Schedule A changes periodically as America's labor needs change, so you should check with the INS, Department of Labor, or a consulate abroad to see if you qualify.

Schedule B lists jobs for which there are too many workers in America. Jobs listed on Schedule B usually are for those that require little or no skill, low pay, and long hours. Getting labor certification based on a Schedule B job is rare—don't bother applying unless you can show you can do some other kind of work. In some cases, a skilled lawyer can argue that you should receive a waiver.

What to File

To apply, you will need to find someone willing to hire you in the United States. Obviously, being in the United States makes this easier than if you write to prospective employers from abroad. Your employer must then file ETA-750, Application for Alien Employment Certification, with the local Department of Labor. The employer should fill out Part A in duplicate and you should complete Part B in duplicate. After the ETA-750 is approved, the Petition for Prospective Alien Employee (Form I-140) should also be filed on your behalf.

The employer must first get labor certification for the position through the *state* Department of Labor, which will process the application and forward it to the federal Department of Labor for its approval. The state employment service categorizes jobs according to the United States Department of Labor's requirements. The employer must then advertise the job in a newspaper.

It can take from one to two years to receive labor certification. Filing the ETA-750 is free.

Filling Out ETA-750

Even if you do not have to get labor certification, your future employer should first fill out Form ETA-750, Part A, Offer of Employment, and file it with the local Department of Labor.

In Part A of ETA-750 the employer should describe the business, job duties, and the qualifications required for applicants. Part A also asks for proof of the employer's efforts to advertise the job and about responses to the ad. Part A also asks the employer to show that he or she has:

- the ability to pay the alien's wage, even before the alien will start work;
- complied with state, federal, and local employment laws such as equal opportunity; and
- not sought alien labor because of a work stoppage or labor dispute with current employees.

Job descriptions can be tricky. In item 13 of Part A, the employer should make sure the description reflects the minimum requirements for the job. The employer may have to show that no one less qualified was hired for the job. Word the description fairly. Sometimes the Department of Labor finds that job descriptions are "unduly restrictive." This means the description was written specifically for the alien. Some finesse may be required to show that no American who could fill the job will take it.

In items 9 through 15, consult the DOT, OOH, and SVP to write the best description. Make sure your description is in line with both the Department of Labor handbooks in regards to minimum requirements and the salary offered. But within those guidelines, aim high.

Part B of the ETA-750, Statement of Qualifications of Alien, should be filled out by you. You should be able to provide supporting documentation such as transcripts, diplomas, and letters from previous employers.

Filling Out I-140

The Petition for Prospective Immigrant Employee (Form I-140) is the final step in receiving approval to work in the United States. Third and Sixth Preference applicants and employers who have received labor certification should file this form.

If you apply under the Third Preference category, you may complete the I-140 yourself or have someone authorized by your employer file it for you. Sixth Preference applicants must have their future employers complete and sign Form I-140.

If your petition for a Third or Sixth Preference category visa is approved, your spouse and children under twenty-one immediately become eligible for visas.

You should file Form I-140 along with supporting documents such as transcripts and diplomas and the Department of Labor's certification.

Discuss the information to be included on these forms with your employer. The ETA-750 asks for a description of the duties the alien will be performing. Both parts of

INSTRUCTIONS FOR FILING A PERMANENT LABOR CERTIFICATION (ETA 750) IN NEW YORK STATE

Submit all forms and attachments in <u>DUPLICATE.</u> Identify all attachments.

I.   If employer and/or alien is represented by an attorney, attorney must submit INS Form G—28. Only the attorney need sign the G—28.

II. If employer or alien is represented by an agent, not an attorney, authorization of agent must be completed on ETA 750 Part A and/or Part B.

III. Federal regulations mandate that the employer make a good faith effort to recruit and consider U.S. workers for the job offered to the alien. <u>Processing time will be considerably shorter if the employer does this recruitment on his own within six months prior to filing the application</u> (except for college and university teachers where competitive recruitment and selection of the alien must occur within 18 months of filing). If conducted, prior recruitment and its results should be documented and submitted with employer's written request to waive otherwise mandatory Job Service recruitment and advertising. Recruitment documentation must specify sources used, dates of contact, results, and job related reasons for failure to hire each job applicant who may have responded. Evidence of recruitment activities, such as copies of advertising should accompany the narrative report. If published advertising was used for recruitment purposes, at least one ad must contain all terms and conditions of employment, including a specific wage offer. Advertising, if placed only in a daily publication, should have appeared more than once and must state the employer's business name.

To be considered for a waiver of the Job Service recruitment and related advertising requirements, the application must also contain documentation and evidence that notices describing the job with full particularity, including wage offer, were posted conspicuously on the employer's premises for at least ten consecutive business days. The notices may not be addressed only to the employees of the firm. Results must be specified. Jobs in private households need not be posted. All other jobs MUST be posted.

Although a job order waiver request may be filed with us, the decision on the waiver as well as on the certification rests with the United States Department of Labor, Employment and Training Administration. Job orders may not be waived for Schedule B occupations. (See Special Situations below.)

IV. A properly completed application will also contain:

A. ETA 750 Part A in duplicate with employer's original dated signature on each.

B. ETA 750 Part B in duplicate with alien's original dated signature on each.

C. Documentation signed and dated by employer as follows:

1. The job is being described without unduly restrictive requirements. Requirements which call for justification include foreign languages; education, training, experience or special qualifications which differ from the norm for the occupation in the U.S.; a live-in requirement; a preference; the duties of more than one occupation.

2. If employer hired alien with less education, training, experience or special requirements for any job within his organization in the U.S., employer must explain why it is not feasible to hire a U.S. worker on the same terms as he originally hired the alien.

3. If the job is covered by a union contract, a copy of that portion of the contract which shows current union scale for the job represented in the application.

4. If unions are a source of U.S. workers, employer must document details of his recruitment through the union.

—2—

V. Special Situations.

Schedule B is a list of occupations including unskilled jobs and those which require little or no educa-tion, training, or experience. Denial of labor certification is mandatory unless the Certifying Officer grants a written request filed by the employer for a Schedule B waiver. Recruitment, including Job Service recruitment cannot be waived for a Schedule B job offer.

Household Domestic Service Workers
Special documentation requirements for live-in household domestic service workers should be requested from this office prior to filing.

All household workers except those who primarily provide health care services must document paid experience of one year or the equivalent in the same duties as those specified in the application for alien employment certification.

College and University Teachers and Aliens of Exceptional Ability in the Performing Arts.
Special documentation requirements apply in these occupational categories. Instructions should be requested from this office prior to filing.

Medical Doctors
Employers seeking certification for medical doctors should check current documentation requirements with this office prior to filing.

VI. General Information.

A. To be considered for permanent certification, the job offer must represent permanent, full time work for an employer other than oneself. The employer must have a specific location in the U.S. to which workers may be referred for employment and a location in the U.S. at which the job will be performed. The application for labor certification must be filed with the state office having jurisdiction over the work site.

B. Please read and review all parts of the application before filing. Errors, inconsistencies, and omis-sions can cause delays of months or even years in the issuance of a labor certification. Be sure to submit all forms and required documentation when filing.

C. Any necessary clarification or amendment of the application will be requested in writing. Response must be received in full within 45 days of the date of request. A late reply results in automatic cancellation and loss of priority date. There are no exceptions to this rule.

D. When documenting requirements such as foreign languages or qualifications which differ from the norm for the occupation, the documentation must show how the requirement is a business necessity as opposed to a preference or convenience of the employer or those he serves. Requirements must relate to satisfactory performance of job duties and be those which would qualify a U.S. worker for the job.

E. Certification will not be issued if there are U.S. workers who are able, willing, qualified and avail—able at prevailing wages and working conditions for the job submitted for alien employment certi-fication. Determinations are made by the Regional Office of the United States Department of Labor, Employment and Training Administration, not by state agencies.

F. Willful misrepresentation of material fact in an Application for Alien Employment Certification is a federal offense punishable by fine, imprisonment or both.

ES 578.1 (8-85)   N.Y.S — Dept. of Labor

OMB Approval No. 44-R1301

| U.S. DEPARTMENT OF LABOR
Employment and Training Administration

APPLICATION
FOR
ALIEN EMPLOYMENT CERTIFICATION | **IMPORTANT: READ CAREFULLY BEFORE COMPLETING THIS FORM**
PRINT legibly in ink or use a typewriter. If you need more space to answer questions on this form, use a separate sheet. Identify each answer with the number of the corresponding question. SIGN AND DATE each sheet in original signature.

To knowingly furnish any false information in the preparation of this form and any supplement thereto or to aid, abet, or counsel another to do so is a felony punishable by $10,000 fine or 5 years in the penitentiary, or both (18 U.S.C. 1001). |

PART A. OFFER OF EMPLOYMENT

1. Name of Alien *(Family name in capital letter, First, Middle, Maiden)*

2. Present Address of Alien *(Number, Street, City and Town, State ZIP Code or Province, Country)* | 3. Type of Visa *(If in U.S.)*

The following information is submitted as evidence of an offer of employment.

4. Name of Employer *(Full name of organization)* | 5. Telephone *(Area Code and Number)*

6. Address *(Number, Street, City or Town, Country, State, ZIP Code)*

7. Address Where Alien Will Work *(if different from item 6)*

8. Nature of Employer's Business Activity	9. Name of Job Title	10. Total Hours Per Week		11. Work Schedule *(Hourly)*	12. Rate of Pay	
		a. Basic	b. Overtime	a.m. / p.m.	a. Basic $ per	b. Overtime $ per hour

13. Describe Fully the Job to be Performed *(Duties)*

14. State in detail the MINIMUM education, training, and experience for a worker to perform satisfactorily the job duties described in Item 13 above.

EDU-CATION *(Enter number of years)*	Grade School	High School	College	College Degree Required *(specify)*
				Major Field of Study

TRAIN-ING	No. Yrs.	No. Mos.	Type of Training

EXPERI-ENCE	Job Offered		Related Occupation		Related Occupation *(specify)*
	Number				
	Yrs.	Mos.	Yrs.	Mos.	

15. Other Special Requirements

16. Occupational Title of Person Who Will Be Alien's Immediate Supervisor ➤ ➤

17. Number of Employees Alien will Supervise ➤

◀ **ENDORSEMENTS** *(Make no entry in section - for government use only)*

Date Forms Received	
L.O.	S.O.
R.O.	N.O.
Ind. Code	Occ. Code
Occ. Title	

Replaces MA 7-50A, B and C (Apr. 1970 edition) which is obsolete.

ETA 750 (Oct. 1979)

18. COMPLETE ITEMS ONLY IF JOB IS TEMPORARY			19. IF JOB IS UNIONIZED *(Complete)*	
a. No. of Openings To Be Filled By Aliens Under Job Offer	b. Exact Dates You Expect To Employ Alien		a. Number of Local	b. Name of Local
	From	To		
				c. City and State

20. STATEMENT FOR LIVE-AT-WORK JOB OFFERS *(Complete for Private Household Job ONLY)*

a. Description of Residence		b. No. Persons Residing at Place of Employment				c. Will free board and private room not shared with anyone be provided?	("X" one)
("X" one)	Number of Rooms	Adults	Children		Ages		☐ YES ☐ NO
☐ House			BOYS				
☐ Apartment			GIRLS				

21. DESCRIBE EFFORTS TO RECRUIT U.S. WORKERS AND THE RESULTS. *(Specify Sources of Recruitment by Name)*

22. Applications require various types of documentation. Please read PART II of the instructions to assure that appropriate supporting documentation is included with your application.

23. EMPLOYER CERTIFICATIONS

By virtue of my signature below, I HEREBY CERTIFY the following conditions of employment.

a. I have enough funds available to pay the wage or salary offered the alien.

b. The wage offered equals or exceeds the prevailing wage and I guarantee that, if a labor certification is granted, the wage paid to the alien when the alien begins work will equal or exceed the prevailing wage which is applicable at the time the alien begins work.

c. The wage offered is not based on commissions, bonuses, or other incentives, unless I guarantee a wage paid on a weekly, bi-weekly or monthly basis.

d. I will be able to place the alien on the payroll on or before the date of the alien's proposed entrance into the United States.

e. The job opportunity does not involve unlawful discrimination by race, creed, color, national origin, age, sex, religion, handicap, or citizenship.

f. The job opportunity is not:

(1) Vacant because the former occupant is on strike or is being locked out in the course of a labor dispute involving a work stoppage.

(2) At issue in a labor dispute involving a work stoppage.

g. The job opportunity's terms, conditions and occupational environment are not contrary to Federal, State or local law.

h. The job opportunity has been and is clearly open to any qualified U.S. worker.

24. DECLARATIONS

DECLARATION OF EMPLOYER ➤ *Pursuant to 28 U.S.C. 1746, I declare under penalty of perjury the foregoing is true and correct.*

SIGNATURE		DATE
NAME *(Type or Print)*	TITLE	

AUTHORIZATION OF AGENT OF EMPLOYER ➤ *I HEREBY DESIGNATE the agent below to represent me for the purposes of labor certification and I TAKE FULL RESPONSIBILITY for accuracy of any representations made by my agent.*

SIGNATURE OF EMPLOYER		DATE
NAME OF AGENT *(Type or Print)*	ADDRESS OF AGENT *(Number, Street, City, State, ZIP Code)*	

PART B. STATEMENT OF QUALIFICATIONS OF ALIEN

FOR ADVICE CONCERNING REQUIREMENTS FOR ALIEN EMPLOYMENT CERTIFICATION: *If alien is in the U.S., contact nearest office of Immigration and Naturalization Service. If alien is outside U.S., contact nearest U.S. Consulate.*

IMPORTANT: READ ATTACHED INSTRUCTIONS BEFORE COMPLETING THIS FORM.

Print legibly in ink or use a typewriter. If you need more space to fully answer any questions on this form, use a separate sheet. Identify each answer with the number of the corresponding question. Sign and date each sheet.

1. Name of Alien *(Family name in capital letters)*	First name	Middle name	Maiden name

2. Present Address *(No., Street, City or Town, State or Province and ZIP Code*	Country	3. Type of Visa *(If in U.S.)*

4. Alien's Birthdate *(Month, Day, Year)*	5. Birthplace *(City or Town, State or Province)*	Country	6. Present Nationality or Citizenship *(Country)*

7. Address in United States Where Alien Will Reside

8. Name and Address of Prospective Employer if Alien has job offer in U.S.	9. Occupation in which Alien is Seeking Work

10. "X" the appropriate box below and furnish the information required for the box marked

	City in Foreign Country	Foreign Country
a. ☐ Alien will apply for a visa abroad at the American Consulate in ———————➤		

	City	State
b. ☐ Alien is in the United States and will apply for adjustment of status to that of a lawful permanent resident in the office of the Immigration and Naturalization Service at ———————➤		

11. Names and Addresses of Schools, Colleges and Universities Attended *(Include trade or vocational training facilities)*	Field of Study	FROM		TO		Degrees or Certificates Received
		Month	Year	Month	Year	

SPECIAL QUALIFICATIONS AND SKILLS

12. Additional Qualifications and Skills Alien Possesses and Proficiency in the use of Tools, Machines or Equipment Which Would Help Establish if Alien Meets Requirements for Occupation in Item 9.

13. List Licenses *(Professional, journeyman, etc.)*

14. List Documents Attached Which are Submitted as Evidence that Alien Possesses the Education, Training, Experience, and Abilities Represented

Endorsements	DATE REC. DOL
	O.T. & C.
(Make no entry in this section — FOR Government Agency USE ONLY)	

(Items continued on next page)

15. WORK EXPERIENCE. *List all jobs held during past three (3) years. Also, list any other jobs related to the occupation for which the alien is seeking certification as indicated in item 9.*

a. NAME AND ADDRESS OF EMPLOYER

NAME OF JOB	DATE STARTED Month / Year	DATE LEFT Month / Year	KIND OF BUSINESS

DESCRIBE IN DETAILS THE DUTIES PERFORMED, INCLUDING THE USE OF TOOLS, MACHINES, OR EQUIPMENT	NO. OF HOURS PER WEEK

b. NAME AND ADDRESS OF EMPLOYER

NAME OF JOB	DATE STARTED Month / Year	DATE LEFT Month / Year	KIND OF BUSINESS

DESCRIBE IN DETAIL THE DUTIES PERFORMED, INCLUDING THE USE OF TOOLS, MACHINES, OR EQUIPMENT	NO. OF HOURS PER WEEK

c. NAME AND ADDRESS OF EMPLOYER

NAME OF JOB	DATE STARTED Month / Year	DATE LEFT Month / Year	KIND OF BUSINESS

DESCRIBE IN DETAIL THE DUTIES PERFORMED, INCLUDING THE USE OF TOOLS, MACHINES, OR EQUIPMENT	NO. OF HOURS PER WEEK

16. DECLARATIONS

DECLARATION OF ALIEN ► ► *Pursuant to 28 U.S.C. 1746, I declare under penalty of perjury the foregoing is true and correct.*

SIGNATURE OF ALIEN	DATE

AUTHORIZATION OF AGENT OF ALIEN ► ► *I hereby designate the agent below to represent me for the purposes of labor certification and I take full responsibility for accuracy of any representations made by my agent.*

SIGNATURE OF ALIEN	DATE

NAME OF AGENT *(Type or print)*	ADDRESS OF AGENT *(No., Street, City, State, ZIP Code)*

the ETA-750 and I-140 ask for descriptions of the alien's qualifications. You should be clear with your employer on your job description and what qualifications you have that will be listed on all forms. Be prepared to back up everything you say about your qualifications. An INS official will ask you about the answers to these questions in the interview, so you should be sure you don't accidentally create any inconsistencies in your file. For example, if the job calls for a college degree and you have only three and a half years of college your application will be rejected even though you feel your years of experience on the job qualify you as much as a college graduate. Your experience on the job may not make up for the lack of degree if it is required.

If anything on your application does not agree with statements made by the employer, the INS may decide to deny your application.

Proving Exceptional Ability for Labor Certification

People in some professions have difficulty proving to the Department of Labor and the INS that they qualify if they claim exceptional ability in a field under the Third Preference category. Though the Third Preference usually is reserved for professionals and leaders in a field with a degree, you may qualify for this category by claiming exceptional ability in your field. Proving it to the court can get complicated, and you may want to hire a lawyer to argue your case. You and your lawyer should assemble documents showing exceptional ability, such as:

- published books or articles in your field;
- books or articles written about you;

- membership in an organization for which your abilities make you eligible.

Also look for material that shows your:

- international stature;
- salary, which matches or exceeds that of others in your field with exceptional ability;
- awards, grants, or other honors in your field;
- affidavits from colleagues, associates, and respected members of your field.

While this section has outlined general requirements for labor certification and applying for permanent residence through the Third and Sixth Preference categories, success with the Department of Labor can be best achieved by an expert in the field.

Refugees and Asylees

Refugees and asylees are those aliens who believe they would face persecution from their government because of their race, religion, nationality, political beliefs, or their involvement in political or social organizations. Those who, for these reasons, apply for a visa to enter the United States from a country other than their own, and from outside the United States, are classified as **refugees**. Those who apply for a permanent visa after they have already entered the United States are classified as **asylees.**

Those seeking refugee or asylum status are not subject to the numerical limits of the Preference System. However, Congress and the President set a limit on the number of refugees who enter the country on a year-by-year basis. A limit of 5,000 people can enter the United States each year for asylum. If the INS thinks you qualify for a visa under one of the categories in the Preference System, it will ask you to apply in that way. Also, because of the limited number of people who can apply for refugee status or asylum, you may find it easier to petition for a visa within the Preference System.

You should consult a lawyer when applying for entry to the United States through either one of these methods. Your case for refugee or asylee status must be a strong one. To show the State Department that you qualify for refugee or asylee status, you must prove you would be in direct physical danger if you returned to your country. The State Department can be strict with their definitions of danger. Your fear must be well founded. Many people from Northern Ireland and Central and South America, for example, have a difficult time proving refugee status even when their governments routinely persecute them. Of the many thousands of applications for refugee or asylee status, the State Department approves about 3 percent every year.

One of the most difficult tasks of the enforcement function of the INS is determining who can qualify for asylum. Under asylum rules, persons must be fleeing political persecution and be in danger. However, the INS and the State Department believe that most people who apply for asylum are fleeing economic hardship. While asylum exists for the humanitarian goal of freeing people around the world from oppression, critics of the system say that asylum is extended mostly to people from countries with which the United States is not friendly.

Refugees: What to File

If you are not in the United States, you can apply for refugee status by filing:

- Form I-590, Registration for Classification as Refugee;
- Form G-325A, Biographic Information; and
- FD-258, a fingerprint chart.

The forms must be filed when you are not in your country of origin. A separate form should be filed for each member of your family. Submitting the forms directly with the INS at one of its offices outside the United States is usually the easiest route. However, you may also file at a consular office of the State Department designated to process the forms.

To prove your refugee status, you should provide proof that you are a victim of persecution. Documents should include:

- military books;
- newspaper clippings;
- passports;
- birth records;
- marriage certificates;
- two passport-size photographs for each family member.

You will also have to be examined by an INS-approved doctor.

If you receive refugee status, you can enter the United States and may work while you're here. After a year, you can apply for adjustment of status to receive permanent resident status by filing Form I-485, Application for Permanent Residence.

Asylees: What to File

Those seeking asylum must file while they live in the United States. You can apply for asylum if you entered the country illegally or are on parole. Like the application for refugee status, you must prove that you

For sale by the Superintendent of Documents, U.S. Government Printing Office
Washington, D.C. 20402

U.S. Department of Justice
Immigration and Naturalization Service (INS)

Petition for Prospective Immigrant Employee

Instructions

Read the instructions carefully. If you do not follow the instructions, we may have to return your petition which may delay final action.

Definitions

Third Preference Immigrant - A prospective employee who is a member of the professions, or who because of exceptional ability in the sciences or arts will substantially benefit the national economy, cultural interest, or welfare of the United States, and whose services are sought by an employer.

Sixth Preference Immigrant - A prospective employee who is capable of performing skilled or unskilled labor, not of a temporary or seasonal nature, for which there is a shortage of employable and willing persons in the United States.

Schedule A - A list of occupations for which it has already been determined that a shortage of U.S. workers exists. This list can be found in Title 20 CFR 656.10.

1. Who can file?

A. You may file this form under Third Preference if you are:

  1) the prospective employer, or
  2) the prospective employee, or
  3) any other person applying on the prospective employee's behalf.

B. You may file this form under Sixth Preference only if you are the prospective employee's prospective employer.

If the petition is approved, the husband or wife and unmarried children under 21 years of age of the prospective employee will automatically be eligible to apply for a visa.

2. What documents do you need?

A. 1) In general, you must give INS certain documents with this form. For each document needed, give INS the original and one copy. **Originals will be returned to you.**

  2) If you do not wish to give an original document, you may give INS a copy. The copy must be certified by:

    a) an INS or U.S. consular officer, or

    b) an attorney admitted to practice law in the United States, or

    c) an INS accredited representative

    (INS still may require originals).

  3) Documents in a foreign language must be accompanied by a complete English translation. The translator must certify that the translation is accurate and that he or she is competent to translate.

B. You must give INS a completed Form ETA–750A&B ''Application for Alien Employment Certification'' bearing the Department of Labor's certification, unless the occupation is currently listed in Schedule A (see definitions).

C. You must document the prospective employee's qualifications:

  1) If the prospective employee's qualifications are based on education, give INS:

    a) diploma(s) and

    b) a certified copy of school transcript(s).

  2) If the prospective employee's qualifications are based on exceptional ability in the sciences or arts, give INS evidence of national or international recognition such as awards, prizes, specific products, publications, memberships in a national or international association that maintains standards of outstanding achievement in a specific field, etc.

  3) If the prospective employee's qualifications are based on a profession requiring a license or other official permission to practice, give INS a copy of the license or other official permission.

  4) If the prospective employee's qualifications are based on technical training or specialized experience, give INS affidavits or published material supporting this training or experience.

  5) For physicians or surgeons, also give INS:

    a) the results of Parts 1 and 2 of the National Board of Medical Examiners Examination, the Visa Qualifying Examination, or Foreign Medical Graduate Examination in Medical Sciences.

    b) evidence of competency in oral and written English.

D. The prospective employer must give INS documentary evidence that establishes ability to pay the offered wage (e.g., latest annual report, last U.S. tax return, profit/loss statement, etc.)

E. Affidavits - These must come from independent sources, such as the prospective employee's former employers or recognized experts familiar with the prospective employee's work. The affidavits must:

    a) identify the person making the affidavit, showing the capacity in which he or she is testifying

    b) give the places and the dates during which the prospective employee gained his or her experience

    c) describe in detail the duties the prospective employee performed, the tools he or she used, how he or she was supervised, and any supervisory tasks that he or she performed. A mere statement, for example, that the prospective employee was employed as a baker, is not adequate.

    d) show the date on which the affidavit was signed.

3. How should you prepare this form?

A. Type or print legibly in ink.

B. If you need extra space to complete any item, attach a continuation sheet, indicate the item number, and date and sign each sheet.

C. Answer all questions fully and accurately. If any item does not apply, please write "N/A".

4. Where should you file this form?

A. If you are in the United States, send or take the completed form and supporting documents to the INS office that has jurisdiction over the place of intended employment.

B. If you are outside the United States, contact the nearest American Consulate to find out where to send the completed form.

5. When will a visa become available?

The availability of an immigrant visa number depends on the number of aliens in the same visa classification who have an earlier priority date (date for which visas are available) on the visa waiting list.

Visa numbers are given out in the order in which Forms ETA-750A&B are filed with the Department of Labor or the order in which they are properly filed with INS in Schedule A cases. Since these numbers are limited each year, it is important to make sure the form is properly filed to put the prospective employee on the waiting list at the earliest possible date. To be properly filed, the form must be complete, the form must be signed, the necessary documents must be attached, and the fee must be paid. For a monthly update on dates for which immigrant visas are available, you may call (202) 647-0508.

6. What is the fee?

You must pay $50.00 to file this form. **The fee will not be refunded, whether the petition is approved or not.** DO NOT MAIL CASH. All checks or money orders, whether U.S. or foreign, must be payable in U.S. currency at a financial institution in the United States. When a check is drawn on the account of a person other than yourself, write your name on the face of the check. If the check is not honored, INS will charge you $5.00.

Pay by check or money order in the exact amount. Make the check or money order payable to "Immigration and Naturalization Service". However,

A. if you live in Guam: Make the check or money order payable to "Treasurer, Guam", or

B. if you live in the U.S. Virgin Islands: Make the check or money order payable to "Commissioner of Finance of the Virgin Islands".

7. What are the penalties for submitting false information?

Title 18, United States Code, Section 1001 states that whoever willfully and knowingly falsifies a material fact, makes a false statement, or makes use of a false document will be fined up to $10,000 or imprisoned up to five years, or both.

8. What is our authority for collecting this information?

We request the information on this form to carry out the immigration laws contained in Title 8, United States Code, Section 1154(a). We need this information to determine whether a person is eligible for immigration benefits. The information you provide may also be disclosed to other federal, state, local, and foreign law enforcement and regulatory agencies during the course of the investigation required by this Service. You do not have to give this information. However, if you refuse to give some or all of it, your petition may be denied.

It is not possible to cover all the conditions for eligibility or to give instructions for every situation. If you have carefully read all the instructions and still have questions, please contact your nearest INS office.

U.S. Department of Justice
Immigration and Naturalization Service (INS)   Petition for Prospective Immigrant Employee   OMB # 1115-0061

DO NOT WRITE IN THIS BLOCK		
Case ID#	Action Stamp	Fee Stamp
A#		
G-28 or Volag#		
Petition was filed on:		Petition is approved for status under section: ☐ 203(a)(3) ☐ 203(a)(6)
_____ (Priority Date)		Section 212(a)(14) certification ☐ Attached ☐ Sched. A, Group _____

A. Information about this petition

This petition is being filed for a: ☐ 3rd Preference Immigrant ☐ 6th Preference Immigrant

(See instructions for definitions and check one block only)

B. Information about employer

1. Name (Family name in CAPS) (First) (Middle)   or   (Company Name)

2. Address (Number and Street)

(Town or City)   (State/Country)   (ZIP/Postal Code)

3. Address where employee will work (If different) (Number and Street)

(Town or City)   (State/Country)   (ZIP/Postal Code)

4. Employer is: ☐ an organization ☐ a permanent resident
(check one) ☐ a U.S. citizen ☐ a nonimmigrant

5. Social Security Number or **IRS employer ID number**

6. Alien Registration Number (if any)

7. Description of Business (Nature, number of employees, gross and net annual income, date established) (If employer is an individual, state occupation and annual income).

8. Have you ever filed a visa petition for an alien employee in this same capacity?
☐ Yes ☐ No   (If Yes, how many?)

9. Are you and the prospective employee related by birth or marriage?
☐ Yes ☐ No

10. Are separate petitions being filed at this time for other aliens?
☐ Yes ☐ No   (If Yes, list names)

11. Title and salary of position offered

12. Is the position permanent? ☐ Yes ☐ No
13. Is the position full-time? ☐ Yes ☐ No
14. Is this a newly-created position? ☐ Yes ☐ No
(If No, how long has it existed?)

C. Information about prospective employee

1. Name (Family name in CAPS) (First)   (Middle)

2. Address (Number and Street)   (Apartment Number)

(Town or City)   (State/Country)   (ZIP/Postal Code)

3. Place of Birth (Town or City)   (State/Country)

4. Date of Birth **5. Sex** **6. Marital Status**
(Mo/Day/Yr) ☐ Male ☐ Married ☐ Single
☐ Female ☐ Widowed ☐ Divorced

7. Other names used (including maiden name)

8. Profession or occupation and years held

9. Social Security Number   **10. Alien Registration Number** (if any)

11. Name and address of present employer (Name)

(Number and Street)

(Town or City)   (State/Country)   (ZIP/Postal Code)

12. Date employee began present employment

13. If employee is currently in the U.S., complete the following:
He or she last arrived as a (visitor, student, exchange alien, crewman, stowaway, temporary worker, without inspection, etc.)

Arrival/Departure Record (I-94) Number   **Date arrived** (Month/Day/Year)

Date authorized stay expired, or will expire as shown on Form I-94 or I-95

14. Has a visa petition ever been filed by or on behalf of this person?
☐ Yes ☐ No   (If Yes, explain)

INITIAL RECEIPT	RESUBMITTED	RELOCATED		COMPLETED		
		Rec'd	Sent	Approved	Denied	Returned

Form I-140 (REV. 3-2-87) Y

C. (continued) Information about prospective employee

15. List husband/wife and all children of prospective employee

Name	Relationship	Date of Birth	Country of Birth	Present Address

16. Employee's address abroad

(Number and Street)	(Town or City)	(Province)	(Country)

17. If your employee's native alphabet is other than Roman letters, write his/her name and address abroad in the native alphabet:

(Name)	(Number and Street)	(Town or City)	(Province)	(Country)

18. Check the appropriate box below and give the information required for the box you checked:

☐ The employee will apply for a visa abroad at the American Consulate in _____
(City) (Country)

☐ The employee is in the United States and will apply for adjustment of status to that of a lawful resident in the office of the Immigration and Naturalization Service at _____ (City) (State) _____. If the employee is not eligible for adjustment of status, he or she will apply for a visa abroad at the American Consulate in _____ (City) (Country)

Warning: The INS investigates employment experience. If the INS finds that employment experience is false, the application is denied and the person responsible for providing false information may be criminally prosecuted.

Penalties: You may, by law, be fined up to $10,000, imprisoned up to five years, or both, for knowingly and willfully falsifying or concealing a material fact or using any false document in submitting this petition.

Your Certification

This petition may only be filed by one of the following:

I am ☐ the employer

☐ the prospective employee (only allowed for 3rd preference)

☐ a person filing on behalf of and authorized by the prospective employee (only allowed for 3rd preference)

I certify, under penalty of perjury under the laws of the United States of America, that the foregoing is true and correct. Furthermore, I authorize the release of any information from my records which the Immigration and Naturalization Service needs to determine eligibility for the benefit that I am seeking.

Print Name _____ Title _____

Signature _____ Date _____ Phone Number _____

Signature of Person Preparing Form if Other than Above

I declare that I prepared this document at the request of the person above and that it is based on all information of which I have any knowledge.

(Print Name)	(Address)	(Signature)	(Date)

G-28 ID Number _____

Volag Number _____

NOTE: Fill in Items 1–5 below so that your petition approval can be recorded by the Immigration Service.

1. Name of Prospective Employee	A#
2. Other Names Used	
3. Country of Birth	4. Date of Birth
5. Name of Prospective Employer	

Action Stamp	Section	Priority Date
	☐ 203(a)(3)	
	☐ 203(a)(6)	Filing Date
		Sent to Consul at:

Petition for Prospective Immigrant Employee
Form I-140 (REV.3-2-87)Y

CHECKLIST

☐ Have you filled in all the information required on the form?

☐ Have you signed the form?

☐ Have you enclosed the Labor Department forms ETA 7-50 A & B?

☐ Have you enclosed all other required documents?

☐ Have you enclosed the fee?

are a victim of persecution, with similar documents. If your application is based on religious persecution, you may have an easier time proving your case. To apply for asylum you must file:

- Form I-589, Request for Asylum in the United States;
- Form G-325A, Biographic Information;
- a fingerprint card; and
- supporting documents as outlined above for refugees.

After you apply, the INS will interview you and send your application on to the State Department. If the State Department approves your request, the INS usually grants its approval, too. Like refugees, you can apply for permanent residence one year after you receive authorization for asylum.

One of the advantages of asylum is that you do not have to file separate requests for members of your family. One of the disadvantages of asylum is that you could wait a long time before receiving approval of your request. The State Department may delay deciding on your request in hopes that the political situation in your country will change.

Some people have waited years for the State Department to rule on their cases. Those familiar with asylum applications say that the State Department may have as many as 100,000 applications for asylum on file. If you do not qualify for refugee status or asylum, but think you can show good reasons why you are the victim of persecution, have medical difficulties, or can argue for family reunification under *extenuating circumstances*, you may apply for humanitarian parole. Although receiving approval for parole is rare, you may want to consider it if your case shows unusual and extenuating circumstances.

You can apply through a consulate or embassy using the normal nonimmigrant visa request forms. Or you can write a letter to the Central Immigration Office in Washington. Whichever application route you take, you should provide detailed evidence of your claim to humanitarian parole. If your request is granted, you should apply for asylum soon after you enter the United States.

As you can see, receiving a visa number and getting approval for your request for permanent residence status are among the most time-consuming and complicated procedures on your way to becoming a United States citizen. Assuming that you do receive your permanent residence status and abide by the rules for maintaining permanent residence, the path to citizenship now is relatively clear. All you have to do is follow the guidelines in the next chapter for applying for naturalization.

U.S. Department of Justice
Immigration and Naturalization Service

OMB NO. 1115-0086
Request for Asylum In The United States

INSTRUCTIONS
READ ALL INSTRUCTIONS CAREFULLY BEFORE COMPLETING THIS FORM

1. General:

Use typewriter or print legibly in block letters with ballpoint pen.

DO NOT LEAVE ANY QUESTIONS UNANSWERED. Where appropriate insert "none" or "not applicable". If you need more space to fully answer any question, use a separate sheet of paper this size and identify each answer with the number of the corresponding question. One form may include an entire family (husband, wife, and children if they are also applying for asylum) except children over age 21 or married, who must file a separate form.

Each applicant age 14 or older must complete the Biographic Information Form G-325A and Fingerprint Chart FD-258.

2. SUBMISSION OF FORM:

Be sure to sign, mail or take this form to the Immigration and Naturalization Service having jurisdiction over your place of residence.

3. FINGERPRINTS:

Fingerprint cards with instructions for their completion are available at the office of the Immigration and Naturalization Service where you intend to file your application. You may have your fingerprints recorded on Form FD-258 at an office of the Immigration and Naturalization Service, other Law Enforcement Offices, Immigration and Naturalization Service Outreach Centers, Charitable and Voluntary Agencies. The card must be signed by you in the presence of the individual taking your prints, who must then sign his name and enter the date in the spaces provided. It is important to furnish all the information called for on the card.

4. PASSPORT INFORMATION:

You will be notified to appear for an interview with an Immigration Officer within 45 days after your form is received. You must bring your passport with you to this interview. If other members of your family are included in your form, they must also appear for the interview and bring their passports.

An immigration officer will interview you regarding asylum and make an evaluation of the propriety of the claim.

You may remain in the United States until a final decision is made on your case (or you are notified otherwise by this Service).

5. UNITED NATIONS:

You may, if you wish, forward a copy of your form and other supporting documents to the: Regional Representative of the United Nations, High Commissioner for Refugees, United Nations, 1718 Connecticut Ave., N.W., Suite 200, Washington, D.C. 20009

6. SUPPORTING DOCUMENTS:

Background materials, such as newspaper articles, affidavits of witnesses or experts, periodicals, journals, books, photographs, official documents, your own statements, etc., must include explanations from you of their relevance to your personal case and situation. Give full citation of your sources, dates, pages, etc.

The burden of proof is upon you to establish that you have a wellfounded fear of persecution on account of your race, religion, nationality, membership in a particular social group or political opinion, and for this reason you are unwilling or unable to return to your country of last residence. To persecute is defined as: "to pursue; to harass in a manner designed to injure, grieve or afflict; to oppress; specifically, to cause to suffer or put to death because of belief".

Answer all questions on this form as to "when", "where", "how", "who", and "why" relating to your claim of persecution.

Attach as many sheets and explanations as necessary to fully explain the basis of your claim.

7. TRANSLATION:

Any document in a foreign language must be accompanied by a translation in English. The translator must certify that he or she is competent to translate and that the translation is accurate.

(over)

Form I-589 (Rev. 12-2-88)N   (Tear off this instruction sheet before submitting application)

8. WORK AUTHORIZATION:

You may request permission to work while your asylum form is pending. submit a written statement with this form explaining your reasons and include the original Form I-94, ARRIVAL AND DEPARTURE RECORD of each person seeking work.

Generally, work authorization, if granted, will be valid during the pendency of the form.

9. PENALTY:

Title 18, United States Code, section 1546, provides,"Whoever knowingly makes under oath any false statement with respect to a material fact in any application, affidavit, or other document required by the immigration laws or regulations prescribed thereunder, or knowingly presents any such application, affidavit or other document containing any such false statement, shall be fined not more than $2,000 or imprisoned not more than 5 years or both."

10. REPORTING BURDEN:

Public reporting burden for this collection of information is estimated to average 1 hour per response, including the time for reviewing instructions, searching existing data sources, gathering and maintaining the data needed, and completing and reviewing the collection of information. Send comments regarding this burden estimate or any other aspect of this collection of information, including suggestions for reducing this burden to: U.S. Department of Justice, Immigration and Naturalization Service (Room 2011), Washington, DC 20536; and to the Office of Management and Budget, Paperwork Reduction Project: OMB No. 1115-0086, Washington, DC 20503.

U.S. Department of Justice

Immigration and Naturalization Service

OMB No. 1115–0086

REQUEST FOR ASYLUM IN THE UNITED STATES

INS Office:
Date:

1. Family Name	First	Middle Name	2. A number (if any or known)

All other names used at any time (include maiden name if married)	3. Sex ☐ Male ☐ Female	4. Marital status ☐ Single ☐ Divorced ☐ Married ☐ Widowed

I was born: (Month) (Day) (Year) in (Town or City) (State or Province) (Country)

Nationality — at birth	At present	Other nationalities

5. If stateless, how did you become stateless?

6. Ethnic group	7. Religion	8. Languages spoken

9. Address in United States (In care of, C/O, if appropriate) (Number and street) (Apt. No.) (City or town) (State) (Zip Code)   10. Telephone number (include area code)

11. Address abroad prior to coming to the United States (Number and street) (City) (Province) (Country)

12. My last arrival in the U.S. occurred on: (Mo/Day/Yr)   As a ☐ Visitor ☐ Student ☐ Stowaway ☐ Crewman ☐ Other (Specify)

At the port of (City/State)   Means of arrival (Name of vessel or airline and flight number, etc.)

I ☐ was ☐ was not inspected   Date authorized stay expires (Mo/Day/Yr)

13. My nonimmigrant visa number is _____, it was issued by the U.S. Consul on_____ (If none, state "none") (Mo/Day/Yr)

at_____ (City, County)

14. Name and location of schools attended	Type of school	From Mo/Yr	To Mo/Yr	Highest grade completed	Title of degree or certification

15. What specific skills do you have?	16. Social Security No. (if any)

17. Name of husband or wife (wife's maiden name)

18. My husband or wife resides ☐ with me ☐ apart from me (if apart, explain why)

Address (Apt. No.) (No. and street) (Town or city) (Province or state) (Country)

Form I-589 (Rev. 12-2-88)N   (OVER)

RECEIVED	TRANS. IN	RET'D TRANS. OUT	COMPLETED

Page 1

19. If in the U.S. is your spouse included in your request for asylum? ☐ Yes ☐ No (If not, explain why)

20. If in the U.S. is spouse making separate application for asylum? ☐ Yes ☐ No (If not, explain why)

21. If in the U.S. are children included in your request for asylum? ☐ Yes ☐ No (If not, explain why)

22. I have_____ sons or daughters as follows: (Complete all columns as to each son or daughter. If living with you state "with me" in last column; otherwise give city and state or foreign country of son's or daughter's residence).

Name	Sex	Place of birth	Date of birth	Now living at :

23. Relatives in U.S. other than immediate family

Name	Address	Relationship	Immigration status

24. Other relatives who are refugees but outside the U.S.

Name	Relationship	Country where presently located

25. List all travel or identity documents such as national passport, refugee convention travel document or national identity card

Document type	Document number	Issuing country or authority	Date of issue	Date of expiration	Cost	Obtained by whom

26. Why did you obtain a U.S. visa?

27. If you did not apply for a U.S. visa, explain why not?

28. Date of departure from your country of nationality (Mo / Day / Yr.)

29. Was exit permission required to leave your country? ☐ Yes ☐ No (If so, did you obtain exit permission ☐ Yes ☐ No (If not, explain why)

30. Are you entitled to return to country of issuance of your passport ☐ Yes ☐ No Travel document ☐ Yes ☐ No Or other document ☐ Yes ☐ No (If not, explain why)

31. What do you think would happen to you if you returned? (Explain)

32. When you left your home country, to what country did you intend to go?

33. Would you return to your home country? ☐ Yes ☐ No (Explain)

34. Have you or any member of your immediate family ever belonged to any organization in your home country? ☐ Yes ☐ No. (If yes, provide the following information relating to each organization: Name of organization, dates of membership or affiliation, purpose of the organization, what, if any, were your official duties or responsibilities, and are you still an active member. (If not, explain)

35. Have you taken any action that you believe will result in persecution in your home country? ☐ Yes ☐ No (If yes, explain)

36. Have you ever been ☐ detained ☐ interrogated ☐ convicted and sentenced ☐ imprisoned in any country? ☐ Yes ☐ No (If yes, specify for each instance: what occurred and the circumstances, dates, location, duration of the detention or imprisonment, reason for the detention or conviction, what formal charges were placed against you, reason for the release, names and addresses of persons who could verify these statements. Attach documents referring to these incidents, if any).

37. If you base your claim for asylum on current conditions in your country, do these conditions affect your freedom more than the rest of that country's population? ☐ Yes ☐ No (If yes, explain)

38. Have you, or any member of your immediate family, ever been mistreated by the authorities of your home country/country of nationality ☐ Yes ☐ No. If yes, was it mistreatment because of ☐ Race ☐ Religion ☐ Nationality ☐ Political opinion or ☐ Membership of a particular social group? Specify for each instance; what occurred and the circumstances, date, exact location, who took such action against you and what was his/her position in the government, reason why the incident occurred, names and addresses of people who witnessed these actions and who could verify these statements. Attach documents referring to these incidents.

39. After leaving your home country, have you traveled through (other than in transit) or resided in any other country before entering the U.S.? ☐ Yes ☐ No (If yes, identify each country, length of stay, purpose of stay, address, and reason for leaving, and whether you are entitled to return to that country for residence purposes.

40. Why did you continue traveling to the U.S.?

41. Did you apply for asylum in any other country? ☐ Yes __ Give details ☐ No __ Explain why not

(over)

42. Have you been recognized as a refugee by another country or by the United Nations High Commissioner for Refugees? ☐ Yes ☐ No   (If yes, where and when)

43. Are you registered with a consulate or any other authority of your home country abroad?   ☐ Yes—Give details ☐ No—Explain why not

44. Is there any additional information not covered by the above questions?   (If yes, explain)

45. Under penalties of perjury, I declare that the above and all accompanying documents are true and correct to the best of my knowledge and belief.

_____   _____
(Signature of Applicant)   (Date)

SAMPLE ONLY

_____   _____
(Interviewing Officer)   (Date of Interview)

ACTION BY ADJUDICATING OFFICER   ☐ GRANTED   ☐ DENIED

_____   _____
(Adjudicating Officer)   (Date)

Advisory opinion requested ☐   _____
                                                                      (Date)

(4)

Becoming a Citizen

KEY TERMS

naturalization ceremony   *Certificate of Citizenship*   *Oath of Citizenship*

Once you have received permanent residence status in the United States, you can begin thinking about becoming naturalized. This means that someone who is not a United States citizen becomes a citizen through the legal procedure of naturalization. Before you can apply for naturalization, you will have to live in the United States as a permanent resident alien for three or five years, depending on whether you received residence through a marriage or a relative or a job. Establishing residency may seem to take a long time, but the years will pass quickly if you keep the final goal in mind.

If there are no problems with the forms you've filed so far, applying for citizenship will be the easiest of all. The application is based on the forms you've already filed, and the interview generally is short. It's never too early to begin preparing yourself for the examination part of your naturalization application.

Review the application for naturalization about three months before you need to fill it out. File the application promptly before the end of your three-year or five-year residency requirement. Knowing what is required on the application will help you avoid creating any problems for yourself. For example, if you received permanent residence status on the basis of a job offer, the INS may think you misled them should you change jobs soon after obtaining your Green Card.

The forms you filled out to become a permanent resident will be reviewed by the INS again. Any differences between the information you provided on these forms and your application for naturalization will be closely examined by the INS.

In this chapter, you'll see how the naturalization process works, what rights you gain when you become a citizen, and how to fill out the application for becoming naturalized.

How Do I Become a Citizen?

If you are a legal permanent resident alien of the United States, you can apply for citizenship once you have fulfilled the residency requirements. You also must meet the requirements for naturalization, such as being a person of good moral character and being willing to take the Oath of Citizenship. While you are a permanent resident, you also should be able to support yourself, either by working or with the help of friends and family. You will have to prove that you are not likely to become a public charge. The requirements for naturalization are described in Chapter Two, pages 30–39, and are reviewed later in this chapter.

Three simple steps lead to naturalization. First, you must fill out an application and provide any supporting documents. These will be much like the ones you used in earlier applications. Then you'll be interviewed by an INS official and asked questions about your application as well as about certain aspects of United States history and Government. If the interview is successful, the INS office will recommend to the court that your application for naturalization be approved. You, along with a number of others, will appear for a hearing, called the **naturalization ceremony**, before a federal

judge. At the ceremony, you will formally pledge an Oath of Allegiance to the United States.

Unless the group being naturalized with you is very large, you should receive your **Certificate of Citizenship** that day. Sometimes the certificate will be mailed to you later. The certificate shows that you have completed the naturalization process. With the certificate, you have the same rights and responsibilities as all other United States citizens.

Your Certificate of Citizenship is an important document. It proves your legal right to all the benefits of citizenship. If you lose it or have your name legally changed, you should apply for a new certificate through an INS office.

Your Rights as a Citizen

As a permanent resident alien in the United States you enjoyed some of the privileges of citizenship. Now, as a citizen, you can take full advantage of the services and legal protection extended to all American citizens. Your new rights include:

- voting in local, state, and federal elections;
- holding any elective office except for President or Vice President of the United States;
- applying for any job available in the United States;
- applying for a United States passport;
- receiving Social Security benefits;
- receiving state and federal aid; and
- petitioning for the immigration of your relatives abroad as a citizen under the Preference System.

Along with these rights, citizens also have certain duties to their country. There is the possibility that you will be asked to serve in the armed forces. Other duties that American citizens sometimes take for granted include being responsible and active members of their communities. The American system works because its citizens voice their opinions about politics and social issues. They become involved in organizations and institutions that tell their government how they think the United States Government can best work for all individuals and groups of people. Individuals vote for elected officials in all levels of government. Some people choose not to vote as a conscious political act. No United States citizen can be forced to participate in any group or to vote. Voting is, perhaps, more a right than a duty.

Within the limits of the law, Americans have the right to voice protest through marches, publications, and political lobbying, individually or in groups. Sometimes political activity pushes the boundaries of the law. Yet one of the most important aspects of this system is that citizens can be critical of it.

Without the participation of its citizens, the American system of government would decay.

Requirements for Citizenship

Before you can apply for naturalization, you should have fulfilled (or be willing to fulfill) the requirements for citizenship. In Chapter Two you will find more detailed explanations of the citizenship requirements, particularly those for permanent residency and eligibility. Use this list as a review to be sure you're ready to apply for citizenship.

1. You must be at least eighteen years old.
2. You must have entered the United States legally and have applied for and become a permanent resident alien.

You must show that you maintained your permanent residence status for a statutory period of years. Maintaining your permanent residence status means that you did not violate any of the regulations concerning your permanent residency. You worked in the job upon which your application was based, or you can show that your marriage to a citizen to gain permanent residence status is true and legal.

If you married a United States citizen to achieve permanent residence status, you must show that you lived here for three years while you had permanent residence status.

If you left the country and were readmitted to the United States, you must not have left for more than half of the five-year or three-year period, and for no longer than one continuous year.

3. You must show that you have lived in the state where you file your petition for naturalization for at least six months before filing.
4. You must show that you intend to live in the United States permanently.
5. You must be a person of good moral character and be loyal to the United States and the principles of the Constitution.
6. You must not have been a member of the Communist Party for at least ten years before applying for citizenship.
7. You must not have broken any immigration laws nor been deported.
8. You must be able to read, write, and speak simple English, and sign your name in English. You should also be prepared to answer questions about United States Government and history.

You may receive a waiver from this requirement if you have a physical handicap making you unable to speak, read, or write. Others who may receive a waiver include those who are over fifty years of age who have lived in the United States for more than twenty years.

9. You must be willing to take the **Oath of Citizenship,** in which you give up your allegiance to all other countries and pledge to support and protect the United States and obey its laws and Constitution. (The Oath appears on page 39.)

After applying for naturalization, it's a good idea to stay in the United States until you have taken the Oath of Citizenship. This is no longer required by law, but you wouldn't want to have any trouble at the border upon your last return from a trip abroad before becoming a citizen.

The Naturalization Application

This is the moment you've been waiting for. If you have fulfilled the permanent residency requirement, you can now apply for naturalization. In many ways, this application is a formality—and much simpler than petitioning to enter the United States or applying for a Green Card. It gives the INS a chance to review your file one last time. You'll also be asked to learn about how the government runs and a little about America's history. You can probably complete the application without the advice of a lawyer. Even so, the INS will review your entire immigration file, from the first visa application to your naturalization application. If you think the INS will see any inconsistencies in your immigration records, consult a lawyer.

What to File

While the application itself is fairly simple, it can take the INS up to one year to process it. The sooner you apply, the higher you will be on the INS's waiting list. While you should not apply before meeting the residency requirement, you may want to gather all the forms and materials before you become eligible.

To apply for naturalization you will need:

- Form N-400, Application to File Petition for Naturalization;
- Form G-325A, Biographic Information;
- Form FD-258, fingerprint card;
- three passport-size photographs of yourself; and
- a filing fee of $60.00.

Other forms you might need include:

- Form N-402, Application to File Petition on Behalf of Child. Not all your children automatically become naturalized with you. If your spouse is a permanent resident alien and does not become a citizen when you do, your child may not become a citizen. It will be easier if a child becomes naturalized with you before he or she turns eighteen; after turning eighteen, the child will have to be naturalized separately. If you are a citizen, you can file this form for a child who is under eighteen. With the form you should also file the Biographic Information sheet, three photographs of the child, and a fingerprint chart if the child is over fourteen. (Cases where children may become naturalized with you are discussed with the instructions for filling out Form N-400 later in this chapter.)
- Form N-426, Request for Certification of Military or Naval Service, if your application is based on your service in the United States military;
- Form G-28, Notice of Appearance of Attorney or Representative, if you want a lawyer to help you with your application;

- Form-600, Application for Certification of Citizenship, if you want your minor children who qualify for citizenship with your application to receive a Certificate of Citizenship. You may also file this form if you think you already qualify for citizenship through a family relation such as a spouse or parent. However, you should check with a lawyer if you are not sure you should use this form.

You can write to the INS office nearest you for the necessary forms, or you can pick them up yourself. INS offices are listed in the appendices of this book. If you write to the INS, type or print your letter, following the model letter that follows. Using the formal business-letter format will help speed up the INS's response.

SAMPLE LETTER REQUESTING FORMS

> Your street address
> Your city, state, zip code
> Date the letter is written

Immigration and Naturalization Service
Street address
City, state, zip code

Dear Sir or Madam:

I would like to apply to become a United States citizen.

Please send the application packet to the above address. The forms I need are:
    Form N-17, Naturalization Requirements and General Information;
    Form N-400, Application to File Petition for Naturalization;
    Form G-325A, Biographic Information;
    Form FD-258, fingerprint chart; and
    (You can list other forms you might need, such as Form N-402, Application to File Petition for Naturalization in Behalf of Child.)

Thank you for your prompt attention. I look forward to receiving the application at your earliest convenience.

> Sincerely,
>
> (Sign your name)
>
>
> Print your name here

There is a fee to file the Application to File Petition for Naturalization. The Petition for Naturalization (Form N-405), filed with the naturalization court after your application is approved, will be processed at no extra charge.

Filling Out the N-400

As with any other form you file with the INS, type or print legibly in ink. You should leave no question unanswered. If a question does not apply to you, write "N/A" in the space provided. If you need more space than the form provides, use a separate sheet of paper. Write your name, the date, the form number, and the item number on it. Sign it and attach it to the form.

Consistency is also important. Your name and other information should appear on this form as it does on other forms filed with the INS and on your Alien Registration Card. Look over the copies of previous forms you filed to be sure you don't accidentally create any inconsistencies in your file that the INS will question.

Carefully read through the directions on the form and those provided in this book. Using the instructions in this book as a guide should answer most of the questions you have as you fill out the form.

Photographs

When you submit the Application to File Petition for Naturalization (Form N-400), you should also include three passport-size photographs of yourself. The requirements for the photographs are specific, so follow the instructions carefully. *Be sure your photographs are taken no more than thirty days before you submit them with the application.* Though most places that take passport photographs are familiar with the format, you may want to check with the photographer that the pictures will meet the requirements. The photographs should be:

- on thin paper, measure 2 inches by 2 inches, and have a non-glossy finish. Machine-made photographs will be rejected;
- black-and-white or color, not machine-colorized;
- a frontal view of your face (do not wear a hat) with 1¼ inch measuring from the top of your head to your chin;
- against a white or light-colored background.

When you get the photographs, write your Alien Registration Number and name *in pencil* on the back of each one. This is required by the INS and helps them keep your photographs and your other application materials together.

FILLING OUT THE APPLICATION TO FILE PETITION FOR NATURALIZATION
(FORM N-400)

You will be asked to pay a fee of $60.00 when you file this form.

1–3 Fill in your name as it appears on your Alien Registration Receipt Card. You must give the INS your Alien Registration number, but you do not have to provide your Social Security number. (If you do not have one, write "N/A" in the space provided.) Not providing your Social Security number will not affect the decision on your application, but it may slow down the investigation.

U.S. Department of Justice
Immigration and Naturalization Service

Instructions to the Applicant

You must be at least 18 years old to file a petition for naturalization. Using ink or a typewriter, answer every question in the application form, whether you are male or female. If you need more space for an answer, write "Continued" in your answer, then finish your answer on a sheet of paper this size, giving the number of the question. Submit this form to the Immigration and Naturalization Service office having jurisdiction over your place of residence.

You will be examined under oath on the answers in this application when you appear for your naturalization examination.

If you wish to be called for the examination at the same time as a relative who is also applying for naturalization, make your request on a separate sheet. Be sure to give the name and the Alien Registration Number of that relative.

---

1. **You must submit the following (Items A, B, C, and D) with the application.**

   A. Photographs of your face:
      1) Three identical unglazed copies, size 2 X 2 inches only.
      2) Taken within the last 30 days.
      3) Distance from top of head to point of chin to be 1 1/4 inches.
      4) On thin paper, with light background, showing front view without hat.
      5) In natural color or black and white, and not machine-made.
      6) Unsigned (but write Alien Registration Number lightly in pencil in center of reverse side).

   B. Fingerprint Chart (Form FD-258):
      Complete all personal data items such as name, address, date of birth, sex, etc. Write your Alien Registration Number in the space marked "Your No. OCA" or "Miscellaneous No. MNU". You must sign the chart in the presence of the person taking your fingerprints and have that person sign his/her name, title and date in the spaces provided. Take the chart and these instructions to a police station, sheriff's office, or an office of this Service, or other reputable person or organization for fingerprinting. (You should contact the police or sheriff's office first since some of these offices do not take fingerprints for other government agencies.) Do not bend, fold or crease the fingerprint chart.

   C. Biographic Information (Form G-325):
      Complete every item in the Biographic Information form furnished with this application and sign your name on the line provided. If you have ever served in the Armed Forces of the United States, you must also submit a completed Form G-325B.

   D. U.S. Military Service;
      If your application is based on your military service, you must submit Form N-426, "Request for Certification of Military or Naval Service."

2. **You must pay sixty dollars ($60.00) to file this form. The fee will not be refunded, whether the application is approved or not.** DO NOT MAIL CASH. All checks or money orders, whether U.S. or foreign, must be payable in U.S. currency at a financial institution in the United States. When a check is drawn on the account of a person other than yourself, write your name on the face of the check. If the check is not honored, INS will charge you $5.00.

   Pay by check or money order in the exact amount. Make the check or money order payable to "Immigration and Naturalization Service". However,

   A. If you live in Guam: Make the check or money order payable to "Treasurer, Guam", or

   B. If you live in the U.S. Virgin Islands: Make the check or money order payable to "Commission of Finance of the Virgin Islands".

3. **Alien Registration Receipt Card**
   Do not send your Alien Registration Receipt Card with this application.

4. **Examination on Government and Literacy:**
   Every person applying for naturalization must show that he or she has a knowledge and understanding of the history, principles, and form of government of the United States. There is no exemption from this requirement, and you will be examined on these subjects when you appear before the examiner.

   You will also be examined on your ability to read, write, and speak English. If on the date of your examination you are more than 50 years of age and have been a lawful permanent resident of the United States for 20 or more years, you will be exempt from the English language requirements of the law. If you are exempt, you may take the examination in any language you wish.

Form N-400 (10/26/89) N

(Continued on Reverse.)

Application to File Petition for Naturalization

Instructions to the Applicant - Continued

5. Oath of Allegiance:

You will be required to take the following oath of allegiance to the United States in order to become a citizen.

I hereby declare, on oath, that I absolutely and entirely renounce and abjure all allegiance and fidelity to any foreign prince, potentate, state or sovereignty, of whom or which I have heretofore been a subject or citizen; that I will support and defend the Constitution and laws of the United States of America against all enemies, foreign and domestic; that I will bear true faith and allegiance to the same, that I will bear arms on behalf of the United States when required by the law; that I will perform noncombatant service in the armed forces of the United States when required by the law; that I will perform work of national importance under civilian direction when required by the law; and that I take this obligation freely without any mental reservation or purpose of evasion; so help me God.

If you cannot promise to bear arms or perform noncombatant service because of religious training and belief, you may omit those statements when taking the oath.

"Religious training and belief means a person's belief in a relation to a Supreme Being involving duties superior to those arising from any human relation, but does not include essentially political, sociological, or philosophical views or merely a personal moral code.

6. The following applies only to applicants who have foreign-born children who are under 18 years of age.

Some or all of your own foreign-born children (not stepchildren) who are not yet citizens may possibly become United States citizens automatically when you are naturalized. This will happen:

A. If the child is a lawful permanent resident of the United States and still under 18 years of age when you are naturalized, and

B. If the child's other parent is already a citizen or becomes a citizen before or at the same time that you become naturalized. If, however, the child's other parent is deceased, or if you are divorced and have custody of the child, then it makes no difference that the child's other parent was or is an alien.

C. If your child is illegitimate and you are the mother, only Section A above applies.

D. If the child is adopted, is in your custody, the adoption was completed before the child's 16th birthday, and if the child is a lawful permanent resident of the United States.

E. If your child is illegitimate and you are the natural father, Section A above applies. You must establish that you were a United States citizen on the date of the child's birth; you must file an affidavit of support valid until the child's 18th birthday; and you must acknowledge paternity in writing, under oath, or have a court order stating that the child is yours.

If you wish, you may apply for a certificate of citizenship for these children on Form N-600, Application for Certificate of Citizenship, with proof of your naturalization.

7. Notice to applicants:

Authority for collection of the information requested in this form and those forms mentioned in the instructions hereto is contained in Sections 309. 328, 329, 332, 334, 335 or 341 of the Immigration and Nationality Act of 1952 (8 U.S.C. 1439, 1440, 1443, 1445, 1446 or 1452). Submission of the information is voluntary inasmuch as the immigration and nationality laws of the United States do not require an alien to apply for naturalization. If your Social Security number is omitted from a form, no right, benefit or privilege will be denied for your failure to provide such number, However, as military records are indexed by such numbers, verification of your military service, if required to establish eligibility for naturalization, may be difficult. The principal purposes for soliciting the information are to enable designated officers of the Immigration and Naturalization Service to determine the admissibility of a petitioner for naturalization and to make appropriate recommendations to the naturalization courts. All or any part of the information solicited may, as a matter of routine use, be disclosed to a court exercising naturalization jurisdiction and to other federal, state, local or foreign law enforcement or regulatory agencies, Department of Defense, including any component thereof, the Selective Service System, the Department of State, the Department of the Treasury, Central Intelligence Agency, Interpol and individuals and organizations in the processing of the application or petition for naturalization, or during the course of investigation to elicit further information required by the Immigration and Naturalization Service to carry out its function. Information solicited which indicate a violation or potential violation of law, whether civil, criminal or regulatory in nature may be referred, as routine use, to the appropriate agency, whether federal, state, local or foreign, charged with the responsibility of investigating, enforcing or prosecuting such violations. Failure to provide any or all of the solicited information may result in an adverse recommendation to the court as to an alien's eligibility for naturalization and denial by the court of a petition for naturalization.

8. Reporting Burden:

Public reporting burden for this collection of information is estimated to average 30 minutes per response, including the time for reviewing instructions, searching existing data sources, gathering and maintaining the data needed, and completing and reviewing the collection of information. Send comments regarding this burden estimate or any other aspect of this collection of information, including suggestions for reducing this burden, to: U.S. Department of Justice, Immigration and Naturalization Service (Room 2011), Washington, D.C. 20536; and to the Office of Management and Budget, Paperwork Reduction Project, OMB No. 1115-0009, Washington, D.C. 20503.

It is not possible to cover all the conditions for eligibility or give instructions for every situation. If you have carefully read all the instructions and still have questions, please contact your nearest INS office.

U.S. Department of Justice
Immigration and Naturalization Service

Application to File
Petition for Naturalization

OMB #1115-0009

Please read the instructions before filling out this form.

This block for government use only.

Section of Law

1. Your name (Exactly as it appears on your Alien Registration Receipt Card)

2. Your Alien Registration Number   3. Your Social Security Number

4. Your name (Full true and correct name, if different from above)

5. Any other names you have used (Including maiden)

6. You may, by law, change your name at the time you are naturalized. If you wish to do so, please print or type that name below, or the name you want your certificate of naturalization issued under.

7. Your date of birth (Month/Day/Year)   8. Your Sex
☐ Male   ☐ Female

9. Your place of birth (City or Town)

(County, Province or State)   (Country)

10. Was your father or mother ever a United States citizen?
(If Yes, explain fully)   ☐ Yes   ☐ No

11. Can you read and write English?   ☐ Yes   ☐ No

12. Can you speak English?   ☐ Yes   ☐ No

13. Can you sign your name in English?   ☐ Yes   ☐ No

14. Date you were admitted for permanent residency (Month/Day/Year)

15. Place you were admitted for permanent residency (City and State)

16. Date your continuous residency began in the U.S. (Month/Day/Year)

17. How long have you continuously resided in the State where you now live? (Number of Months)

18. Do you intend to reside permanently in the United States?
(If No, explain fully)   ☐ Yes   ☐ No

19. Have you served in the United States Armed Forces?
(If Yes, complete all of #19.)   ☐ Yes   ☐ No
Branch of Service (Indicate if Reserve or National Guard)
☐ Inducted   ☐ Enlisted

Location where you entered (City and State)

Service began (Month/Day/Year)

Service ended (Month/Day/Year)

Service number

Rank at discharge

Type of discharge

Reason for discharge (Alienage, conscientious objector, other)

20. At what addresses in the United States have you lived during the last 5 years? List present address *first*.

Street Address	City, county and State	From (Month/Day/Year)	To (Month/Day/Year)
			Present

21. What employment have you held during the last 5 years? List present or most recent employment *first*. (If none, write "None".)

Name and Address of Employer	Occupation or Type of Business	From (Month/Day/Year)	To (Month/Day/Year)

Form N-400 (10/26/89) N

22. What is your present marital status?

☐ Married ☐ Widowed ☐ Divorced ☐ Single

23. Complete the following *regarding your husband or wife if you are currently married.*

First (given) name	Date married (Month/Day/Year)	Date of birth (Month/Day/Year)	Country of birth
Place he or she entered the U.S.	Date entered the U.S. (Month/Day/Year)	His or her Alien Registration Number	Present immigration status
Date naturalized (Month/Day/Year)	Place naturalized	Present address (street and number)	City and State or country

24. Complete the following if you were previously married

Total number of times you have been married

Name of prior husband or wife	Date of marriage (Month/Day/Year)	Date marriage ended (Month/Day/Year)	How marriage ended	INS Status
				☐ Alien ☐ Citizen
				☐ Alien ☐ Citizen
				☐ Alien ☐ Citizen

25. Complete the following if your present husband or wife was previously married.

Total number of times your husband or wife has been married

Name of prior husband or wife	Date of marriage (Month/Day/Year)	Date marriage ended (Month/Day/Year)	How marriage ended	INS Status
				☐ Alien ☐ Citizen
				☐ Alien ☐ Citizen
				☐ Alien ☐ Citizen

26. Complete all columns for each of your children. (If child lives with you, state "with me" in Location column; otherwise, give the City and State of that child's residence.)

Indicate your total number of children

Given name	Date of birth	Country of birth	Date of entry	Port of entry	Location	Alien Registration No.	Sex
							☐ Male ☐ Female
							☐ Male ☐ Female
							☐ Male ☐ Female
							☐ Male ☐ Female
							☐ Male ☐ Female
							☐ Male ☐ Female
							☐ Male ☐ Female

27. Complete the following with regard to each absence you have had from the United States for a period of six months or less since you entered for permanent residence. (If none, write "None".)

Ship, airline, railroad, or bus company, or other means used to return to the United States.	Returned at (Place or port of entry)	Date departed	Date returned

28. Complete the following with regard to each absence you have had from the United States for a period of six months or more since you entered for permanent residence. (If none, write "None")

Ship, airline, railroad, or bus company, or other means used to return to the United States.	Returned at (Place or port of entry)	Date departed	Date returned

Form N-400 (10/26/89) N

29. The law provides that you may not be regarded as qualified for naturalization, if you knowingly committed certain offenses or crimes, even though you may not have been arrested. Have you ever, in or outside the United States:

    (If you answer "Yes" to a) or b), give the following information as to each incident.)

a) knowingly committed any crime for which you have not been arrested?

    ☐ Yes   ☐ No

b) been arrested, cited, charged, indicted, convicted, fined or imprisoned for breaking or violating any law or ordinance, including traffic regulations?

    ☐ Yes   ☐ No

Where (City, State and Country)	Date of Offense	Nature of Offense	Outcome of case, if any

30. List your present and past membership in or affiliation with every association, fund, foundation, party, club, society or similar group in the United States or in any other place, and your foreign military service (If none, write "None".)

Name of organization	Location of organization	Membership from	Membership to

31. Are you now, or have you ever, in the United States or in any other place, been a member of, or in any other way connected or associated with the Communist Party? (If "Yes", attach full explanation)

    ☐ Yes   ☐ No

32. Have you ever knowingly aided or supported the Communist Party directly, or indirectly through another organization, group or person? (If "Yes", attach full explanation)

    ☐ Yes   ☐ No

33. Do you now or have you ever advocated, taught, believed in or knowingly supported or furthered the interests of Communism? (If "Yes", attach full explanation)

    ☐ Yes   ☐ No

34. During the period March 23, 1933 to May 8, 1945, did you serve in, or were you in any way affiliated with, either directly or indirectly, any military unit, paramilitary unit, police unit, self-defense unit, vigilante unit, citizen unit, unit of the Nazi Party or SS, government agency or office, extermination camp, concentration camp, prisoner of war camp, prison, labor camp, detention camp or transit camp, under the control or affiliated with:

a) the Nazi Government of Germany?

    ☐ Yes   ☐ No

b) any government in any area occupied by, allied with, or established with the assistance or cooperation of, the Nazi Government of Germany?

    ☐ Yes   ☐ No

35. During the period of March 23, 1933 to May 8, 1945, did you ever order, incite, assist, or otherwise participate in the persecution of any person because of race, religion, national origin, or political opinion?

    ☐ Yes   ☐ No

36. Were you born with, or have you acquired in some way, any title or order of nobility in any foreign state?

    ☐ Yes   ☐ No

37. Have you ever been declared legally incompetent or have you ever been confined as a patient in a mental institution?

    ☐ Yes   ☐ No

38. Are deportation proceedings pending against you, or have you ever been deported or ordered deported, or have you ever applied for suspension of deportation?

    ☐ Yes   ☐ No

39. When was your last federal income tax return filed?

    (year) _____

40. Since becoming a permanent resident of the United States, have you filed an income tax return as a nonresident? (If "Yes", explain fully).

    ☐ Yes   ☐ No

41. Since becoming a permanent resident of the United States, have you failed to file an income tax return because you regarded yourself as a nonresident? (If "Yes", explain fully).

    ☐ Yes   ☐ No

42. Have you ever claimed in writing, or in any other way, to be a United States citizen?

☐ Yes ☐ No

43. Have you ever deserted from the military, air or naval forces of the United States?

☐ Yes ☐ No

44. Have you ever left the United States to avoid being drafted into the Armed Forces of the United States?

☐ Yes ☐ No

45. Do you believe in the Constitution and form of government of the United States?

☐ Yes ☐ No

46. Are you willing to take the full oath of allegiance to the United States? (See instruction #5)

☐ Yes ☐ No

47. If the law requires it, are you willing to bear arms on behalf of the United States? (If "No", attach a full explanation)

☐ Yes ☐ No

48. If the law requires it, are you willing to perform noncombatant services in the Armed Services of the United States? (If "No", attach a full explanation)

☐ Yes ☐ No

49. If the law requires it, are you willing to perform work of national importance under civilian direction? (If "No", attach a full explanation)

☐ Yes ☐ No

50. Did you ever apply for exemption from military service because of alienage, conscientious objections, or other reasons? (If "Yes", attach a full explanation)

☐ Yes ☐ No

51. Did you ever register under United States Selective Service laws or draft laws? (If "Yes", complete the following)

☐ Yes ☐ No

| Date registered |
| Selective Service Number |
| Local Board Number |
| Present classification |

52. The law provides that you may not be regarded as qualified for naturalization, if, at *any* time during the period for which you are required to prove good moral character, you have been a habitual drunkard; advocated or practiced polygamy; have been a prostitute or procured anyone for prostitution; have knowingly and for gain helped any alien to enter the United States illegally; have been an illicit trafficker in narcotic drugs or marijuana; have received your income mostly from illegal gambling, or have given false testimony for the purpose of obtaining any benefits under this Act. Have you ever, *anywhere*, been such a person or committed any of these acts? (If you answer yes to any of these, attach full explanation.)

☐ Yes ☐ No

This block is to be completed by the person preparing form if other than the applicant.

I declare that this document was prepared by me at the request of the applicant and is based on all information of which I have any knowledge.

Signature X	Signature of Applicant X
Address	Mailing Address
Telephone Number	Date	Telephone Number	Date

Do not fill in blanks below these lines; *This application must be sworn to before an officer of the Immigration and Naturalization Service.*

AFFIDAVIT

I do swear that I know the contents of this application, comprising pages 1 to 4, inclusive, and the supplemental forms thereto.

(Form Numbers _____)

subscribed to by me, that the same are true to the best of my knowledge and belief, that corrections numbered:

_____ to _____

were made by me or at my request, and that this application was signed by me with my full, true and correct name, **so help me God.**

_____
(Complete and true signature of applicant)
(Demonstrate applicant's ability to write English)

Non Filed

_____
(Date, reasons)

Subscribed and sworn to before me by applicant at the preliminary investigation

_____

_____

At

_____

This _____ day of _____, 19 _____

I certify that before verification of the above applicant stated in my presence he or she had (heard) read the foregoing application, corrections therein and supplemental form(s) and understood the contents thereof.

_____
(Naturalization Examiner)

4–6   If you wish to change your name since you applied for permanent residency, this is the place to do it. If you got married or want to legally change your name, you can save yourself legal trouble later by doing it now. If you have a maiden name, fill in your complete maiden name in question 5.

7–10   These questions ask when you were born, what gender you are, and where you were born. Fill in where you were born exactly as it appears on other INS forms.

10   If you answer "yes" here, attach an explanation describing why you think your parent was a citizen.

11–13 The official who interviews you will ask you to prove that you can read, write, and speak simple English. You also should be able to sign your name in English.

   You can receive a waiver if you are over fifty years old and have lived in the United States for more than twenty years, or if you are physically unable to speak, read, or write.

14–16 Your answers to these questions will help the INS determine if you have fulfilled the permanent residency requirement of five or three years, which is necessary to be eligible to complete this form.

   Write the city and state where you entered the United States with permanent residence status. This may not be the same place where you were first admitted to the United States. The date you were admitted for permanent residency should be the date stamped on your visa or Arrival/Departure Record, not the date you received the visa.

   If the date you were admitted for permanent residency differs from the date you began continuous residence, attach a full explanation.

17–18 Write in the number of months (*not* years) you have lived in the *state* where you now live. You must live in the state where you file this form for at least six months before applying for naturalization.

18   Check "yes" to qualify for citizenship. The INS includes this question because some newly naturalized citizens have left the United States shortly after they received citizenship. For example, if you get a job offer you cannot refuse in another country after you become a citizen, you risk losing your naturalized status if you decide to take the job. You will have to prove that you fully intend to stay in the United States, especially if you live abroad within one year of receiving citizenship.

19   Most people will check "no" to this question. If you have served in the United States military in any capacity, answer all of question 19 completely. You should also submit Form N-426, Request for Certification of Military or Naval Service, if you are applying for citizenship because you served in the armed forces.

20   The INS needs to know where you lived as a permanent resident alien. List your current address first, exactly as it appears on any other INS forms, and all other addresses in reverse chronological order.

   Be sure to include the *county,* as well as the city and state, in which you lived.

21   List your employment history for the past five years. If your application for permanent residency was based on employment, you should list the information about that job exactly as it appears on the I-140, Petition for Prospective Alien Employee. If there are any differences between the job you said you would hold and the job you actually had, you may be accused of fraudulently obtaining your permanent residence status. If the INS does find you guilty of fraud, your application will be denied and you may lose your permanent residence status.

22–25 These questions ask about whether or not you are now married. If you check "widowed," "divorced," or "single" in question 22, simply write "N/A" in the first square provided in question 23.

23   If you are married, complete all the information about your spouse here. Carefully review this information with your husband or wife to be sure you answer all the questions correctly.

24   If you were previously married, provide the required information about each of your previous partners. Bring a copy of the divorce decree with you to the interview. Many examiners ask to review them for evidence of good moral character. Don't forget to write in the total number of times you have been married.

25   Write in how many times your current spouse has been married and provide information about each one of them. Go over this information with your current partner.
      Once again, be sure to list all names exactly as they appear on other INS documents.

26   List the names, dates of birth, and the other information requested about each of your children under the age of eighteen, whether they are aliens or citizens. Children under the age of eighteen may become naturalized with you if:
      • your child is under eighteen and a legal permanent resident;
      • your child's other parent becomes naturalized or is already a citizen when you become naturalized. Whether or not the other parent is an alien, the child may be naturalized with you if you have custody of him or her because the other parent has died or you and the other parent are divorced;
      • you are the mother of an illegitimate child who is under eighteen and is a legal permanent resident;
      • your adopted child is a legal permanent resident and was under the age of sixteen when the adoption became final. The child should have lived with you for at least two years;
      • you are the father of an illegitimate child and can prove that you were a citizen when the child was born. You also have to provide affidavits of support and swear under oath that you are the father, or have a court order showing that you are the father.
      Note: For children who do not qualify for naturalization with your application, you

should file Form N-402, Application to File Petition for Naturalization in Behalf of Child.

 If you want any of your children to receive a Certificate of Citizenship, you should also file Form N-600, Application for Certificate of Citizenship, for each child.

27–28 Record all trips you took outside the United States, no matter what their length. Your answers about travel outside the United States will help verify that you have maintained your permanent residence status. For each question, fill in the kind of transportation you took when you returned to the United States. Fill in the exact date of entry as it appears in your Arrival/Departure Record, Form I-94.

27 Write "None" if you did not leave the United States at all while you were a permanent resident. If you did travel across the border as a permanent resident, enter the kind of transportation you used when you reentered the United States after the trip. Write the date of your return as it appears in your Arrival/Departure Record.

28 Write "None" in the space provided if you did not leave the United States for more than six months at one time since you received permanent residence status. If you were outside the United States for more than six months, you should support your claim that you maintained permanent residence status by showing that you applied for and received a reentry permit, Form I-131. The examiner will ask you why you stayed out longer than six months, to ascertain if you broke your continuous residence claim.

29 If your answer to either 29(a) or (b) is yes, you should consult a lawyer. You should record all arrests, indictments, and convictions in this space. Even if you received a traffic ticket, tell the INS about it here. (Having traffic tickets will not affect your eligibility, but the INS will note if you paid the tickets as a reflection of good moral character.) You should provide supporting documents such as official conviction records and records of court proceedings.

 Where the INS is concerned, honesty is the best policy. Your application *will* be investigated. Though the eligibility requirements for citizenship say that you should not have been convicted of a crime, you may still be able to become a citizen if you have committed a minor crime. Getting around this rule is difficult, however, and you should hire a lawyer to help you.

30 List all organizations you belong to, including social and cultural clubs, political parties, and others. List your present memberships first and earlier involvements last, beginning with the most recent organization you left.

 Your demonstrated involvement in the community will work to your advantage in the eyes of the INS. Are you a member of a parent-teacher organization? Do you belong to a church or to a sports team? Do you do any volunteer work for any nonprofit groups such as the Girl Scouts or Boy Scouts, a soup kitchen, a local benevolent society? Include them here.

You also should indicate where and when you served in the armed forces of another country.

31–38 Your answers to these questions tell the INS that you have not violated any of the eligibility rules for citizenship. Most people will answer "no" to these questions. If you honestly cannot answer "no," you should consult an immigration expert for help with your application.

31 If you were a member of the Communist Party at any time, answer "yes." Attach proof showing that you were a member more than ten years ago or that you were forced to become a member, and you probably will still be eligible for citizenship.

31–33 If you answer "yes" to these questions, your application will be denied.

34 If you answer "yes" here, show affidavits of support stating that you did not directly persecute people on the basis of race, religion, national origin, or political opinion.

35 A "yes" answer here will mean loss of your permanent residency status and being deported.

36 American citizens cannot hold titles or claim nobility in any other country. Seek legal help if you do. You may have to renounce any titles you held in your native country.

39–41 When you became a permanent resident and began working in the United States, you should have checked with the Internal Revenue Service about filing a tax return. In general, you should file a tax return for every year that you are a permanent resident alien. Many examiners ask to see your tax forms, so bring copies with you to the interview.

39 Enter the last tax year prior to filing this application.

40 If for some reason you filed as a nonresident while you were a permanent resident alien, you should explain this fully. Ask your tax preparer or a lawyer to help you.

41 Answering "yes" means you have abandoned your permanent residence status and jeopardized your application.

42–44 Your answers here show the INS that you have not misrepresented your alien status, and that you have not neglected your responsibility to serve in the United States military.

If you check "yes" to any of these questions, you should consult a lawyer.

45–46 Answering "yes" to your belief in and support of the United States Constitution and to your willingness to take the Oath of Allegiance lets the INS know that you fulfill these eligibility requirements for becoming a citizen.

46 If you answer "no" because you do not wish to bear arms, attach a statement showing that you cannot bear arms in good conscience because of your religious training and beliefs. Ask your religious organization to write a letter in your support, explaining the principles that prevent you from bearing arms and stating that you are a member of that group.

47–49 Part of the Oath of Allegiance—and one of the eligibility requirements—is that you are willing to serve in the United States armed forces. If you do not want to bear arms, you may omit this from the Oath of Allegiance. However, you will have to explain why you will not serve in the military on a separate sheet of paper attached to your application. The same is true if you do not want to serve in a noncombatant capacity in the military, or if you cannot conscientiously serve the United States under the direction of nonmilitary governmental employees.

50–51 These questions show your history both with foreign military groups and those of the United States. If you answer "yes" to question 50, you may be ineligible for citizenship and should get legal counsel.

If you registered for the Selective Service, sometimes called the draft, tell the INS when you registered and provide the other information requested about your draft registration. By law you should have registered with the Selective Service when you became a permanent resident alien if you were born during or after 1963. Every male alien between the ages of eighteen and twenty-six should register with the Selective Service.

52 This is the final question about your eligibility for citizenship. It deals with the requirement for being a person of "good moral character." Unless you are an alcoholic; a polygamist; a prostitute; have helped an alien enter the United States illegally or been convicted of a crime involving narcotic drugs or marijuana; earn most of your money from gambling; or have lied about any immigration-related subject, you should check "no" to this question.

Signature If you want to change your name when you become a citizen, print or type your name as you want it to be in this space. Below that, sign your name as it is now legally. Naturalization is a court action. Legally, the court can change your name when you become a citizen.

Beneath your signature, you should print or type your current address (exactly as it appears in question 20), your phone number, and the date you completed the application. The space below this will be filled out when you are interviewed by an immigration officer.

Fingerprint Chart

Three important considerations for Form FD-258, the fingerprint chart:

1. Do not bend or fold the card at any time before or after you are fingerprinted;
2. Sign the card only in the presence of the official who fingerprinted you. He or she will sign the card then, too, and should provide his or her title and the name of his or her office or agency;
3. Only the FD-258 fingerprint chart sent to you by the INS may be submitted with your application. If you lose it or get a set of bad fingerprints, you must get another one from the INS.

The back of the card shows examples of proper fingerprints. Note that the joints of the finger as well as the fingertip should appear. The lines of the print should be clear. Smeared prints are not acceptable.

You can be fingerprinted at an INS office, by a sheriff's office, or at a local police station. If you get your fingerprints from a sheriff's office or police station, call ahead of time to see if you need to make an appointment and if it will cost anything.

Before you go in to be fingerprinted, type or print your name in the space provided at the top center of the chart. Fill in your address in the space at left marked "Residence of Person Fingerprinted." The spaces below this, including the date, should be completed by the person who fingerprints you. To the right, fill in your Alien Registration Number in the space marked "Your No. *OCA*" or "Miscellaneous No. *MNU*." In the set of boxes to the far right, write in your sex ("F" or "M"), race, height, weight, eye and hair color, and date and place of birth in the spaces provided. To avoid any confusion, take the instructions about the fingerprint chart on Form N-400, Application to File Petition for Naturalization, with you. Also take some identification with you, such as your Alien Registration Receipt Card.

Biographic Information, Form G-325A

The final document you should fill out to complete your application provides information about you and your employer. You will be making two copies when you fill it out, so be sure you press down hard if you write in ink, or use a typewriter. The information you provide on this form should exactly match the same kind of information you provide on the N-400 or any other INS document.

Top of form. On the first line, fill in your name (last, first, and middle), gender, and nationality. Under "File Number" write in your Alien Registration Number.

On the second line include any other names you have used, including your maiden name. You should also fill in the city and country where you were born and your Social Security number if you have one. Write "N/A" if you do not have one.

The third, fourth, and fifth lines ask for information about your parents and husband or wife. List your father first (again, last name first) and your mother below that. Include your mother's maiden name. If you do not know where either of your parents was born, write "unknown" in that space.

Fill in the information on line four for your current spouse. You will provide information about previous husbands or wives in the spaces provided below this line.

If you are not married or do not have any previous spouses, write "none" in the spaces provided.

Middle of form. This section asks where you have lived in the United States. Begin with your current address and list the most

APPLICANT

LEAVE BLANK

SIGNATURE OF PERSON FINGERPRINTED

RESIDENCE OF PERSON FINGERPRINTED

DATE | SIGNATURE OF OFFICIAL TAKING FINGERPRINTS

EMPLOYER AND ADDRESS

REASON FINGERPRINTED

TYPE OR PRINT ALL INFORMATION IN BLACK

LAST NAME NAM   FIRST NAME   MIDDLE NAME

ALIASES AKA

ORI
NYINSNY00
USINS
NEW YORK, NY

CITIZENSHIP CTZ

YOUR NO. OCA

FBI NO. FBI

ARMED FORCES NO. MNU

SOCIAL SECURITY NO. SOC

MISCELLANEOUS NO. MNU

FBI   LEAVE BLANK

DATE OF BIRTH DOB
Month Day Year

SEX | RACE | HGT. | WGT. | EYES | HAIR | PLACE OF BIRTH POB

LEAVE BLANK

CLASS

REF.

1. R. THUMB | 2. R. INDEX | 3. R. MIDDLE | 4. R. RING | 5. R. LITTLE

6. L. THUMB | 7. L. INDEX | 8. L. MIDDLE | 9. L. RING | 10. L. LITTLE

LEFT FOUR FINGERS TAKEN SIMULTANEOUSLY | L. THUMB | R. THUMB | RIGHT FOUR FINGERS TAKEN SIMULTANEOUSLY

FEDERAL BUREAU OF INVESTIGATION
UNITED STATES DEPARTMENT OF JUSTICE
WASHINGTON, D.C. 20537

APPLICANT

1. LOOP

CENTER OF LOOP

DELTA

THE LINES BETWEEN CENTER OF LOOP AND DELTA MUST SHOW

2. WHORL

DELTAS

THESE LINES RUNNING BETWEEN DELTAS MUST BE CLEAR

3. ARCH

ARCHES HAVE NO DELTAS

FD-258 (REV. 12-29-82)

TO OBTAIN CLASSIFIABLE FINGERPRINTS:

1. USE BLACK PRINTER'S INK.
2. DISTRIBUTE INK EVENLY ON INKING SLAB.
3. WASH AND DRY FINGERS THOROUGHLY.
4. ROLL FINGERS FROM NAIL TO NAIL, AND AVOID ALLOWING FINGERS TO SLIP.
5. BE SURE IMPRESSIONS ARE RECORDED IN CORRECT ORDER.
6. IF AN AMPUTATION OR DEFORMITY MAKES IT IMPOSSIBLE TO PRINT A FINGER, MAKE A NOTATION TO THAT EFFECT IN THE INDIVIDUAL FINGER BLOCK.
7. IF SOME PHYSICAL CONDITION MAKES IT IMPOSSIBLE TO OBTAIN PERFECT IMPRESSIONS, SUBMIT THE BEST THAT CAN BE OBTAINED WITH A MEMO STAPLED TO THE CARD EXPLAINING THE CIRCUMSTANCES.
8. EXAMINE THE COMPLETED PRINTS TO SEE IF THEY CAN BE CLASSIFIED, BEARING IN MIND THAT MOST FINGERPRINTS FALL INTO THE PATTERNS SHOWN ON THIS CARD (OTHER PATTERNS OCCUR INFREQUENTLY AND ARE NOT SHOWN HERE).

THIS CARD FOR USE BY:

LEAVE THIS SPACE BLANK

1. LAW ENFORCEMENT AGENCIES IN FINGERPRINTING APPLICANTS FOR LAW ENFORCEMENT POSITIONS.*

2. OFFICIALS OF STATE AND LOCAL GOVERNMENTS FOR PURPOSES OF EMPLOYMENT, LICENSING, AND PERMITS, AS AUTHORIZED BY STATE STATUTES AND APPROVED BY THE ATTORNEY GENERAL OF THE UNITED STATES. LOCAL AND COUNTY ORDINANCES, UNLESS SPECIFICALLY BASED ON APPLICABLE STATE STATUTES DO NOT SATISFY THIS REQUIREMENT.*

3. U.S. GOVERNMENT AGENCIES AND OTHER ENTITIES REQUIRED BY FEDERAL LAW.**

4. OFFICIALS OF FEDERALLY CHARTERED OR INSURED BANKING INSTITUTIONS TO PROMOTE OR MAINTAIN THE SECURITY OF THOSE INSTITUTIONS.

INSTRUCTIONS:

*1. PRINTS MUST FIRST BE CHECKED THROUGH THE APPROPRIATE STATE IDENTIFICATION BUREAU, AND ONLY THOSE FINGERPRINTS FOR WHICH NO DISQUALIFYING RECORD HAS BEEN FOUND LOCALLY SHOULD BE SUBMITTED FOR FBI SEARCH.

2. PRIVACY ACT OF 1974 (P.L. 93-579) REQUIRES THAT FEDERAL, STATE, OR LOCAL AGENCIES INFORM INDIVIDUALS WHOSE SOCIAL SECURITY NUMBER IS REQUESTED WHETHER SUCH DISCLOSURE IS MANDATORY OR VOLUNTARY, BASIS OF AUTHORITY FOR SUCH SOLICITATION, AND USES WHICH WILL BE MADE OF IT.

**3. IDENTITY OF PRIVATE CONTRACTORS SHOULD BE SHOWN IN SPACE "EMPLOYER AND ADDRESS". THE CONTRIBUTOR IS THE NAME OF THE AGENCY SUBMITTING THE FINGERPRINT CARD TO THE FBI.

4. FBI NUMBER, IF KNOWN, SHOULD ALWAYS BE FURNISHED IN THE APPROPRIATE SPACE.

MISCELLANEOUS NO. - RECORD: OTHER ARMED FORCES NO., PASSPORT NO. (PP), ALIEN REGISTRATION NO. (AR), PORT SECURITY CARD NO. (PS), SELECTIVE SERVICE NO. (SS), VETERANS' ADMINISTRATION CLAIM NO. (VA).

✿U.S.G.P.O. 1989-172-720

---

recent addresses next. These should match the addresses listed on the N-400.

Unlike the N-400, this form asks for your last address outside the United States. Fill in the last address where you lived for more than one year.

Bottom of form. The last part of the form concerns your employment history.

Fill in your current job as it appears on other INS forms and list your most recent jobs before that below it. You'll notice that you should also include the last job you held while outside the United States.

Check the box that applies to the form you are filling out. If it is the N-400, check "Naturalization."

FORM G-325A

BIOGRAPHIC INFORMATION

OMB No. 1115-0066

Approval expires 4-30-85

(Family name)	(First name)	(Middle name)	☐ MALE ☐ FEMALE	BIRTHDATE (Mo.-Day-Yr.)	NATIONALITY	FILE NUMBER A-
ALL OTHER NAMES USED (Including names by previous marriages)			CITY AND COUNTRY OF BIRTH			SOCIAL SECURITY NO. (If any)

	FAMILY NAME	FIRST NAME	DATE, CITY AND COUNTRY OF BIRTH (If known)	CITY AND COUNTRY OF RESIDENCE .
FATHER				
MOTHER (Maiden name)				

HUSBAND (If none, so state) OR WIFE	FAMILY NAME (For wife, give maiden name)	FIRST NAME	BIRTHDATE	CITY & COUNTRY OF BIRTH	DATE OF MARRIAGE	PLACE OF MARRIAGE

FORMER HUSBANDS OR WIVES (if none, so state) FAMILY NAME (For wife, give maiden name)	FIRST NAME	BIRTHDATE	DATE & PLACE OF MARRIAGE	DATE AND PLACE OF TERMINATION OF MARRIAGE

APPLICANT'S RESIDENCE LAST FIVE YEARS. LIST PRESENT ADDRESS FIRST.

STREET AND NUMBER	CITY	PROVINCE OR STATE	COUNTRY	FROM MONTH	YEAR	TO MONTH	YEAR
						PRESENT TIME	

APPLICANT'S LAST ADDRESS OUTSIDE THE UNITED STATES OF MORE THAN ONE YEAR

STREET AND NUMBER	CITY	PROVINCE OR STATE	COUNTRY	FROM MONTH	YEAR	TO MONTH	YEAR

APPLICANT'S EMPLOYMENT LAST FIVE YEARS. (IF NONE, SO STATE.) LIST PRESENT EMPLOYMENT FIRST

FULL NAME AND ADDRESS OF EMPLOYER	OCCUPATION (SPECIFY)	FROM MONTH	YEAR	TO MONTH	YEAR
				PRESENT TIME	

Show below last occupation abroad if not shown above. (Include all information requested above.)

THIS FORM IS SUBMITTED IN CONNECTION WITH APPLICATION FOR: ☐ NATURALIZATION ☐ STATUS AS PERMANENT RESIDENT ☐ OTHER (SPECIFY): Are all copies legible? ☐ Yes	SIGNATURE OF APPLICANT	DATE
	IF YOUR NATIVE ALPHABET IS IN OTHER THAN ROMAN LETTERS, WRITE YOUR NAME IN YOUR NATIVE ALPHABET IN THIS SPACE:	

PENALTIES: SEVERE PENALTIES ARE PROVIDED BY LAW FOR KNOWINGLY AND WILLFULLY FALSIFYING OR CONCEALING A MATERIAL FACT.

APPLICANT: BE SURE TO PUT YOUR NAME AND ALIEN REGISTRATION NUMBER IN THE BOX OUTLINED BY HEAVY BORDER BELOW.

COMPLETE THIS BOX (Family name)	(Given name)	(Middle name)	(Alien registration number)

Check the box labeled "Yes" to verify that your answers on the duplicate beneath the carbon paper are readable.

In the heavily outlined black box beneath the word "APPLICANT," write your last name, first name, and Alien Registration Number again.

When you have filled out the entire form, sign it in the space provided exactly as it appears on your N-400 and all other INS forms. Write in the date. Below that box, you may write your name in your native alphabet—for example, Russian or Chinese—if it does not use Roman letters.

Filing Your Application

When you have answered all the questions on the form, and completed your fingerprint chart and photographs, make copies of the forms for yourself. Tear off the instructions on Form N-400 (this is the first page) to keep for your records, and take or mail the application and supporting documents to the INS office nearest you. Be sure to include the Biographic Information Sheet, fingerprint chart, photographs, and any other supporting documents in the envelope. Your application will be handled by many INS officials. It's best not to fold any of them (particularly the fingerprint chart). Use a large (at least nine-by-twelve-inch) envelope and mail it directly at a post office. You might want to mail your application by certified mail. This way you will get a receipt telling you if and when the INS received your application.

Once you have filed your Application to File Petition for Naturalization, admire the work you have done and prepare to wait for up to one year. Some offices will process your form more quickly, but a long wait is not unusual. If you haven't begun to do so already, you can study United States history and Government to prepare for your interview. It may take many weeks or months for the INS to call you for an interview.

In the interview, an INS official will ask you to prove that you fulfilled the permanent residency requirement. He or she may also ask you about other aspects of your eligibility and the information you provided on the forms. Review your copy of your application just before the interview. You should be familiar with all of the information you have provided on the application. The examiner will also ask you about United States Government and history, and make sure that you meet the language requirement.

When you successfully complete the examination, the INS official will ask you to sign the affidavit on the last page of Form N-400. Your signature tells the court that you swear under oath that all the information you have provided is true. The examiner will then help you file the Petition for Naturalization (Form N-405) with the clerk of the naturalization court.

The court clerk will fill in the name of the court and your name and address and ask you to sign it. The Petition for Naturalization is a legal document that you sign to swear that you have truthfully met all of the requirements for becoming a United States citizen.

The Naturalization Ceremony

The final, and for many people, the most exciting step toward naturalization is the naturalization hearing. After filing your petition with the court, you may wait anywhere from a few weeks to a few months before you receive a letter called Notification to Appear for Final Hearing, Form N-445. In some places, hearings (often called naturalization ceremonies) are held only a few times a year. In other places they may be held more often.

The Notification to Appear for Final Hearing tells you when and where you should appear before a federal judge to become naturalized. This is the last form you'll have to fill out before becoming a citizen. By now the questions will be familiar to you. One last time you will be asked if you are a person of good moral character, are or have been a Communist, and if you have committed any crimes. The form also asks if you have traveled outside the United States since you filed your petition for naturalization. (Remember that, while you may travel abroad after you file your petition, it's unwise to do so.) These questions are mostly a formality, but you should answer them truthfully.

What to Bring to the Ceremony

The naturalization examiner at the court will ask you for the Notification to Appear for Final Hearing, and he or she may ask you questions about your answers.

The front of the form lists the other documents you should bring to the hearing:

- the form itself, N-445, with all the questions answered;
- your Alien Registration Card; and
- any other INS documents you have, including a Reentry Permit or Refugee Travel Document.

Check the space next to each item to be sure you bring them with you and to show the examiner that you brought them.

When you have filled in all the necessary information, write in the city and state where you signed the form, the date, and your full address. Sign the form and head for your naturalization hearing.

At the Ceremony

Depending on the judge, the naturalization ceremony itself can be quite simple or elaborate. No one, least of all you, takes it lightly. It represents the end of your labors to come to America. It announces the beginning of a new commitment and opportunity in your life—United States citizenship.

The opening of the court, when the court crier announces the judge and that the court is in session, begins the ceremony. Sometimes the United States flag will be presented by a color guard and an invocation (a prayer) will be delivered by one or more clergy from various religious groups. Then the candidates—you and all the others in the room who have successfully fulfilled the requirements for citizenship—will be presented. In the rare event that only a few people will be naturalized, the judge may ask you questions about where you are from and why you want to become a citizen. The court wants you to know that naturalization is a momentous occasion, and that you will soon become part of the American community. If the judge asks any questions at all, they are merely a formality. Usually, however, the candidates are presented to the judge as a group. A representative from the INS will testify that each of the candidates is ready and qualified for citizenship.

Then the most impressive part of the ceremony takes place. The clerk of the court or the judge will read the Oath of Citizenship. You may be asked to repeat the Oath after him or her, or you may simply say "I do" after the Oath has been read.

Finally, the judge or someone designated by the court may make a short speech about what American citizenship can and will mean to you. You may also be asked to recite the Pledge of Allegiance.

When it's all over, you will receive the document that makes all of the waiting and ceremony worth it—your Certificate of Citizenship. You may leave the ceremony with your certificate in hand, or if the group is large, it will be mailed to you later.

Regardless of when you actually receive the Certificate of Citizenship, you are a United States citizen when you leave the ceremony that day. Now you can lead a full life as an American. You can enjoy the right to vote and the benefits of full protection under the United States Constitution. You can feel proud of your accomplishment. Welcome!

CHAPTER FIVE

Preparing for the Exam

At last you are ready to prepare for the naturalization interview and examination. When you meet with an INS examiner to review your application for citizenship, he or she will ask you questions about the process of becoming a citizen, and about some aspects of United States history and Government. Except for signing your name and writing a few simple phrases in English, the entire exam is given orally. The examiner observes your ability to understand and speak English as you answer the questions.

Many of the questions will deal with your application. Review your documents carefully before your interview. You should be able to answer any questions about the information you provide on the Application to File Petition for Naturalization (Form N-400) and your other INS documents. The examiner will question you *under oath* to be sure that you:

- meet the residency requirements;
- are a person of good moral character;
- do not belong to any subversive organization or the Communist Party;
- understand United States history and Government; and
- can speak, read, and write simple English.

The examiner may also ask you to describe the process of becoming a United States citizen, what it means to have good moral character, and what the Oath of Citizenship means. Be sure you are familiar with these before your interview (the Oath appears on page 39).

This chapter describes the aspects of government and history you should know. By the time you are finished preparing for the exam, you will understand the principles of the Constitution, how government works, and something about American history.

The INS publishes a list of questions on United States history and Government. Each section in this chapter is followed by questions drawn from this list, which the examiner may ask you. Read each section to get a basic understanding of the events and concepts, and study the questions to be sure you can answer each one confidently. Also spend some time reviewing the special sections throughout the chapter that describe important United States patriotic symbols such as the national anthem and American flag.

It may seem like you have an overwhelming amount of material to learn before your exam. While it is important to understand how the government works and why and how America was founded, most examiners are most interested in questioning you about your application. Relax, take a deep breath, and let yourself enjoy the story of America's government and history.

Part I
The Constitution and United States Government

KEY TERMS

Constitution
Republic
amendments
Bill of Rights
Legislative branch
Judicial branch
Executive branch

checks and balances
Congress
House of Representatives
Senate
impeach
bill

veto
Supreme Court
Chief Executive
Cabinet
Vice President
Electoral College

The key terms for each part of this chapter—The Constitution, United States Government, State and Local Government, and United States History—express the concepts the examiner will ask you about. However, you should also be familiar with the other terms in italic type, too numerous to list, that are included in this chapter.

The original European settlers, along the East Coast of the United States, came here seeking economic prosperity, religious freedom, and escape from political persecution. Not all came willingly (the slave trade thrived in early America), but those who did formed the original thirteen colonies. The colonies rebelled from Great Britain during the American Revolutionary War because they wanted the freedom to participate in and criticize government, and to worship and conduct business as they pleased. These are some of the rights guaranteed by the Constitution.

The *supreme law of the land,* the **Constitution** describes the structure of the United States Government. When it took effect in 1789, the Constitution provided the framework upon which the laws of the United States are based. Our form of government is known as a **Republic**, or *democratic republic.* Abraham Lincoln expressed this idea when he paraphrased the Declaration of Independence, and said that the United States' form of government is "of the people, by the people, and for the people." (The Declaration of Independence described the wrongs of the British government under King George III committed against the colonies and declared war on Great Britain.) One of the first aims of the writers of the Constitution was to form a government that truly represented the wishes and needs of its people.

The men who originally formed the United States Government recognized that the needs of the country and its people might change over time. Changes to the Constitution called **amendments** protect the rights of citizens and modify the structure of the Constitution. The first ten amendments called the **Bill of Rights** were adopted in 1791. These ten amendments specifically protect each American's rights to:

- freedom of speech, press, religion, peaceable assembly (and protest), and the voice to ask for changes in the government. It also separates the power of the church (religion) and the state (government), meaning that even the power of religion cannot usurp the laws of government. This is called *separation of powers.*
- own and keep guns.
- not have soldiers quartered, or housed, in their homes during peacetime without their permission.

- privacy. In other words, government may not unreasonably enter or search people's belongings and property without a legal document from a court.
- a fair trial. A person may not be tried for more than one crime at a time, nor can someone be forced to testify against him or herself.
- a quick and public trial by a jury of his or her peers. The state will provide a lawyer if the person cannot afford one.
- trial by jury in most cases.
- fair punishment for a crime. The government may not hurt prisoners or impose excessive fines.
- no rights outlined in the Constitution may be used to restrict other rights people may have.
- state and local governments. Any power not outlined in the Constitution belongs to the states or to the people.

Since these first ten amendments were added to the Constitution, many other changes to the Constitution have shaped the way the law works, politics, and the way we live today. The *Thirteenth Amendment* abolished (outlawed) slavery after the Civil War between the North and South. As social and cultural reform continued from the mid-nineteenth into the twentieth century, women won suffrage (the right to vote) with the *Nineteenth Amendment* in 1920. After President Franklin D. Roosevelt was elected to four successive terms (serving from 1933 to 1945) in office, the *Twenty-second Amendment* limited the President's term in office to two periods of four years each beginning in 1951. The *Twenty-sixth Amendment* lowered the voting age to eighteen. Other amendments guaranteed due process, allowed the government to collect income taxes, and desegregated schools, housing, the military, and government. In all, the Constitution has twenty-six amendments, only sixteen after the Bill of Rights.

Checks and Balances: How Government Works

The Constitution protects the rights of United States citizens and describes how the government is organized. It informs how Americans elect officials, and make, interpret, and enforce laws. Divided into sections called *articles*, the Constitution spells out a specific system of government divided into *three branches*. Each of the branches has power over a particular aspect of government, from making laws to enforcing them. The **Legislative branch** *makes* the laws, the **Judicial branch** *interprets* the laws, and the **Executive branch** *enforces* the laws. No branch has power over another and they work independently of each other. With this system of **checks and balances** government strives to truly represent the wishes of its people.

The Constitution provides for three levels of government. Power is shared by the *federal*, or *national*, form of government and *state and local governments*. (See page 141 for a discussion of how state government operates.) Federal government oversees areas of national interest. The powers of the national government are separate from those of state government. The primary responsibilities of the federal government include defense, foreign relations, immigration and naturalization, and trade with other nations and between the states. It also has the power to make money, to collect taxes, and to collect money for public programs such as Social Security. Sometimes a state's interests and laws may not agree with the Constitution. However, no state law can contradict or conflict with the Constitution.

The Constitution was written to allow for changes in America's needs. This is the process of amendment. When an amendment is added to the Constitution, each state must approve that amendment as adopted by Congress. A Congressional committee or the President may propose an amendment. The House of Representatives and Senate debate and reword the amendment as necessary. When the amendment passes, by a two-thirds vote of both houses of Congress, it is sent to the state legislatures for *ratification*, or approval. To become an amendment, three-fourths of the state legislatures must approve it. Sometimes, a vote of two-thirds of the state legislatures may prompt Congress to call a special national convention to approve an amendment. The same process for ratifying the amendment applies to a national convention.

The writers of the Constitution recognized that it needed to be flexible enough to allow for changes in its structure. It also provided a strong framework upon which the laws that govern its citizens can be made, without danger of autocratic rule. Under the Constitution, laws are always open to interpretation.

In large measure, the "supreme law of the land" reflects the social and political climate of America at any given time. When the judges on the Supreme Court agree on a strict interpretation of the Constitution, the federal government is limited to doing only what is stated specifically in the Constitution. More often, the Constitution is interpreted loosely, and the government can legally expand its powers as needed. In 1973, for example, the Supreme Court tried a case in

Government Branches and Checks and Balances

*Makes laws
Can override a veto
Approves presidential
appointments
Impeaches officials*

LEGISLATIVE BRANCH

CONGRESS

Makes
the Laws

House of
Representatives

Senate

*Senate approves
or disapproves
appointments*

*Vetoes or
signs laws*

*Declares laws
unconstitutional*

EXECUTIVE BRANCH

PRESIDENT

Enforces
the Laws

Vice President

Executive
Departments and
Agencies

Appoints justices

JUDICIAL BRANCH

SUPREME
COURT

Interprets
the Laws

Federal Courts

*Declares acts
unconstitutional*

which a Texas woman fought for the right to have an abortion. The ruling made it difficult for states to make laws restricting abortions. In 1989, that ruling was modified by another Supreme Court decision that allowed states to restrict a woman's access to affordable abortion. A loose interpretation of the Constitution allows the federal government to create and *repeal* (or revoke) laws as the need arises. Whether we agree with Supreme Court decisions or not, the system seems to work because of America's strong federal government and loose interpretation of the Constitution.

Legislative Branch

On the federal level, the branches of the government work under a system of checks and balances. The Legislative branch, **Congress,** is made up of two "houses" of elected government officials called the **House of Representatives** and the **Senate,** which make federal laws. This form of legislature is called *bicameral,* meaning "two houses." Congress also has the power to declare war, regulate the value of money and coin it, and levy and collect taxes.

Each house has its own responsibilities as outlined in the Constitution. The House of Representatives introduces legislation dealing with the budget and taxes and has the power to **impeach** public officials, or charge them with crimes as government officials. The Senate's special duties include deciding the guilt or innocence of impeached officials, approving Presidential appointments, and ratifying treaties between the United States and other governments.

Congressional representatives are elected to the House of Representatives for a term of two years. The number of representatives from each state is determined by that state's population. States with large populations have more representatives than states with smaller populations. In all, there are *435 representatives.* The Senate seats *100 senators;* each state elects two to represent it for a term of six years. To be elected to the House of Representatives, a person must be at least twenty-five years old, a United States citizen for at least seven years, and reside in the state where he or she is elected. Senators must be at least thirty years old, citizens for at least nine years, and a resident of his or her state.

Each house conducts its business in its own room of the Capitol Building in Washington, D.C. The Vice President of the United States presides over the proceedings of the Senate, while a Speaker elected by the congressional representatives presides over the House of Representatives. In addition, each house has its own committees that study, write, and amend legislation dealing with a particular area. Both houses, for example, have committees for Agriculture, Armed Services, Budget, Small Business, and Veterans' Affairs, among others. The Senate has committees for Commerce, Science, Transportation; Finance; and Labor and Human Resources. Standing (or permanent) House committees include Education and Labor; Science, Space, and Technology; and Ways and Means.

The officials elected to both houses of Congress represent their *constituents*, the voters, from their home states. A congressional representative represents the residents of his or her congressional district within a state, while a senator represents all the people residing in his or her state.

How Congress Makes Laws

A representative in the House or a senator may introduce a **bill** (the document that will eventually become law) in his or her respective house. It is assigned a number or title by the clerk of the House of Representatives and sent to the committee of the Senate or the House that is responsible for the particular area the bill relates to (e.g., a bill providing aid to farmers would go to the committee on Agriculture). The committee debates the bill, listens to the opinions of interested people and members of the Congress, and sometimes offers amendments to the bill. The bill is then voted on by the committee and, if passed, the bill is sent back to the clerk of the House.

If the bill is unacceptable to the committee, they may *table*, or ignore, it. Or, if they send it back to its house with no recommendations or changes, the bill usually will not become law. When a bill goes back to its house with recommendations from a committee, that house then debates it and suggests amendments. After debating it, the house votes on the bill.

If the bill passes, it is sent to the other house, where it is again debated, amendments made, and a vote taken. If the bill is not passed by the second house, the bill dies. If it passes with amendments, a joint congressional committee (composed of members of both the House and the Senate) tries to reach a compromise between the two versions of the bill. Both houses must agree to all a bill's amendments before it can become a law.

When a bill passes both houses of Congress, it is sent to the President to be signed into law. If the President signs the bill, it immediately becomes law. If the President does not sign it, after ten days it will become law if Congress is still in session. If after ten days Congress adjourns and the President has not signed the bill, it does not become law. This is known as a *pocket veto*.

The President may also **veto** (or refuse to approve) a bill. He may send it back to the house that originally produced the bill with suggestions for revision. The bill is then debated again in light of the President's comments and a roll-call vote is taken. To *override* the President's veto, both houses must pass it with a two-thirds vote.

Judicial Branch

The Judicial branch of government refers to the federal court system. As described in the Constitution, the highest court in the land, the **Supreme Court**, is charged with explaining and interpreting the laws passed by Congress. It makes the final decision as to whether or not a law violates the principles of the Constitution. It also may declare proclamations or acts of Congress unconstitutional.

The Supreme Court is the highest court in the federal court system. The *District Courts*, the lowest federal courts, try cases in which someone has broken a federal law. Beneath the Supreme Court, the *Circuit Courts of Appeals* hear *appeals* (requests for a new hearing in a higher court) from the lower courts. For example, when an issue or a person is tried in district court and the ruling is considered unfair, an appeal may be made to have the case heard in a higher federal court.

The federal courts also settle disputes between different states or persons from different states, and between individuals and the federal government. Federal courts may also settle legal arguments between states and federal government and between states and foreign governments or citizens. The federal court also has the power to naturalize people as United States citizens.

The nine *justices*, or judges, who sit on the Supreme Court meet every year in the Supreme Court Building in Washington, D.C., usually from October through June.

They are appointed by the President, and the Senate must approve their appointment. The head of the court, the *Chief Justice*, is also appointed by the President. Decisions are made by a majority vote of the justices. A justice is appointed for life, and Congress determines his or her salary. As with other public officials, a justice may be impeached for breaking the law.

The Supreme Court makes the final decision on all cases. Once the Court has ruled on a case, the decision cannot be changed. However, the Court may hear a new case and make a decision that revises an earlier one. As we saw earlier, abortion is one example. The history of civil rights legislation, on which the Supreme Court originally ruled that African-Americans and whites have "separate but equal" public facilities, provides another example. The "separate but equal" principle was struck down by the Court in 1954. Most of the cases the Supreme Court hears are appeals from the lower courts. Sometimes they try cases involving foreign diplomats. The most important thing to remember about the Supreme Court is that it can declare a state or federal law unconstitutional, meaning it can no longer be a law because it conflicts with the principles of the Constitution.

Executive Branch

The Constitution describes a third branch of government responsible for enforcing the laws of the United States under the Constitution. *George Washington*, the general who led the colonies' armed forces during the Revolutionary War, was elected president and was sworn in the same year the Constitution took effect in 1789.

The Executive branch of the government includes the office of the President of the United States and the departments and agencies under it. The Executive branch is responsible for enforcing the laws and administering (or overseeing the operation of) the federal government. The President has many responsibilities. While the President is often perceived as the top authority in government (and is sometimes referred to as the **Chief Executive**), the structure of the Executive branch (and the checks and balances system) ensures that he or she would never have absolute power over the other branches of government. The important powers of the President include being the leader of the country and *commander in chief* of the military, appointing Cabinet members and Supreme Court justices, making treaties with foreign countries, and pardoning people convicted in federal courts.

CHECKS ON THE JUDICIAL BRANCH

- The President may pardon anyone convicted of a crime.
- The President appoints Supreme Court Justices, and the Senate must approve the appointment.
- Congress determines the number of judges and their salaries.
- Congress may decide which cases should begin with the Supreme Court.

EXECUTIVE DEPARTMENTS

Every administration supports different programs funded and administered by the government. The other branches also oversee certain government-run agencies. Congress oversees the General Accounting Office (GAO), Government Printing Office (GPO), Library of Congress and the Copyright Royalty Tribunal, among others. The Supreme Court and the judicial branch oversee the courts. Every President forms his or her own *executive agencies*. Such agencies, which advise the President, include the Office of Management and Budget, Council of Economic Advisors, National Security Council (NSC), Council on Environmental Quality, and others dealing with policy, drugs, transportation, and technology.

Separate and longstanding *executive departments* include the following departments.

State Advises the President on foreign policy based on reports from CIA and Foreign Service offices around the world. Also issues visas through its consulates and embassies. Ambassadors may also help negotiate treaties and agreements with other countries under the President or the Senate's direction.

Treasury Recommends fiscal policy and budget to the President. The Customs Service, the United States Mint, and the Secret Service (which protects the President and other federal officials) also fall under this department. The Internal Revenue Service (IRS) collects taxes from citizens and businesses.

Defense Recommends defense needs and strategy and coordinates with four other departments—the *Army, Air Force, Navy,* and *Marine Corps.* Assists with national security policy and has been known to negotiate arms limitations agreements.

Justice Investigates and prosecutes federal law violators. Various agencies include the Federal Bureau of Investigation (FBI), Drug Enforcement Administration (DEA), and Immigration and Naturalization Service (INS). The Justice Department also administers the federal prison system and such areas as the Freedom of Information Act and Privacy Act.

Interior Responsible for public lands and parks, such as Yellowstone National Park and Native American reservations. The department's Fish and Wildlife Service protects America's natural resources.

Agriculture Works with farmers to produce efficient crops. Provides loans to small farms

---

Though the President is commander in chief and the Chief Executive, the checks and balances system limits the power of the office. For example, the President can order military troops into action, but cannot declare war. Only Congress has the power to declare war. The President is not above the law, either. The House of Representatives may impeach (or accuse) the President of committing crimes as a public official. The Senate may then try and convict or acquit the President of the crimes. If found guilty, the President must leave office. The House of Representatives began impeachment proceedings against President Richard M. Nixon (1969–1974) in 1974 for crimes relating to the break-in of the Democratic National Headquarters at the Watergate Apartments in Washington, D.C., in 1972. Nixon resigned shortly afterward.

and may buy certain crops if the free-market price drops below a certain level in its programs to support commodity and price. Also offers such nutrition programs for low-income people as Food Stamps and programs for women, infants, and children.

Commerce Offers research, publications, loans, and technical assistance to develop domestic and international business in the United States. Conducts the Census every ten years. It also researches our national resources and provides services such as the National Weather Service and oceanographic studies.

Labor Enforces federal labor law ensuring safe conditions, minimum wage, overtime pay, equal opportunity and nondiscrimination, and other civilian rights and benefits. Also provides job training programs and regulates labor unions. Offers grants to students for post-secondary (after college) study and work–study.

Health and Human Services Researches disease and supports health programs such as those combatting alcohol and drug abuse. Administers Social Security, aid to the blind, dependent children, and refugees, and provides Welfare.

Housing and Urban Development Enforces nondiscrimination in housing and provides housing and improved living conditions for various income levels. Offers low-interest loans to homeowners and develops low-cost housing.

Transportation Researches policy and programs for safe and convenient transportation. The Coast Guard enforces laws at sea, including regulations on vessels. Offers financial and technical assistance for the development of mass transit systems.

Education Researches the condition of education and schools in America and recommends new strategy. Offers bilingual, vocational, and adult education programs, and loans for work–study.

Energy Researches energy sources and provides information on energy conservation. Sets rates and grants licenses to energy producers.

Veterans Affairs Administers programs for veterans of the United States military. Offers loans for education, family, and medical services. Especially offers compensation to disabled veterans.

Enforcing the laws of the United States requires the work of many people in departments and agencies under the Executive Office. Members of the **Cabinet** assist the President with running the government. The Cabinet is composed of the heads, or *Secretaries*, of the executive departments. Though the Constitution does not require that a President have a Cabinet, George Washington had four Cabinet members.

Today there are fourteen departments including the Department of State, the Department of the Treasury, Department of Defense, Department of Justice, Department of the Interior, and other departments from agriculture and labor to education, energy, and transportation. (See sidebar, "Executive Departments," above.) The *Attorney General of the United States* heads the Department of Justice, and is one of the most important

Cabinet members. The Attorney General is responsible for the three government agencies that enforce the law, including the Central Intelligence Agency (CIA), Federal Bureau of Investigation (FBI), and the Immigration and Naturalization Service (INS).

Appointed by the President and approved by the Senate, the Cabinet members help the President carry out the duties of the Executive Office. Independent agencies beneath these departments help fulfill the specific responsibilities of each department. New agencies are created as the needs of the nation change. Examples include the Commission on Civil Rights, the Small Business Administration, and NASA (the space program). A separate group of Executive agencies is also appointed by the President to serve as boards of advisors.

Also under the office of the President, the **Vice President**, elected with the President, presides over the Senate. The Constitution originally said that the Vice President would be the person who received the second highest number of votes in a national presidential election. Obviously, this meant that the President would have to work with his campaign opponent. Since an 1804 amendment to the Constitution, the President and Vice President have run together in general elections on the same *ticket*.

The Vice President's important duties include advising the President and becoming President should the current President die or become unable to perform his or her duties. The Vice President participates in Cabinet meetings and serves on the National Security Council.

Both the President and Vice President must meet certain requirements to be elected. They must be natural-born citizens of the United States, thirty-five years old when they take office, and they must have lived in the United States for at least fourteen years.

Presidents are elected for four-year terms and may not serve more than two as stated in the Twenty-second Amendment to the Constitution. Two months after a President is elected in November, he or she is *inaugurated* (sworn in) on January 20, after which the official term of office begins. At the inauguration ceremony, the President takes the *Oath of Office*, in which he or she swears to fulfill the duties of President and uphold the principles of the Constitution.

Congress passed laws setting forth the *lines of succession* should the President not be able to complete the term of office. The Vice President first acts as President. If the Vice President dies or resigns from office, the Speaker of the House of Representatives becomes President. If he or she cannot fill the office, the acting president of the Senate, the President *pro tempore* (meaning "of the time being") of the Senate, then becomes President. Last in line is the Secretary of State.

How a Presidential Election Works

A presidential election operates slightly differently from any other type of election in the United States. The President and Vice President are the only officials not elected by a direct, or popular, vote of the people. Though there can be any number of political parties in the United States, there is essentially a two-party system. The Republicans and Democrats each nominate a Presidential *candidate* at their respective national conventions. The candidates then choose someone to run for Vice President on the same ticket in the *general election*.

Presidential elections are held every four years on the first Tuesday after the first Monday in November. While United States citizens may vote for the candidate they want on that day, the President is actually elected by the **Electoral College.** The electors are nominated at the national conventions of the Republican and Democratic parties. On election day, some states list the names of the nominated electors while others list the names of the presidential candidates. Either way, the party that receives the highest number of votes sends its electors to the Electoral College.

The number of electors from each state is based on that state's number of senators and representatives. There are *538 electors* in all, representing 100 senators, 435 representatives, and three from the District of Columbia. The members of the Electoral College meet in December, after the general election, in their state capitals or at another place designated by their state legislatures. Traditionally, electors vote for their party's candidate, though they are not required by the Constitution to do so. In 1824, 1876, and 1888, for example, candidates who had not received the popular vote won the electoral vote and thus the presidential election.

When the electoral votes are cast, they are sent to the President of the United States Senate (the Vice President). In a joint session of Congress on January 6, the President of the Senate opens the sealed electoral votes and counts them. To be elected, the candidate must receive a majority of the electoral votes, or 270 electoral votes.

CHECKS ON THE EXECUTIVE BRANCH

- Congress checks the Executive branch with its power to refuse to provide money in the budget proposed by the President.
- Congress may refuse to approve presidential appointments; it can also refuse to create or abolish departments or agencies the President requests.
- The Senate may reject treaties negotiated by the President.
- The House of Representatives may impeach the President, and the Senate can try and convict the President.
- The Judicial branch checks the President through the Supreme Court's power to declare presidential actions unconstitutional.

Review Questions for The Constitution and United States Government

What is the form of government of the United States?

A Republic, or democratic republic, means that the people have the right to elect officials and govern themselves. Abraham Lincoln called this a government "of the people, by the people, and for the people."

What is the "supreme law of the land"?

The Constitution outlines the power of the federal government. It is called the "supreme law" because state and local laws must not conflict with the Constitution.

When did the Constitution take effect?

After the colonies won the Revolutionary War, the United States Government as outlined in the Constitution took effect in 1789.

What is the Bill of Rights, and what does it say?

The first ten amendments to the Constitution are called the Bill of Rights because they protect and guarantee the rights of American citizens to, among other things, freedom of speech, religion, peaceable assembly, and the right to a fair trial.

What other amendments are there to the Constitution? How have they changed the rights of Americans?

The Thirteenth Amendment abolished slavery.

The Nineteenth Amendment gave women suffrage, the right to vote.

The Twenty-second Amendment limited the President to two four-year terms in office.

The Twenty-sixth Amendment lowered the voting age to eighteen.

Other amendments deal with other voting rights, segregation and civil rights, and the business of government.

How can the Constitution be amended? How many amendments have been added to the Constitution?

When both the Senate and the House of Representatives adopt an amendment by a two-thirds vote, it is sent to the state legislatures for ratification. For it to become law, three-fourths of the state legislatures must approve the amendment.

There are twenty-six amendments in all, sixteen have been ratified since the Bill of Rights.

Checks and Balances: How Government Works

What is a federal, or national, government? What are its powers?

A federal, or national, government refers to the government representing all the states. It deals with issues of concern to the country as a whole such as defense, taxes, war, immigration, and trade with other nations.

What are the three levels of government?

The federal (or national) government oversees the workings of all the states, the state and local governments rule on all areas of concern to a state's residents.

What are the branches of government? What does a system of checks and balances mean?

The Legislative, Judicial, and Executive branches run government according to a system of checks and balances. The Legislative branch (the Congress) makes the laws, the Judicial branch (the Supreme Court) interprets the laws, and the Executive branch (under the office of the President) enforces the laws. No one person or government body absolutely controls government.

Legislative Branch

What does the Legislative branch do?

Its primary function is to make federal laws. It also can declare war, provide for coining money and regulate its value, and levy and collect taxes.

What is Congress?

The Congress, comprised of the House of Representatives and the Senate, makes up the Legislative branch of government. Representatives and senators are elected by American citizens registered to vote.

How are representatives elected and what qualifications must they have?

The members of the House of Representatives are elected by voters in their respective districts. To be eligible for election, a candidate must be twenty-five years old, a citizen for seven years, and live in the state where he or she is elected.

How are senators elected and what qualifications must they have?

Senators are elected by a direct vote in their respective districts. To be eligible for election, a candidate must be twenty-five years old, a citizen for seven years, and live in the state where he or she is elected.

How many members does each house of Congress have?

Currently there are 435 representatives in the House. The number of representatives from each state is determined by that state's population. The bigger the state, the more representatives it has. The senate seats 100 senators, two from each of the fifty states.

How long do congressmen and senators serve in office?

Members of the House of Representatives are elected for two-year terms. Senators' terms last for six years.

Who presides over each house of Congress?

The House of Representatives elects a Speaker to preside over its sessions. The Vice President leads the business of the Senate.

How Congress Makes Laws

What is a "bill"?

The proposed legislation introduced by a representative or senator in Congress that will become a law is called a bill. Usually bills are debated and amended before they become law.

How does a bill become law?

After a bill is introduced to the House of Representatives or the Senate, it is debated, amended, and voted on. If it passes, it is sent to the other house for approval. Both houses must agree on all amendments to the bill.

When both houses have passed the bill, it is sent to the President to be signed into law.

When can a bill become law without the President's signature?

If the President vetoes a bill, it goes back to the House. Both houses of Congress must pass the bill by a vote of two-thirds to override the veto. If the President does not sign the bill within ten days and Congress is still in session, the bill becomes law.

Judicial Branch

What is the purpose of the Judicial branch?

The Judicial branch interprets and explains federal laws according to the principles of the Constitution.

What is the highest federal court and how many members does it have?

The Supreme Court, the highest court in America, has nine members. Eight of the justices are called associates. The Chief Justice leads the court.

How does a person become a Supreme Court justice?

The President appoints the justices, who are approved by the Senate.

How long can a person be a Supreme Court justice?

Appointments to the Supreme Court last a life time or until the justice resigns.

Can a federal judge be removed from his or her position?

Congress may impeach and convict a judge of committing crimes and misdemeanors as a public official. This is the only way a federal judge can be removed.

What important duties does the Supreme Court have?

The court decides whether laws passed by Congress agree with the Constitution. It also hears appeals from the lower federal courts.

Where and when does the Supreme Court meet?

The justices meet in the Supreme Court Building in Washington, D.C. The Court usually convenes in October and recesses in June.

What are the other federal courts?

Congress established the Circuit Courts to hear appeals beneath the Supreme Court, and the District Courts to try cases involving federal law.

What power does Congress have over the Supreme Court?

The Senate may decide not to approve a presidential appointment to the court. Congress also determines how many justices sit on the court and how much they are paid.

Executive Branch

What is the purpose of the Executive branch?

This branch of government enforces the laws of the United States.

Who heads the Executive branch?

The President of the United States, sometimes called the Chief Executive, is ultimately responsible for running the Executive branch.

What are some of the President's important duties?

As the Chief Executive, the President enforces the laws of the United States with the help of the departments in the Executive branch. The President appoints Cabinet members (the heads of the executive departments) and appoints justices to the Supreme Court. During war, the President is commander in chief of the armed forces. The President makes treaties with other countries and has the power to grant pardons to people who have been convicted in federal courts.

Can the President declare war?

Only the Congress may declare war, though the President may send troops into action.

How can the President be removed from office?

The President may be impeached (or accused) of committing crimes as a federal official. After the President is impeached, he or she is tried for the crimes.

Who has the power to impeach the President?

The House of Representatives has the power to impeach a President.

Who tries impeached officials?

Only the Senate may try and convict impeached elected officials.

What does "impeachment" mean?

Impeachment is an accusation of serious misconduct or crimes by a government official while performing his or her duties.

What other offices make up the Executive branch?

The thirteen executive departments and the Vice President are part of the Executive branch.

What is the Cabinet?

The Secretaries, or heads, of the executive departments advise the President on policy and running the government.

Who sits on the Cabinet?

The Vice President and the executive department heads sit on the Cabinet. Some of the department heads are the Attorney General (head of the Department of Justice), the Secretary of State, Secretary of Treasury, Secretary of Defense, Secretary of Interior, Secretary of Agriculture, and the Secretary of Transportation.

How does someone become a Cabinet member?

The President appoints Cabinet members. The appointments must be approved by the Senate.

What are the duties of the Vice President?

The Vice President presides over the Senate, sits on the Cabinet, and serves on the National Security Council.

What is the term of office for the President of the United States?

Presidents are elected for four-year terms and may not serve more than two consecutive terms, as set forth by the Twenty-second Amendment to the Constitution.

When does the President begin his or her term of office?

A term begins officially on January 20 at the Inauguration Ceremony when the President takes the Oath of Office.

What qualifications must a person meet to be elected President?

To become President of the United States, a person must be at least thirty-five years old, a natural-born citizen of the United States, and have lived in the United States for at least fourteen years.

Who becomes President should the President become unable to fulfill his or her duties?

The Vice President becomes acting President in the event that a President dies, resigns, or is removed from office. The laws of the line of succession say that if the Vice President cannot take office, the Speaker of the House, the President pro tempore of the Senate, and the Secretary of State are the next in line for the presidency.

How is a President elected?

Though American citizens vote in the general election, the Electoral College actually elects the President.

Is the President elected by a popular vote of the people?

The President and Vice President are elected by representatives from each state called "electors," not by a direct, popular vote of the people.

Who are electors?

Electors are nominated by their party at a national convention. On election day, they are elected from each state when people cast their votes. The electors cast their votes, called "electoral votes," on behalf of the people of their state for President and Vice President.

How many electors does each state have?

Each state has as many electors as it has senators and representatives in Congress.

What is the total number of votes cast for President and Vice President?

In all there are 538 votes: 435 for the House of Representatives, 100 for the Senate, and 3 for the District of Columbia.

How many votes must a candidate receive to be elected President?

A President and Vice President must receive a majority, or 270, of the electoral votes to win the election.

Who was the first President of the United States?

George Washington was sworn in as America's first President in 1789.

How many Presidents have we had up to and including the current President?

President George Bush took office in 1989 to become the forty-first President of the United States.

Part II:
State and Local Government

<table>
<tr><td colspan="3" align="center">**KEY TERMS**</td></tr>
<tr><td>*local government*</td><td>*county*</td><td>*mayor*</td></tr>
<tr><td>*bicameral*</td><td>*board of supervisors*</td><td>*ordinances*</td></tr>
<tr><td>*governor*</td><td>*city charter*</td><td>*city council*</td></tr>
<tr><td>*lieutenant governor*</td><td></td><td></td></tr>
</table>

As the Constitution describes them, the states operate independently of the federal government. Each state has its own constitution. State and local governments answer the needs of the people to which the federal government cannot respond. Though the federal government may fund some public welfare programs, the powers not vested in the national government belong to the states. Schools, housing, police protection, intrastate transportation, and business all fall under the province of state and local government.

Just as the federal government has authority over fifty individual states, state government has authority over smaller districts called counties, each with their own **local government**. Within county government, there are town, municipal (or city), and village governments. These governments operate independently of state government, but must comply with the laws and constitution of that state. The state provides funding for education, roads, and some health care, but local governments usually administer the programs.

State Government

State governments function as microcosms of the federal government. Smaller models of the federal government, they are *republican*; each has three branches of government that fulfill the same duties as the Legislative, Judicial, and Executive branches on the federal level. The three-branch system ensures checks and balances.

The smaller population of states makes the people's direct vote, or *direct democracy*, easier on the state and local level. State constitutions give people the power to vote on state laws, the constitution, and amendments to it. In some states they also can vote to *recall* (or impeach) a public official, such as the governor, for crimes as a public official. (Arizona recently recalled its Governor Meekham for racist remarks and mismanagement of funds.) In some western states, citizens can introduce legislation or an amendment to the constitution by submitting a *petition* describing their proposal with a required number of signatures. In a direct democracy, this is called an *initiative*. In other states, citizens vote on

BRANCHES OF FEDERAL, STATE, AND LOCAL GOVERNMENTS

	Federal	State	City
Executive	President	Governor	Mayor
	Vice President	Lieutenant	City Commissioner
	Cabinet	Governor	and Assistants
	Executive	Governor's Advisor	
	Departments		
Legislative	Congress	Bicameral	City Council or
	House of	Legislatures,	Commission
	Representatives	a House and	
	Senate	Senate in all states	
		except Nebraska	
Judicial	Supreme Court	State Supreme	City Courts
	Circuit Court	Court	Family Court
	of Appeals	Appellate Courts	Small Claims
	District Courts	District and	Traffic
		Superior Courts	Justice of the Peace

referenda dealing with changes to the constitution or legislation.

The state constitutions govern how each branch of government operates. State constitutions also have their own declaration (or bill) of rights and describe how to amend their constitutions, just as the Constitution does.

The Constitution of the United States, however, is the supreme law. Nothing in state or local amendments or law may contradict the Constitution or rulings by the Supreme Court. Historically, though, changes in federal law begin on the state and local level when people demand change. For example, before the 1960s local laws in southern states prohibited African-Americans from voting. They also suffered from substandard housing and education under the Supreme Court's 1896 "separate but equal" ruling in *Plessy v. Ferguson*. When activists challenged these conditions, state and local courts ruled in favor of the *status quo*.

After two decades of protest, the government finally responded to activists such as Martin Luther King, Jr., and the Southern Christian Leadership Conference (SCLC), the National Association for Colored People (NAACP), and the Coalition for Racial Equality (CORE), among others. The Supreme Court's 1954 ruling on desegregating schools in *Brown v. Board of Education* and passage of the 1964 Civil Rights Act, introduced by President John F. Kennedy and passed under President Lyndon B. Johnson, soon forced the states to protect their citizens' civil rights.

Each of the branches of state government is organized in much the same way as the Legislative, Judicial, and Executive branches of the federal government. The *legislative branch* of state government makes the laws. Many state laws govern unemployment, disability insurance, and worker's compensation. Most state legislatures are **bicameral**, having both a house of representatives and a senate. (Nebraska, Guam, and the Virgin Islands have *unicameral* legislatures with just one house of representatives.) The lieutenant governor, elected by the people, presides over the senate in state government.

Many state electoral systems offer voters direct democracy. The people vote directly for their legislators, generally four-year terms for senators and two-year terms for representatives. Like the federal system, the number of representatives from districts in a state may be based on an area's population. Other states may have a specific number of representatives for a geographic area regardless of population. Still other states may require that voters elect representatives for the entire state, not just for their local area.

The state court system also resembles the federal structure. The *judicial branch* is headed by the state supreme court, which explains state laws and rules on legal disputes between citizens and the state. The court also decides if a person is guilty or innocent of breaking state law. Some states have intermediate *appellate courts*. Most states have district, superior, circuit, or common pleas courts beneath the supreme court. On the local level, there may be county and municipal courts, a justice of the peace, and other special courts for traffic violations, small claims, or juvenile court.

Cases heard by the state court system can be *civil* or *criminal*. Civil cases deal with legal matters such as wills and estates, divorce, and property or damage claims. Criminal trials involve crimes such as theft and murder. State judges are elected by the people. In most serious cases an accused person may be tried by a jury. Depending on the case and the state, either the jury or the judge decides on the punishment a criminal should receive. In all cases, however, the judge makes the final decision on the *sentence*, or punishment, of a person found guilty by the court.

A **governor** heads the *executive branch*. The governor executes state law and proposes new legislation. Governors advise their legislatures on laws the state needs and can call special sessions of the legislature. Governors sign bills into law and can pardon or change the sentences of persons convicted of state crimes. Governors also have authority over the state's *National Guard*, statewide peacekeeping forces. They usually are called upon when local police departments cannot control civil unrest (or riots).

Like the President, the governor has a kind of vice president called a **lieutenant governor**. As with presidential elections, a governor runs with a lieutenant governor on the same ticket. If the governor dies or leaves office, the lieutenant governor becomes acting governor. The lieutenant governor also presides over the state senate. A governor also has a group of advisers like the President's Cabinet. These advisers may be elected by the people or appointed by the governor. The state's auditor or comptroller oversees the state's finances, the treasurer collects state taxes and pays the state's bills, its attorney general represents the state in court, and the secretary of state keeps records and publishes state laws.

Voters elect governors by direct vote for four-year terms. As with presidential terms, some states limit the number of years a governor may serve. Each state has its own *qualifications for governor*, but usually he or she must be over thirty years old, a natural-born citizen of the United States, and a resident of the state for at least five years.

County and City Governments

Within a state's borders, **county** borders are governed by a **board of supervisors** or *commissioners*. Town, city, and village governments cooperate with county and state government to oversee any areas not covered by the states or federal government. County governments may maintain parks, run a sheriff's office, regulate or administer garbage disposal, look after roads, oversee the schools, regulate business, and often have authority over water supply.

Each state's constitution provides that each city have a **city charter** describing the city's government. The city has the power to protect its people with a police force and has its own court system. The head of city government, called the **mayor** or *city manager*, has many of the same kinds of powers as the governor. The mayor's duties include introducing legislation and enforcing city laws, called **ordinances.** Town and city governments police traffic and parking, dispose of garbage, have zoning laws, and regulate the construction of buildings. City government varies widely, but must have some kind of **city council** elected from local neighborhoods to make city laws.

Review Questions for State and Local Government

How are the fifty states governed?

Each state has its own constitution that describes the structure of its government. Of course, the state constitution may not conflict with the Constitution of the United States.

Who formed each state's constitution?

Under the Constitution of the United States, the people elected representatives to write their state constitutions. In most states, the people vote on its amendments.

What is a direct democracy?

In a direct democracy, the people cast their votes directly for public officials.

What powers does state government have?

On its own and in cooperation with the federal government, state government provides schools, police protection, public assistance programs, regulates working conditions and business, and makes laws.

What are some of the laws state government passes?

Among other things, state law governs unemployment, disability insurance, and worker's compensation.

Who makes state laws?

The legislative branch, usually having a house of representatives and a senate, makes the laws. The governor often recommends legislation.

How are state legislators elected?

The people cast a direct vote for legislators to the house of representatives or the senate. The apportionment of representatives differs from state to state.

What is the most important office in state government?

The governor, the chief executive of the state, leads the executive branch of state government.

Who elects governors and for how long?

The people vote directly for their governor. A governor serves a term of four years.

Who presides over the state senate?

The lieutenant governor leads the senate. He or she runs with the governor on the same party ticket.

County and City Governments

What are the forms of local government?

Beneath the state level, county, city, town, and village governments govern areas that are not covered by the state or federal governments.

What is a county and who runs its government?

Counties are districts within a state run by a board of supervisors or commissioners elected by the people.

What is the constitution of a city, and what are its laws?

City government is described in the city charter. City laws are called ordinances.

Who heads city government?

A mayor or city manager leads city government.

Who makes the city's laws or ordinances?

A city council makes the laws. Council members are elected from local neighborhoods.

What do city ordinances usually cover?

City laws protect citizens, administer and regulate garbage disposal, provide zoning and construction ordinances, and police traffic and parking.

Part III:
United States History

KEY TERMS

Christopher Columbus
Jamestown, Virginia
thirteen colonies
taxation without representation
Boston Tea Party
Revolutionary War

Declaration of Independence
Thomas Jefferson
Independence Day
George Washington
Articles of Confederation
American Flag

Pledge of Allegiance
national anthem
Abraham Lincoln
Civil War
Emancipation Proclamation

Traditionally, the United States' textbook history begins with Europe's exploration and colonization of North America during the fifteenth and sixteenth centuries. It then covers the development of the economy, politics, and government of the United States. Of course Native Americans inhabited the land long before that time, and the social and cultural fabric of American life changed many times over the years.

The INS probably will be most interested in what you know about the Revolutionary War for Independence and the Civil War between the northern and southern states. The questions the INS uses focus on these events and on United States government. You may also be asked about patriotic symbols and songs as well as about your knowledge of the current government. For instance, they might ask if you can name our top federal and state officials or what you know about America's past Presidents and political parties.

This chapter reviews the most important events in United States history. If you're interested in knowing more, you can order *United States History: 1600–1987* from the Superintendent of Documents, United States Government Printing Office, Washington, D.C., 20402.

Early America: Exploration and the Colonies

Before Europeans discovered America, several groups of Native Americans (the American Indians) inhabited the region of North America now known as the United States. Scholars differ on the origins of these peoples, though one popular theory says they migrated here between 10,000 and 20,000 years ago. The eastern portion of the Soviet Union and Alaska may have once been connected by a spit of land known as the Bering Land Bridge. Perhaps Native Americans traveled across that bridge and settled along the Pacific Coast from Alaska into the American Northwest, eventually moving inland.

Another theory is that they migrated from South America. Scientists recently discovered human remains in a cave in South America dating to 32,000 years ago. Still other scholars wonder if Norse, Phoenician, and African travelers visited North America's East Coast. In creation myths and legends some Native American tribes date their origins to six million years ago.

Whatever their origin, tribes and family groups from west to east hunted, planted, bartered, and thrived. Many of the Pacific Coast tribes (Haida, Kwakiutl, Modoc, Tlingit, and Tsimshian) fished and whaled on the open ocean while the Plains tribes (Blackfoot, Crow, Cheyenne, and Lakota) were nomadic, following the huge herds of bison that provided clothing and food. The Great Basin and Plateau tribes (Shoshone, Paiute, Ute, Nez Percé, Bannock, Walla Walla, and Yakima) were farmers and nomads. The Northern and Southern Woodlands tribes (Oneidas, Onandogas, Iroquois, Chickasaw, Cherokee, Creek, Choctaw, Natchez, Apalachee, Timucua, and later, after several tribes were destroyed in Florida, the Seminole) hunted and farmed. In the Southwest, the Navajo, Hopi, Pima, Papago, and Zuni thrived in a desert climate.

Much of the cultural richness that existed in pre-colonial North America is lost to the history of Europe's economic war on American soil. After the Italian explorer **Christopher Columbus** opened American shores to exploration, Native American life radically changed as the Spanish, Portuguese, French, and British became interested in North and South America's resources. The Native Americans were decimated by war and disease, and their civilizations sometimes completely destroyed.

Funded by Spain's Queen Isabella, Columbus's celebrated ships—the *Nina*, *Pinta*, and *Santa Maria*—set off in search of a shipping route to India in 1492. When he landed in the Caribbean, Columbus believed that he had found a sea route to India, but navigators following him quickly realized he had actually discovered a new continent. Nonetheless, according to Europeans then and American history textbooks today, Columbus "discovered" America.

To Europe, the continents north and south of the Caribbean represented a New World. Many countries—notably Britain, Spain, and France—warred constantly, and they needed new resources to feed their people and fund their wars. The Spanish first conquered the civilizations of Central America, decimating many native tribes within 100 years of their arrival. Later, they explored North America. Juan Ponce de León claimed the southeast for his country in 1513. Spain also explored portions of the Southwestern United States, introducing the horse to Native American Plains tribes. Britain explored the northern regions of North America with the voyages of John Cabot in 1497 and Henry Hudson in 1609. French navigator Samuel de Champlain sailed inland on the St. Lawrence River in 1609, and the French claimed what is now Canada and the region stretching from New Orleans up the Mississippi and west to the plains. The French and Spanish brought missionaries, and Christianity eventually challenged and altered traditional tribal religion and culture. Europe had conquered North America for settlement by the 1700s.

Columbus's voyage reflected Europe's need to expand. Its rival powers—the Spanish, French, and English—struggled to control trade on the oceans and tap America's abundant resources. The French and Spanish looked to the New World for profitable trapping and trading. For many English people, America also offered an escape from economic hardship and religious and political persecution.

THE UNITED STATES AND ITS TERRITORIES

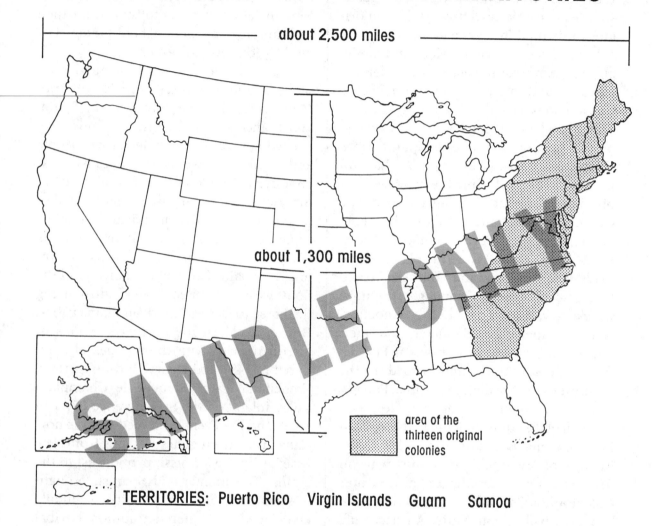

about 2,500 miles

about 1,300 miles

area of the thirteen original colonies

<u>TERRITORIES</u>: Puerto Rico   Virgin Islands   Guam   Samoa

The English and French fought for control of the eastern seaboard of what is now the United States. The French, interested in trapping, settled the northern regions. The English established settlements south of what is now the Canadian border from Maine and New York down the coast to Georgia.

The English were the first to settle colonies. The first successful settlement, established in 1607 in **Jamestown, Virginia**, was not the first attempt. Many settlers had died from malnutrition and exposure in the northern regions in earlier attempts. During the 1600s, however, the original **thirteen colonies** rapidly took shape, with *Virginia* being the first.

The next group of British settlers, the Pilgrims, landed in Plymouth, Massachusetts. The Pilgrims sought religious freedom from the Church of England and wrote their own government charter, the *Mayflower Compact*, in 1620. The Mayflower Compact is the first document written to govern people in North America that specifically set forth the power of the people to cast a vote and make decisions in government by majority rule.

Only half the Pilgrims who arrived in Massachusetts survived the first year, yet a colony had been established. Later, the Puritans arrived with hundreds more colonists. The colony became known as the *Massachusetts Bay Colony*.

The other eleven colonies quickly took shape. In 1623, *New Hampshire* opened for settlement. King Charles I gave what is now *Maryland* to Lord Baltimore in 1632. *Connecticut* and *Rhode Island* were founded in 1635 and 1636 by people in search of religious and political freedom. Settled in 1663, *North and South Carolina* became separate colonies in 1729. In 1664, the British Navy captured New Amsterdam from the Dutch and renamed it *New York*. *New Jersey* became a colony the same year. In 1681, William Penn, who believed in separation of church and state, settled *Pennsylvania*. *Delaware* was given to Penn in 1682, but it became a separate colony in 1704 (though it remained under Pennsylvania's control until 1776). Finally, James Oglethorpe settled the last colony, *Georgia*, in 1732. He founded his colony as a haven for debtors from England. Many of these people came as *indentured servants*, paying for their passage by working for seven years. Others were given a piece of land to farm. By the 1770s, 3 million people lived on the North American coast.

France and England warred constantly between 1689 and 1763, and they eventually fought over control of the colonies. During the *French and Indian War* (1754–1763), the colonists fought with the British to bring the British-French rivalry to an end. The *"Mother Country"* Britain had secured its rule of the colonies.

With the defeat of the French, King George III of England now turned his attention to the colonies. The British government carried a tremendous war debt, and the *Parliament* (Britain's legislature) responded to its economic difficulties by imposing trade tariffs on the colonies. However, the colonists had firmly established their own legislatures and parliaments. Soon the Mother Country and her offspring clashed over taxes and the colonists' right to self-government.

King George had encouraged the British colonies to grow, but was too busy fighting the French to strictly control the colonial governments, which rapidly developed to govern increasing numbers of pioneers and settlers.

Colonial governments still answered to King George. Except in Connecticut and Rhode Island, the king appointed governors (who could veto laws) in the colonies. Though colonial government provided a framework for democracy, it was not complete. For instance, only men who owned land could vote. Yet colonial governments (and the men who owned the land) soon became frustrated with Britain's absentee rule.

The original thirteen colonies had enjoyed relative freedom in business and government before the French and Indian War; they had fairly strong governments of their own by the 1770s. But after the war, Parliament forced the colonies to trade only with British ships and pay high taxes on goods traded with foreign ships. By law, the colonists also had to house, or *quarter*, British troops when asked, which was illegal in Britain. Britain also levied high taxes to pay its war debts. The *Stamp Act* of 1765 was the first of the tax acts, followed by the *Townshend Acts* in 1767, which taxed glass, painter's lead, paper, and tea. The colonies protested, but their protests were unheard in Britain's Parliament because they had no representation there. The colonies rallied around the cry **no taxation without representation**.

The final blow to the colonies came with the *Tea Act of 1773*, which taxed the colonies for tea imported by the British East India Company. Up and down the coast, the colonies boycotted tea, tried to block harbors, and protested the tax. In Massachusetts, a band of protestors called the *Sons of Liberty* boarded British ships in the harbor and dumped all the tea overboard into the water. This became known as the **Boston Tea Party.** Debt-ridden Britain punished the colonies with legislation called the *Intolerable Acts;* in response the colonists quickly organized the *First Continental Congress* in 1774.

At the First Continental Congress, twelve of the thirteen colonies signed a Declaration of Rights, asking the King to repeal the Intolerable Acts which restricted their freedoms. Patrick Henry echoed the sentiments of many colonists in a stirring speech in which he declared, "Give me liberty, or give me death."

King George III responded to Congress's written protest by sending troops to Lexington, Massachusetts, where the colonial *militia* had begun storing supplies. Despite Paul Revere's and William Dawes's nighttime ride from Boston to warn the militia— "The British are coming, the British are coming!"—the *Minute Men* at Lexington were taken by surprise on April 19, 1775,

and eight of them were killed. The British troops then advanced to Concord. Here, the Americans fired back. "The shot heard round the world," as a poet once called it, was the shot that began the **Revolutionary War.**

The American Revolution

Colonial leaders such as Benjamin Franklin, Patrick Henry, Thomas Jefferson, and John Adams strongly believed that the colonies should separate from England and function as one independent state. Other colonists were unsure about separating from England. They thought that perhaps their protest would convince England to grant them the same rights as British citizens. However, when England hired Hessians (mercenary German soldiers) to fight the war, angry Americans banded together. Public sentiment was also swayed by revolutionary thinkers such as *Thomas Paine*. His pamphlet *"Common Sense"* offered a persuasive argument for forming an independent democratic republic. Even so, many *Tories* (also called *Loyalists),* who remained loyal to England, stayed in the colonies after the war started.

In May 1775, representatives from all thirteen colonies gathered at a *Second Continental Congress* in Philadelphia to form a new government. They also prepared for war. Though members of the Congress debated fiercely, they finally decided they had no choice but to declare independence from Great Britain. They adopted the **Declaration of Independence** on *July 4, 1776* in Philadelphia to announce their solidarity and declare war on England.

The Declaration of Independence provided a strong ideological basis for a new democracy. First, it stated that all men are created equal. It also said that government should be by and for the people, meaning that the government should carry out the wishes of its people as expressed by their vote. The Declaration listed the crimes King George III had committed against the colonies, from attempting to dissolve and control colonial governments and sending troops to America without the colonists' consent, to cutting off trade with other nations. The representatives finally declared "That these United Colonies are, and of Right ought to be Free and Independent States; that they are Absolved from all Allegiance to the British Crown, and that all political connection between them and the State of Great Britain, is and ought to be totally dissolved; and that as Free and Independent States, they have full Power to levy War, conclude Peace, contract Alliances, establish Commerce, and to do all other Acts and Things which Independent States may of right do."

Thomas Jefferson, a farmer and lawyer who had strong beliefs in the power of the people to govern themselves, drafted this eloquent document, which we celebrate every **Independence Day** (or *Fourth of July*), our nation's birthday. In the Declaration of Independence he wrote that all people have "certain inalienable Rights, that among these are Life, Liberty, and the pursuit of Happiness."

The Continental Congress also enlisted **George Washington** as the commander-in-chief of the army and began to raise money for supplies. General Washington, an officer who had fought during the French and Indian War, had a difficult task before him. As a young government, the Continental Congress had little money to support its army. The army itself was composed of many smaller volunteer militia units throughout the colonies. Soldiers were ill-trained, and often left the army to return to their farms and families.

Without a strong central government and limited arms, the Americans struggled against trained, uniformed, and better-equipped British forces. However, the British were at war with the French and Spanish, which drained their army. In addition, the colonial *sharpshooters* fought a kind of guerrilla warfare, which the British, fighting in foreign territory, could not defeat. In the first year of the war, the colonists celebrated their victories. On the shores of Lake Champlain, Ethan Allen (of the Green Mountain Men militia) and Benedict Arnold took British troops at *Fort Ticonderoga* by surprise. In Boston, the Continental Army held British troops for two days in the *Battle of Bunker Hill*. Though the Americans eventually retreated, the British suffered heavy casualties.

While the Americans continued to win during the early months of 1776, in August General Washington's 10,000 soldiers lost Long Island to the British. In October, American troops were defeated by British *General William Howe* at White Plains, New York. The British also held Manhattan Island and northern New Jersey. Hoping to squeeze the British army, Washington won a very important victory when he and his winter-ravaged troops crossed the Delaware River to Trenton to capture 1,400 Hessians. Washington soon made his way to Princeton, New Jersey, where American soldiers won an important victory over General Lord Cornwallis in January of 1777. To the north, British *Major General John Burgoyne* recaptured Fort Ticonderoga in July. He and 5,000 men later surrendered at Saratoga,

---

THE PLEDGE OF ALLEGIANCE

The examiner will expect you to recite the **Pledge of Allegiance**. When it is said, citizens stand with their right hands over their hearts and military personnel salute the flag. The Pledge reads:

I pledge allegiance to the flag of the United States of America, and to the Republic for which it stands, one nation, under God, indivisible, with liberty and justice for all.

New York, as they attempted to move south on October 17, 1777.

While the battle raged, the Continental Congress met in 1777 to form a stronger national government and adopt its first constitution, called the **Articles of Confederation**. They also adopted the original **American flag** (see box, p.153), at this session. The Articles of Confederation laid the groundwork for the Constitution but it differed in important ways. While the Articles provided for a central or national government, they gave most powers to the states. The government as outlined in the Articles did not provide a court system to settle disputes or an executive office such as the presidency. The national government could not print money, collect taxes, or recruit an army. The Articles also made it difficult to pass laws or amend the Articles themselves. In short, the states had too much power and the central government had too little power, which made uniting the war-torn colonies even more difficult.

Though the Continental Army had won strategic battles in the first three years of war, by 1778 the colonial government called on the French, already at war with Britain, for help. With their support Washington dealt the final blow to the British army. In 1781, British troops under *General Lord Cornwallis* retreated to *Yorktown, Virginia*. The French landed 3,000 soldiers to stop British troops from moving in to assist Cornwallis. Troops under George Washington and French General Comte de Rochambeau joined at Williamsburg, Virginia, in September. When the siege of Yorktown began on October 6, 1781, the Continental Army boasted 8,846 soldiers supported by 7,800 Frenchmen. Cornwallis's soldiers numbered only 6,000.

On *October 19, 1781*, Lord Cornwallis surrendered. The American Revolutionary War finally came to an end. The British cabinet recognized the Continental Congress as an independent government in 1782. Representatives of Great Britain and the new United States signed the *Treaty of Paris* in *1783*, bringing the war to its official close. The Treaty of Paris gave America the Eastern Seaboard from Maine to Georgia and stretched the country's inland territories to the Mississippi River. A new nation set about repairing the damages of war and strengthening its government.

Creating a New Government

In 1787, the *Constitutional Convention* met to write a better constitution for the new country. The Constitution of the United States called for a strong national government with a three-branch system of checks and balances. It provided a process of making changes in the Constitution (called amendments), which the Articles of Confederation did not include.

Before the Constitution went into effect in 1789, the United States government had already planned a westward expansion. To govern its new lands, the Continental Congress adopted the *Northwest Ordinance*, in 1787, which outlined a procedure for establishing state governments in the area west of New York and north of the Ohio River. The Ordinance provided for public schools, outlawed slavery, and guaranteed civil liberties.

Delegates to the Constitutional Convention represented the interests of their states. Those from the North and South differed on the questions of slavery and taxes. The primarily urban north wanted to protect its developing industry. The southern colonies relied on plantation farming and on slaves for labor. They wanted to export their goods to other countries. When Congress discussed how many representatives should sit in the federal legislature, the northern states argued that slaves should not be counted as part of the population. The southern states wanted to count them as part of the population to increase their voting power in the House, but didn't want them to be counted for tax purposes. The Convention compromised, stipulating that five slaves counted as three free people for determining the number of representatives from a state, but that slaves did not count for taxes. The South also worried that the government would have the power to impose export tariffs, which might make their goods too expensive on the international market. The Convention decided to give Congress the power to levy import taxes and regulate foreign trade, but not to tax exports.

THE AMERICAN FLAG

The first **American flag** adopted by the Second Continental Congress in 1777 offered the Revolutionary army a red, white, and blue banner symbolizing the United States. Sometimes called the "Stars and Stripes," it had thirteen alternating red and white stripes representing the original colonies, and thirteen stars against a blue background representing the first thirteen states.

Red, white, and blue stand for courage, truth, and justice. Since the end of the Revolutionary War, thirty-seven stars have been added to the flag, representing all fifty states. During the flag's early years, stripes were added as states joined the Union. (Congress voted in 1794 to add two stripes and two stars to represent the two new states of Vermont and Kentucky. This flag is believed to be the one originally nicknamed the "Star Spangled Banner.") In 1818 Congress decided to keep the thirteen stripes and add a star to the field for every state. The star is added the July 4 after the new state is adopted.

Once the delegates ironed out their differences and voted to adopt the Constitution, they returned to their state governments to begin the process of ratifying the Constitution. While the smaller states quickly approved it, *Federalist* (favoring the Constitution) sentiment was not widespread in some larger states, which made for heated debate. In New York, where the anti-Federalist movement was strong, Alexander Hamilton, James Madison, and John Jay wrote compelling essays describing the advantages of the government as outlined in the Constitution. These are referred to as *The Federalist Papers*, which offer some of the best writing about the Constitution.

Finally, New Hampshire became the last state to ratify the Constitution, and the government of the United States of America officially began in 1789. The first order of business was electing a President. George Washington, a hero of the Revolution with a reputation for fairness and honesty, was unanimously elected by the Electoral College. He served as President until 1797 and is known as the *Father of our Country*. As a delegate to the Constitutional Convention, Washington had encouraged compromise. As a leader, he inspired all who worked with him. His dedication to uniting the new nation made him a good choice for President.

During the early years of the presidency many precedents were set that influence how our government works today. For example, Washington formed a panel of advisors to help him execute the various responsibilities of the presidency. *John Adams*, the Vice President, sat on the first Cabinet along with Thomas Jefferson, Secretary of State (responsible for foreign policy); *Alexander Hamilton*, Secretary of the Treasury (responsible for the federal budget and minting); *Henry Knox*, Secretary of War (responsible for the Army and Navy); and *Edmund Randolph*, Attorney General (responsible for legal matters). The president's Cabinet today includes the heads of many more executive departments, yet Washington provided the basic structure for this executive advisory board.

Not all of Washington's policies met with approval. One of the most controversial acts of the first presidential administration involved establishing a National Bank to pay the country's war debts. At the same time, the nation needed to develop a sound economy with stable currency that would encourage business to develop. As Secretary of the Treasury, Alexander Hamilton devised the plan for the National Bank. Washington endorsed his proposal. With the memory of Britain's autocratic rule still fresh in their minds, however, many people objected to the National Bank. They believed it gave the federal government too much power.

Political disagreements over these and other financial issues led to the development of the two-party political system that dominates American politics today. The *Federalists*, led by Alexander Hamilton and John Adams, were primarily large landowners and wealthy men, mostly from New England. They supported a strong federal government. The *Democratic-Republicans*, led by Thomas Jefferson and James Madison, represented the farmers and others in the working class. They believed in states' rights and a weaker federal government. The Democratic-Republicans were strongest in the southern and western portions of the early United States. Today's Republican and Democratic parties derive from these early political parties.

Another important political precedent of the time involved foreign policy. The Federalists and the Democratic-Republicans both believed that the United States should remain neutral in international matters. Americans developed an *isolationist* policy in world affairs. America might have trade bonds with another country such as England or France, but many believed it should not involve itself with another country's political affairs. In his farewell address at the end of his second and final term, Washington said, "It is our true policy to steer clear of permanent alliances with any portion of the foreign world." For the most part, the United States would focus on its expansion and development for the next one hundred years, and avoid alliances with foreign countries save for trade.

However, both Britain and France seized United States ships in an attempt to control trade. The second President, *John Adams* (1797–1801), successfully negotiated treaties with both nations, which maintained America's trading routes and saved the young country from a costly war. Adams recognized that the country had too few resources to win a war, and focused on developing its territories to the west.

Expansion and Civil War

With the states united under a strong federal government, millions of immigrants poured into the country seeking freedom and the protection of the Constitution. People from Ireland, England, and the European continent came for rich farmland; some came to escape political persecution or poverty.

Settlers in wilderness territories quickly organized state governments based on the model provided by the Northwest Ordinance and joined the United States. Vermont, Kentucky, and Tennessee were admitted in 1791, 1792, and 1796. In 1803, Ohio became the first state to be admitted from the Northwest Territory. Louisiana (1812), Indiana (1816), Illinois (1818), and Alabama (1819) also were admitted to the United States.

In 1801, the Democratic-Republican party won control of the presidency. Under its third president, *Thomas Jefferson* (1801–09), the United States government actively pursued the exploration, acquisition, and development of the lands west of the Mississippi River. America wanted control of the Mississippi to ship goods from state to state and to other nations. The Mississippi and Missouri Rivers were also important routes west. The United States offered to buy New Orleans from the French. Badly in need of money, France sold the *Louisiana Territory* to the United States for $15 million. America doubled in size and now reached west from New Orleans and the Mississippi into Texas and the Midwest.

In 1804, Jefferson sent Meriwether Lewis and William Clark to explore the newly acquired territory. The *Lewis and Clark Expedition*, guided by the Native American woman Sacagawea, explored the Missouri River and traveled up the Columbia River to the Pacific Ocean. The trip took over a year.

While Jefferson's acquisitions and exploration set an example for following Presidents to push the United States west, foreign countries still threatened America's borders. During the early 1800s, American ships enjoyed profitable trading with both Britain and France. However, Britain and

THE NATIONAL ANTHEM

In a famous battle of the War of 1812, the British bombed Fort McHenry in Baltimore, Maryland, for twenty-five hours in 1814. This battle inspired Francis Scott Key to write the words to "The Star Spangled Banner," America's **national anthem**. Watching the bombardment from a ship, he scribbled the first stanza of the song on the back of an envelope.

In 1931, an act of Congress adopted the song as America's national anthem. The flag that flew over Fort McHenry is in the Smithsonian Institution in Washington, D.C. It is called the "Star Spangled Banner" and has fifteen stripes and stars reflecting the addition of Kentucky and Vermont.

France still warred with each other and both countries blockaded and captured American ships. Britain also forcibly enlisted American sailors to fight in their navy. In one of his last acts as President, Jefferson retaliated in 1809 by signing the *Non-Intercourse Act*, which prohibited British and French ships from entering American harbors. Though the act soon was repealed because of its economic consequences, America sent a clear message to the world: Its right to free trade would not be curtailed.

President James Madison (1809–17) had to negotiate high tensions between Britain, France and the United States. After passing more successful legislation outlawing trade with Britain, America finally declared war on Britain in 1812. During the *War of 1812* the American Navy proved its strength against the once-supreme ruler of the seas. In the first year, "Old Ironsides" (as the ship *Constitution* was known) won two important battles, and American ships captured two British vessels on Lake Erie. Before the war ended in 1814, however, the British seized Washington, D.C. and burned the Capitol, the White House, and the Navy Yard. When the British sailed to Baltimore, Maryland, American forces turned them back. Here *Francis Scott Key* witnessed a nighttime battle that inspired the words to the National Anthem (see box above).

When America signed a favorable *Treaty of Ghent* with the British in 1814, it had many effects on the young nation. It strengthened isolationist sentiments and feelings of nationalism. It also separated Native Americans from their British ally and helped open the West to the United States. Many Indians had fought with the British against the United States because the United States was forcing them out of their homelands and into the West. The Shawnee lost their chief *Tecumseh* in 1813 during a battle, and 900 of 1,000 Creeks were killed in Alabama in 1814.

The United States bought Florida from Spain in 1819 for $5 million. Florida tribes, decimated early on by the Europeans, had banded together to form the Seminole nation. Before the United States negotiated the agreement with Spain, American forces led by Andrew Jackson quelled Seminole resistance in 1818 and captured two Spanish forts in Florida.

As the United States aggressively expanded, it worried that European powers once again would try to intrude in North America. Reacting to rumors that Austria, Prussia, France, and Russia planned to recolonize Latin America, *President James Monroe* (1817–25) issued a statement in 1823 that said America would view foreign intervention in North America as a military threat. The *Monroe Doctrine* also articulated the United States' isolationist stance: It would not interfere with any foreign nation's internal affairs.

During the 1820s and 1830s, the United States poured its energy into opening the West for settlement and commerce. Jedediah Strong Smith discovered a pass through the Rocky Mountains that would make overland travel to the Pacific Coast easier. The Erie Canal cut the travel time from the East Coast to Buffalo by one-third when it was completed in 1825. In 1828, the Baltimore & Ohio, the first passenger railroad, began operating. During the mid-1830s Texans struggled with Mexico for control of the territory. At the siege of the *Alamo* in 1836, every American in the fort died. Months later, General Samuel Houston won Texas's independence from Mexico at the Battle of San Jacinto.

The government also formalized its policy of moving Native Americans out of settled areas with the passage of the *Indian Removal Act* in 1830 under *President Andrew Jackson* (1829–37). By 1838, the last of the American Indians East of the Mississippi moved West in what became known as the *Trail of Tears*.

As the country grew, differences arose between various regions of the country over land policy, taxes, and slavery. When Missouri and Maine asked to join the union in 1819, northern legislators wanted to admit them as free states without slaves. Southerners, already in the minority in the House because of the South's lower population, opposed the action. The Dutch had first brought African slaves to America in 1619, and southern farmers relied on the *slave trade* to supply laborers for their huge plantations. Though importing slaves was outlawed in 1808, the slave trade thrived. (About 250,000 slaves entered the United States illegally between 1808 and 1860.) Economic conditions in the industrialized North did not depend as heavily on slaves.

To resolve their differences, Congress passed the *Missouri Compromise* in 1820. The Compromise admitted Missouri as a slave state and Maine as a free state. It also said that all states admitted north of the 36°30' parallel would be free, and those south of that border would be admitted as slave states. The Missouri Compromise allowed the nation to grow and maintained the union, but the differences between the North and South continued to increase.

During the 1840s, America strove to expand its western border to the Pacific. The United States believed it was its *Manifest Destiny* to govern all the land between the Atlantic and Pacific Oceans. Texas was annexed from Mexico in 1845, Britain agreed to give the United States the *Oregon Territory* to the 49th parallel in 1846, and Mexico ceded the Southwest in 1848.

Neither Britain nor Mexico gave up their territories peacefully. British ships threatened the islands of the Pacific Northwest and Alaska. Texas fought all-out war with Mexico. Angered by the annexation of Texas, Mexico refused to sell California and New Mexico to the United States. Between 1846 and 1848, the United States battled with Mexico in the *Mexican-American War* over control of the region. At its conclusion, Mexico ceded the remaining portion of Texas as well as California and New Mexico to the United States for $15 million.

Finally, the *Gadsden Purchase* of 1853 gave America all the land north of the Rio Grande. The United States controlled the territory of what is now the contiguous forty-eight states.

Yet before Congress appropriated the funds to buy its last bit of land in North America, northern and southern legislators clashed once again over admitting states as slave or free. California wanted to join the United States as a free state. The South, in danger of losing its voting power in Congress, realized the terms of the Missouri Compromise of 1820 no longer would protect their voting interests if states could decide on their own to be slave or free. Southern legislators opposed admitting California as a free state. Doing so would upset the even balance between slave and free states.

In 1850, Henry Clay introduced legislation, *The Compromise of 1850*, that resolved the differences between the North and South for a short time. As a result of this compromise, Utah and New Mexico became territories. A vote of the people (known as *popular sovereignty*) would decide if they would become slave or free states. One part of the Compromise legislation, the *Fugitive Slave Act*, made capturing and convicting a runaway slave much easier. (Slaves did not enjoy due process under the Constitution: A slave could not testify in his or her own defense; slaves also didn't have the right to a trial by jury.)

Abolitionists (those who believed in outlawing slavery) grew increasingly active during this period. By 1838 the *Underground Railroad* was providing an escape route for slaves in the South. Between 1838 and 1860 it smuggled as many as 1,000 slaves each year to freedom in the North. Activists for change in the structure of American society became more vocal. Lucretia Mott and Elizabeth Cady Stanton, who were both abolitionists and feminists, organized the *Seneca Falls New York Women's Rights Convention* in 1848. (Though feminists who wanted the right to vote and abolitionists worked hand-in-hand throughout the middle years of the nineteenth century, slaves would win freedom and suffrage long before women.) Reflecting the attitudes of North and South about slaves, Harriet Beecher Stowe's *Uncle Tom's Cabin* created instant controversy when it was published in 1852. About this time, the African-American Frederick Douglass traveled through the North speaking against slavery and organizing abolitionists.

As activists in the East lobbied for changes in slavery law, Congress quarreled over whether to admit the Kansas and Nebraska territories to the union as free or slave states. In 1854, Congress passed the *Kansas–Nebraska Act*, which gave popular sovereignty to these as well as any new territories annexed by the United States. Abolitionists and their foes staged a series of violent protests. Tensions were so high that the territory became known as "bleeding Kansas," and hundreds of "Beecher's Bibles" (Sharps rifles) were shipped to Kansas. The militant abolitionist *John Brown* joined Kansas's Free State forces to protest the proslavery settlers. In 1856 he led a raid in which five slavery advocates were brutally murdered. (In 1859, John Brown was tried and hanged for treason after his raid of an arsenal at Harpers Ferry, West Virginia.)

Neither the Supreme Court nor the military courts favored abolition. The Supreme Court's pro-slavery 1857 *Dred Scott* decision would stand for many years after slaves won freedom. Dred Scott lived in freedom for seven years in the North. When he returned to the South, he again became a slave. When he filed a case with the Supreme Court to win his freedom, the Court refused to recognize it. As a slave, Scott was not a citizen. He did not deserve the due process in the court system. The Supreme Court's ruling set the tone for the deep racism that dominated post–Civil War and twentieth-century America.

In this political climate America prepared for the presidential election of 1860. The new Republican Party nominated **Abraham Lincoln**, a pioneer lawyer born in Kentucky and trained in Illinois. Lincoln opposed slavery, but politically he could not commit to abolishing it right away. Still, southern voters saw Lincoln as a serious threat. If he were elected, the South vowed to *secede* in protest, separating its government from the *Union*, or United States.

After Lincoln's victory over Stephen A. Douglas of Illinois, South Carolina became the first state to formally declare secession from the Union in December of 1860. The stage was set for a lengthy battle when representatives from South Carolina, Alabama, Mississippi, Florida, Georgia, and Louisiana met on February 4, 1861, to form the *Confederate States of America*. In April 1861 southern troops fired on northern troops at Fort Sumter, South Carolina and began America's **Civil War**. Lincoln quickly responded by blockading southern ports.

Most of the other slave states—Texas, Arkansas, Tennessee, North Carolina, and Virginia—quickly joined the Confederacy. Yet the southern line was not clear-cut. Missouri and Kentucky, both slave states, did not secede. In Virginia, those living in the northwestern mountainous region disagreed with their state government in Richmond, now the capital of the Confederacy. The United States adopted West Virginia as an independent state in 1863 as the country fought its civil war. Even families split over their loyalty to North or South.

The war between the Union and Confederate armies lasted four years. *General Ulysses S. Grant* commanded the Union Army in the west during the early years of the war. After his successful campaign in Tennessee and Mississippi, Lincoln assigned Grant full command of the *Yankee* army. A West Point–trained officer, *General Robert E. Lee*, was chosen to lead the southern *Rebels*. The Civil War proved one of the bloodiest ever, the armies clashing in battles lasting days and weeks that left thousands dead. Though the Confederate Army won many battles during the first year of the war, the South's spirits dampened when General Lee and his troops failed to invade the North through Maryland. At the *Battle of Antietam* in 1862 Lee and his army were forced to retreat. More soldiers were killed or wounded at Antietam than in any other battle of the war: The North lost 2,108 with 9,549 wounded; the South lost 2,700 with over 9,000 wounded.

This turning point was followed by several decisive victories for the Union troops in the South under General Grant. After Grant's successes at Shiloh, Tennessee, Vicksburg, Mississippi, and Lookout Mountain, Tennessee, Union *General William T. Sherman* led his troops on their infamous march to the sea. They swept through the South, burning private homes and land, and destroying major southern cities such as Atlanta. The march left a trail of devastation that helped break the South's fighting spirit.

At the war's midpoint, President Lincoln used his power as President to free slaves in the states still loyal to the Union. The **Emancipation Proclamation** of 1863 did not affect those slaves living in southern states. Some questioned the President's right to invoke such power without Congress's approval. Later, in 1865, passage of the Thirteenth Amendment guaranteed slaves' constitutional freedom.

Following the Emancipation Proclamation, northern and southern soldiers fought for six days at *Gettysburg,* Pennsylvania in one of the war's most vicious engagements. Both sides suffered heavy losses, but Confederate troops finally retreated. In November, Lincoln issued his famous *Gettysburg Address* in which he reiterated the strengths of the Union and said that its unified, democratic government "shall not perish from the earth." Gettysburg became a national cemetery honoring both southern and northern soldiers.

At the start of Lincoln's second term as President in 1865, the South had few resources left to win the war. Sensing the close of the war at hand, Lincoln offered a hopeful message in his *Second Inaugural Address* to the nation. "With malice toward none," he said, "with charity for all, with firmness in the right as God gives us to see the right, let us strive on to finish the work we are in, to bind up the nation's wounds. . . to do all which may achieve and cherish a just and lasting peace among ourselves and with all nations."

Though General Lee surrendered to General Grant at Appomatox Courthouse in Virginia on *April 9, 1865,* the wounds of war would not heal for many years. Southern sentiment against former slaves thrived. Angry citizens formed the Ku Klux Klan soon after the Confederacy's defeat. The assassination of President Lincoln five days after Lee surrendered shocked both North and South: The country faced many difficult years ahead.

Following the Civil War, the United States focused on rebuilding the South with *Reconstruction* legislation. Many northern legislators believed the South should be harshly punished for the war. Against the wishes of *President Andrew Johnson* (1865–69), legislators refused to recognize southern Congressmen when they returned to the Capitol. The legislature asked the southern states to grant slaves citizenship and the right to vote before they could rejoin the Union. Tennessee was the only state to do so, and the other southern states were occupied by Union forces. The Fourteenth and Fifteenth Amendments, which guaranteed to former slaves citizenship and the right to vote, were passed soon after in 1868 and 1870. Though the Reconstruction period ended in 1877, differences between North and South remained pronounced for many years.

Through the latter half of the nineteenth century, huge waves of immigrant labor fed America's industrialization. At the same time, prospectors and settlers pushed west to settle the territories and establish states. In the West, Native Americans were pushed onto reservations. By the close of the nineteenth century when American workers felt threatened by cheaper Chinese labor, Congress passed the Chinese Exclusion Act. American cities grew rapidly with industrialization, and by the twentieth century, the farm population began to drop.

World War I and the Depression

Between 1890 and 1910, immigration skyrocketed, and Congress attempted to distinguish the desirable immigrants from the undesirable. During the first years of the twentieth century, the conditions in urban slums were blamed on the hard-working immigrants from Poland, Greece, and Italy rather than on the economic and social conditions of the country. The United States began to wonder if it could support such a diverse population. Congress's 1911 Dillingham Commission report claimed that immigrants from Eastern Europe and Asia simply did not assimilate well and would not make good citizens.

With industrialization and the end of the Victorian era in Europe, the United States changed dramatically in the cultural, social, and political spheres. Prohibitionists (people who want to outlaw liquor) gradually won states in the East and West. Labor unions became increasingly powerful in American politics. The pace of the American day picked up with the invention of the electric light bulb, the telephone, and later, assembly-line production in factories.

In Europe, France, Great Britain, Russia, and Italy fought Germany and Austria-Hungary in *World War I*. Maintaining its isolationist stance, America struggled to remain neutral. But when the Germans introduced the submarine, the United States reasoned that it could not tolerate unrestricted warfare. Ocean-going passenger liners as well as war ships were watched by German submarines. America entered the war in 1917, three years after it had begun. America's military success during the war helped establish it as a world power. After negotiations lasting over a month, Germany officially surrendered on November 11, 1918. Virtually all of America took to the streets in celebration.

The period after World War I was a time of change. Congress passed the first immigration quota laws during the 1920s. Jeannette Rankin became the first woman elected to Congress, and the National Women's Party was founded in 1916 to fight for *Women's Suffrage* (the right to vote). Women finally won the vote in 1920 with ratification of the Nineteenth Amendment. A year earlier, Congress had ratified the Eighteenth Amendment, introducing the Prohibition era. The economy suffered after the costly war, and the United States once more isolated itself from Europe. But hemlines rose, jazz reached a wide American audience, and spirits were high. The upward spiral would quickly plummet at the close of this turbulent decade.

The *Great Depression* of the 1930s tested America's economic strength. During the 1920s, businesses had earned huge sums of money on the stock market. A few wealthy men controlled the capital of the whole nation. The activities of the American stock exchange had an effect on the world economy. In 1929, business bought fewer capital goods, unemployment rates rose, construction was down, and blue-chip stocks did not perform well. Banks raised their interest rate for loans, and a flood of money from foreign investors allowed buyers to double their money by buying "call loans," or stocks on margin. Beginning in October, the stock market plummeted.

Millions of people lost their jobs, banks all over the nation closed, and America's borders were virtually sealed to immigrants. The optimism and policy of "voluntary cooperation" of Republican *President Herbert Hoover* (1929–33) did not feed farmers or

162 CITIZENSHIP MADE SIMPLE

give jobs to the unemployed. Between 1929 and 1932, farmers lost money as prices for their goods fell. Some killed livestock that was too expensive to feed, others grew more than needed, glutting the market with produce they could not sell. "Hoovervilles," makeshift shanty towns built by the homeless and unemployed, sprung up outside cities all over the country.

Democrat *Franklin Delano Roosevelt* took office as President in 1933 and vowed to put America back on its feet. (In a shift in America's party politics, the Democrats would control the presidency until the election of Dwight D. Eisenhower in 1952.) Roosevelt announced a four-day bank holiday, helping to ease the banking crisis. He quickly introduced economic reforms that would help farmers keep their farms and inject new health into the American economy. His *New Deal* legislation, begun in 1933, called for immediate relief, a program of recovery for the nation, and reform measures to prevent such disasters in the future. Five million people went back to work in programs such as the government-authorized Tennessee Valley Authority, which built an impressive network of dams. The Federal Securities Act regulated the stock market, and the National Industrial Recovery Act created the Public Works Administration. Roosevelt also established the National Labor Board and appointed the first woman cabinet member, Secretary of Labor Frances Perkins.

The United States as a World Power: World War II and After

Roosevelt remained President for an unprecedented twelve years. He is credited with pulling America out of the Depression.

He also provided strong leadership when Japan drew America into *World War II* (1941–45) on December 7, 1941, with the surprise attack on a United States naval base at *Pearl Harbor*, Hawaii. In 1939, German leader Adolf Hitler had invaded Poland, and France and England quickly went to war with Germany. Later the Soviet Union would join the *Allies* against the *Axis* powers of Germany, Italy, and Japan. As it had in World War I, America tried to remain neutral. But the Allies faced a difficult war and the United States joined them in 1941. As commander in chief, Roosevelt successfully led the United States toward victory with the Allies. In June 1944 the Allies launched the *D-Day Invasion* in the final push to defeat Hitler. Unfortunately, Roosevelt died of a brain hemorrhage in April 1945, just a month before Germany surrendered.

Harry Truman (1945–53) took over the presidency anxious to win the war still being fought with Japan in the Pacific. He approved the use of the atomic bomb—the first was dropped on Hiroshima and another on Nagasaki a few days later. Devastated, Japan surrendered in August 1945.

After World War II the United States emerged as a world leader with a growing economy and a powerful military. Though the United States supported the formation of the *United Nations* in an attempt to use diplomatic channels to avoid war between nations, it viewed countries controlled or influenced by the communist-ruled Soviet Union as a threat to democracy. America fought the *Korean Conflict* against Communist North Korea and had chilly relations with the Soviets. The *Cold War* with Communist Russia escalated during the 1950s. Senator Joseph McCarthy exploited people's fears by accusing hundreds of public figures of supporting communism.

The Cold War did not improve when *John F. Kennedy* (1961–63) became President in 1961. Kennedy believed the Soviets were shipping arms to Cuba. In response, he ordered the unsuccessful invasion of Cuba known as the *Bay of Pigs* in 1961. During this time, Americans feared nuclear war might break out.

An Era of Change: From the 1960s Forward

The 1960s were a time of rapid change in the United States. In a race with the Soviets for space technology, the President called for landing a man on the moon by the end of the decade. He and his brother, *Attorney General Robert F. Kennedy*, also grappled with the urgent question of *civil rights*. They negotiated with civil rights leaders, including Roy Wilkins from the National Association for the Advancement of Colored People (NAACP) and *Dr. Martin Luther King, Jr.* of the Southern Christian Leadership Conference (SCLC).

In many southern states, civil rights demonstrators challenged state and federal laws that had been passed during the late nineteenth and early twentieth centuries. These *Jim Crow laws* created a situation in the South where African-Americans lived with substandard conditions in housing, education, and public facilities despite the Supreme Court's "separate but equal" ruling in *Plessy v. Ferguson* in 1896. From boycotting segregated buses in Montgomery, Alabama, to sit-ins at all-white lunch counters in cities all over the South, King and his followers agitated for "freedom now," the right to vote, and economic and social equality for all Americans. Black Americans had waited too long for their rights to be heard in government and to be treated as equal human beings. The Supreme Court's *Brown v. Board of Education* in 1954, which desegregated schools, was a major victory for civil rights advocates. Later, President Kennedy passed some civil rights legislation, but was assassinated in 1963. During the presidency of *Lyndon B. Johnson* (1963–69) the *Civil Rights Act of 1964* was enacted outlawing segregation in housing, schools, and public accommodations.

American involvement in the war in Vietnam contributed to the growing turbulence of this decade of social and political change. Television brought the *Vietnam War* into American homes and public opinion was divided about America's role in the war. Many students and other activists demonstrated against the war. At Kent State University, the Ohio National Guard killed four students in protests that lasted several days.

In 1968, Robert F. Kennedy was killed as he accepted the Democratic nomination for President. Dr. King was assassinated the same year.

The next decade brought an end to the Vietnam War. Activism for civil rights continued, and the modern feminist movement grew during the early 1970s. The Senate approved the Equal Rights Amendment (ERA), which would have barred discrimination against people on the basis of their sex. (The ERA was never ratified.) The Supreme Court's decision in the case of *Roe v. Wade* guaranteed a woman's right to abortion in 1973. The movement for gay and lesbian rights also gained ground during the seventies.

But the 1970s also brought a political crisis. President *Richard M. Nixon* (1969–74) was accused of knowing about an illegal break-in by employees of his campaign during the 1972 presidential election. The break-in was at the Democratic Party headquarters at the *Watergate* apartments in Washington, D.C. The American public questioned the ethics of its own President and the House began impeachment proceedings against Nixon. He resigned in 1974, the first President ever to resign from office.

The American economy fell into *recession* under Republican *Gerald Ford* (1974–77). He was faced with the difficult task of leading a country depressed by the Watergate scandal. Not surprisingly, the Democratic candidate *Jimmy Carter* (1977–81) won the next election in 1976. Though Carter negotiated successful arms limitation agreements with the Soviet Union, his administration was criticized for its weak foreign policy. During his term, Iran held fifty-two Americans hostage for over a year. His failure to present a strong international profile led to a new era in American politics.

Republican *Ronald Reagan* (1981–89) from California swept the 1980 election, promising voters that he would make America strong again. He said he would build up the military to give America leverage in arms negotiations with the Soviets and reduce taxes to strengthen the economy. Internationally, Reagan talked tough with the Soviets during the early 1980s, but later opened arms negotiations with Soviet President Mikhail Gorbachev. At home, Reagan's tax and budget reforms pared down government spending and encouraged private enterprise. While some people benefited from his policies, others criticized the government for turning a deaf ear to the problems of unemployment and housing for the nation's poor.

The popularity of Ronald Reagan perhaps reflected America's need for a strong leader. Reagan relied on a fatherly image and an optimistic attitude to sway public opinion. His policies were far more conservative than those of the previous administration. He appointed conservative judges to the Supreme Court, including the first woman Supreme Court justice, Sandra Day O'Connor. Those concerned with funding AIDS research and caring for AIDS patients were largely dissatisfied with his administration's response. Many viewed his policies as a backlash against the more liberal sixties and seventies. Even in the face of the politically damaging *Iran-Contra Affair*, in which America sent arms to Iran in an attempt to secure the release of hostages being held by Arab kidnappers, at the close of his administration, Reagan continued to be a popular President.

George Bush, who was Vice President to Ronald Reagan, easily won the presidential election in 1988. Even with the failure of many United States savings banks, an increasing national debt, and a faltering economy, Bush optimistically faces the years ahead. As a leading power in world politics, the Bush administration will have to answer to global concerns about the environment and keep pace with the many changes taking place in Eastern Europe. One of the key issues of his administration is drugs. In 1989, United States forces invaded Panama and extradited Panamanian President Manuel Noriega on drug trafficking charges. Another issue of concern to the President is abortion. The Supreme Court ruled in 1989 that the states had some more power to regulate abortion, a major setback for advocates of a woman's right to reproductive freedom.

Based on the foundation laid by the writers of the Constitution and America's early Presidents, American politics will continue to change focus as the needs of America's people and the world change. As the United States evolved from thirteen colonies to a nation, as it suffered civil and world war, it underwent many transformations. Advances were made in the areas of civil rights, sexual equality, and equal opportunity. Yet the country still grapples with the questions of racism, sexism, and homophobia; with unemployment, poor test scores in schools, and widespread poverty. In foreign policy, the 1990s heralded a close in a chapter of the Cold War as countries in Eastern Europe broke free of communist rule. America continues to redefine itself as shifts in the world economy force it to reevaluate and restructure its own economy.

The United States struggles with the same domestic and foreign issues that affect most countries, developed or underdeveloped. Its hope lies in the ability of the Constitution, its republican form of government, and its leaders to adapt to a nation's—and a world's—changing needs.

Review Questions for United States History

Early America: Exploration and the Colonies

Who discovered America and when?

In 1492 Christopher Columbus sailed the ocean blue to discover the New World. This Italian sailor sought a sea route to India. He thought he had found it, but actually landed in the Caribbean.

What was the first successful English settlement in America?

Founded in 1607, Jamestown, Virginia, was the first successful settlement in America.

How many original colonies were there? Can you name them?

Thirteen colonies declared war on Britain in 1776. They were: New Hampshire, Massachusetts, Rhode Island, Connecticut, Delaware, New York, New Jersey, Pennsylvania, Maryland, Virginia, North and South Carolina, and Georgia.

Why did the colonies go to war with the "Mother Country," Great Britain?

The colonists fought Britain's taxes on American trade—taxation without representation. The colonies were forced to pay taxes when they had no representatives in British government.

What was the Boston Tea Party?

A group of revolutionary colonists called the Sons of Liberty threw tea off British ships in Boston Harbor, Massachusetts, in protest of the Tea Act in 1773. Their act is the most famous incident of the colonists' boycott of tea shipped by the British East India Company to America.

What is the Declaration of Independence?

The Declaration declared the colonies' independence from Great Britain in 1776. The thirteen colonies that signed the Declaration eventually became the first thirteen states of the United States.

Who wrote the Declaration of Independence?

Thomas Jefferson, a farmer and lawyer from Virginia, wrote most of the Declaration.

When is our nation's birthday?

We celebrate Independence Day on July 4, the anniversary of the Declaration of Independence. The Fourth of July is a national holiday.

When and where was the Declaration of Independence signed?

The Second Continental Congress accepted the Declaration in Philadelphia on July 4, 1776, but all the delegates did not sign it until a month later.

What was the Revolutionary War?

King George III of England sent troops to the colonies and taxed them without representation. The colonies rebelled. Britain already was at war with France and Spain, and France soon entered the war on the American side. Initially the Americans were at a disadvantage, but after a long, costly war colonial forces under George Washington finally defeated British troops under Lord Cornwallis at Yorktown, Virginia, in 1781. Two years later, in 1783, Great Britain recognized the independent United States when they signed a treaty.

What were the Articles of Confederation?

The Articles of Confederation was the first document to set up self-government of the states under a central government. The Articles did not give the national government enough power. The government did not have the power to stop disagreements between the thirteen states. In 1787, Congress met to write the Constitution of the United States.

Expansion and Civil War

Why do people choose to come to the United States to live?

Some people immigrate for economic opportunity or to escape political persecution. Most people come to share in the freedom offered to them under the United States Government.

Who was the President during the Civil War?

Abraham Lincoln, sometimes called "Honest Abe," was elected the sixteenth President in 1861. The Civil War started shortly after he took office.

When was the Civil War and what was its cause?

The Civil War began in 1861 over the issue of States' Rights. The southern states wanted the right to allow slavery and seceded from the Union. The Union Army won the war in 1865.

When and why was slavery introduced in America?

The Dutch first brought African slaves to America in 1619. Farmers in Virginia and other parts of the South depended on the slave trade to run their large plantations.

What was the result of the Civil War?

During the war, President Lincoln issued the Emancipation Proclamation, in 1863, abolishing slavery. When the North won the war in 1865, the Thirteenth Amendment was ratified, making slavery illegal. The end of the war also reunited the North and the South, saving the United States of America.

The American Flag and the National Anthem

What is the name of the American national anthem?

"The Star Spangled Banner" is the United States' national anthem.

Who wrote the national anthem and when?

Francis Scott Key wrote the words to the song as he watched the British bomb Fort McHenry in Baltimore, Maryland, in 1814.

What are the colors of the American flag? What do they represent?

Red stands for courage, white stands for truth, and blue stands for justice.

How many stripes are on the flag? What do they stand for?

There are thirteen stripes—seven red and six white—on the flag, representing the original thirteen states.

How many stars are on the flag? What do they represent?

The fifty white stars on the flag represent the fifty states of the United States. The first American flag had thirteen stars representing the thirteen original colonies. A star is added for every state that joins the Union.

What is the Pledge of Allegiance?

"I pledge allegiance to the flag of the United States of America, and to the Republic for which it stands, one nation, under God, indivisible, with liberty and justice for all."

How many states are there in the United States, and what is the capital of the United States?

There are fifty states. Washington, D.C., also called the District of Columbia, is the capital and is not a state.

What are the territories of the United States?

Puerto Rico, the Virgin Islands, Samoa, and Guam are territories that have not been ratified as new states.

How big is the continental United States?

The United States is about 2,500 miles across from the Atlantic Coast to the Pacific Coast. From Canada to Mexico, it is about 1,300 miles.

GLOSSARY

adjudicate   To legally judge a document or case.

adjustment of status   The process by which temporary visitors to the United States change their visa status.

advance parole   When an alien is admitted to the United States temporarily while their case for immigration is heard.

alien   Anyone in the United States who is not a natural-born citizen.

appeal   A request for a new hearing in a higher court.

appellate court   A court that hears appeals and can override lower court decisions.

apportionment   How something is distributed, as with the number of representatives in Congress.

asylee (asylum)   An alien in the United States who applies for permanent residency because of a well-founded fear of persecution should they return to their country of origin.

beneficiary   Someone who receives the benefits or proceeds from something. Aliens for whom permanent resident aliens or citizens petition for immigrant status are called beneficiaries.

bill   The proposed document that Congress votes on to become law.

campaign   Persons running for elected office campaign to convince voters to vote for them.

candidate   A person who runs for elected office.

charter   A legal document or grant that establishes a local government or corporation. It defines the organization's purpose, duties, and rights.

checks and balances   A form of government in which each of the three branches—Legislative, Judicial, and Executive—limit the power of each of the other branches.

civil   The rights of individuals to personal freedoms and property. Civil court cases try those who have violated the civil rights of another person.

civil rights   The rights of a person within a particular society under its government.

consular processing   The term for filing for a visa to travel or reside in the United States from American consulates or embassies abroad.

criminal   Court cases in which a person has committed a serious crime such as murder or burglary.

deport   The legal expulsion of a foreign national from the United States.

direct democracy   A form of government in which citizens cast their votes directly for a candidate or legislation.

discrimination   Treating someone differently (usually badly) because of their race, religion, national origin, sexual orientation, physical or mental disability, economic status, or other characteristic.

excludability   A set of rules in immigration law that set forth the reasons why a person may be excluded from entering the United States.

foreign-born   Anyone who is not a citizen.

foreign national   Another term for someone who is not born in the United States and is not a citizen.

general election   An election on the state or national level that involves all voters.

Green Card   A slang term for the Alien Registration Receipt Card, which shows that an alien is a permanent resident alien.

illegal alien   An alien who has violated the terms of his or her visa or who entered the country illegally.

immigrant   The INS uses the word "immigrant" to describe aliens who enter the

United States with a visa permitting them to reside here permanently.

impeach To charge a public official with committing a crime.

inaugurate To place in office with a formal ceremony.

jury A group of citizens chosen by the court to hear a case in court. The jury decides on a person's guilt or innocence and sometimes recommends punishment.

legislate To make laws (*legislation* is the procedure of making laws).

levy To collect something, as a tax.

line of succession The order in which people succeed, or take over, an office.

National Guard A state military force that is on call for the state or federal government. The guard is often called upon during natural disasters.

naturalization The legal process by which an alien becomes a citizen.

nonimmigrant alien The INS uses this term for aliens who enter the United States with temporary visas.

overstay An alien who stays in the United States after his or her visa expires.

pardon To forgive, excuse from punishment, someone who has committed a crime.

petitioner One who formally asks for something in writing.

permanent resident alien An alien who has applied for and received this immigrant status from the INS. A permanent resident alien may live and work in the United States; the alien may also become a citizen after meeting certain requirements.

Preference System The system devised by Congress and the INS to admit immigrant aliens to the United States. The system limits the number of immigrant visas issued each year to all countries.

preside To oversee or lead a meeting; to be in charge of something.

pro tempore Temporarily, for the time being.

public charge Someone who relies on the government for housing, food, or other care.

quota system A system for limiting the number of immigrants based on percentages of aliens from each country already in the United States.

ratify To formally approve or affirm, as when the state legislatures ratify an amendment to the Constitution.

refugee An alien abroad who applies to become a permanent resident alien because he or she faces persecution in their home country.

repeal To take back, recall. Usually used in reference to a law that has been overturned.

representative democracy A form of government in which the people elect officials to make decisions for them in government. Sometimes the people vote directly on the issues, rather than having officials vote on their behalf in the legislature.

republic A government that is democratic and representative.

sham marriage A marriage between people that is not true and valid.

table To postpone or delay, as when a Congressional committee delays making a decision on a bill.

temporary visa The visa issued to aliens who want to visit the United States for a limited time.

veto The power of the President to stop a bill from becoming law.

visa The document or stamp in a passport that allows a visitor to enter the United States.

Choosing a Lawyer

With this book in hand, you can file many of the forms with the INS yourself. However, if your case is complicated, you will have to call on the services of a lawyer. Attorneys in different places run their businesses slightly differently. To practice law in the United States, attorneys must pass a bar exam in the state where they practice. The state bar may disbar, or stop a lawyer from practicing law, for illegal or unethical practices. Beyond that, lawyers have different policies for charging fees and collecting them. Here are a few things to keep in mind as you search for an attorney to help you with immigration and naturalization.

First, find out what experience the lawyer has with immigration law and procedure. The lawyer will act on your behalf with the INS and the government. Membership in an affiliate of The American Bar Association called the American Immigration Lawyers Association is a good indication the attorney specializes in immigration law. Your prospective lawyer should give you some idea of the chances for your success, though no lawyer can guarantee that you will win your case. If an attorney does make such a guarantee, quickly find another one.

Many law firms handle thousands of clients. While large offices may have the advantage of lower fees, they may not take the time to offer personalized service and answer all your questions. Ask a prospective attorney a lot of questions. Do you feel comfortable with the answers you get? Does it seem as though the lawyer will take time to answer your questions every step of the way? In some cases you may pay hefty sums for a lawyer's services. You will want one who will be with you every step of the way.

Many firms specialize in different areas of immigration law. Some deal only with immigration services (the INS) and will not be effective when dealing with a consulate or embassy abroad. Ask about the lawyer's (and the firm's) experience with cases like yours. What other kinds of cases do they most often handle?

Lawyers charge for their services by different methods. Some charge a fixed rate for a particular service, called a "retainer," while others charge by the hour. In many cases, clients will pay for "disbursements" (extra expenses) related to their cases such as phone calls, copying documents, filing fees, messengers, and the like. Ask for estimates of these costs. When a lawyer charges a retainer for a specific job, you will probably have to pay more if you lose the case. If the lawyer charges by the hour, ask for an estimate of the amount of time your case requires.

You and your lawyer should have a comfortable working relationship. If you call your lawyer three times a day and take a lot of his or her time, expect to pay more. Your lawyer should be willing to answer all your questions under the fees you agree to pay, but some clients get nervous about their case and dominate the lawyer's time. Trust your attorney to get the job done as quickly and efficiently as legally possible.

INS Regional and District Offices

Regional offices probably will refer you to a district or sub-office nearest you. In most cases, district offices can process your documents and send you forms and information. You may also file at some sub-offices listed in Appendix Three. Write or call the INS office nearest you to be sure you file your forms with the correct office.

Address all correspondence to: Immigration and Naturalization Service.

The following states do not have INS offices. Write to or call the district office listed:

State	District Office
Alabama	Atlanta, GA
Arkansas	New Orleans, LA
Delaware	Philadelphia, PA
Iowa	Omaha, NE
Kansas	Kansas City, MO
Mississippi	New Orleans, LA
New Hampshire	Boston, MA
North Dakota	St. Paul, MN
South Dakota	St. Paul, MN
West Virginia	Philadelphia, PA
Wyoming	Denver, CO

Regional Offices

Northern Region

Federal Building
Fort Snelling
Twin Cities, MN 55111
612-854-7754

Eastern Region

Federal Building
Elmwood Avenue
Burlington, VT 05401
802-951-6524

Southern Region

First International Building
1201 Elm Street
Room 2300
Dallas, TX 75270
214-767-6014

Western Region

Terminal Island
San Pedro, CA 90731
213-514-6537

District Offices

Alaska

Federal Building, United States
  Courthouse
701 C Street, Room D-251
Lock Box 16
Anchorage, AK 99513
907-271-5029

Arizona

Federal Building
230 North 1st Avenue
Phoenix, AZ 85205
602-261-3122

California

300 North Los Angeles Street
Room 1000
Los Angeles, CA 90012
213-894-2119

880 Front Street
Room 1-513
San Diego, CA 92188
619-557-5570

Appraisers Building
630 Sansome Street
San Francisco, CA 94111
415-556-4411

Colorado

1787 Federal Office Building
1961 Stout Street
Denver, CO 80202
303-844-3526

District of Columbia

4420 North Fairfax Drive
Arlington, VA 22203
703-235-4055

Florida

7880 Biscayne Road
Miami, FL 33138
305-536-5741

Georgia

Room 1408
Richard A. Russell Federal Building
77 Forsythe Street, SW
Atlanta, GA 30303
404-221-5158

Hawaii

P.O. Box 461
595 Ala Moana Boulevard
Honolulu, HI 96809
808-546-8979

Illinois

Dirksen Federal Office Building
219 South Dearborn Street
Chicago, IL 60604
312-353-7334

Louisiana

Postal Service Building
Room T-8005
701 Loyola Avenue
New Orleans, LA 70113
504-589-6533

Maine

76 Pearl Street
P.O. Box 578
Portland, ME 04112
207-780-3354

Maryland

E.A. Garmatz Federal Building
101 West Lombard Street
Baltimore, MD 21201
301-962-2120

Massachusetts

John Fitzgerald Kennedy Federal
    Building
Room E-132
Government Center
Boston, MA 02203
617-565-3077

Michigan

Federal Building
333 Mount Elliot Street
Detroit, MI 48207
313-226-3290

Minnesota

27 New Post Office Building
180 East Kellogg Boulevard
St. Paul, MN 55101
612-725-7107

Missouri

9847 Conant Avenue
Kansas City, MO 64106
816-891-0603

Montana

Federal Building
301 South Park, Room 512
Drawer 10036
Helena, MT 59626
406-449-5288

Nebraska

Federal Office Building, Room 1008
106 South 15th Street
Omaha, NE 68102
402-221-4651

New Jersey

Federal Building
970 Broad Street
Newark, NJ 07102
201-645-4400

New York

68 Court Street
Buffalo, NY 14202
716-849-6760

26 Federal Plaza
New York, NY 10278
212-206-6500

Ohio

Anthony J. Celebrezze Federal Building
1240 East 9th Street, Room 1917
Cleveland, OH 44199
216-522-4770

Oregon

Federal Office Building
511 Northwest Broadway
Portland, OR 97209
503-221-2271

Pennsylvania

Room 1321, United States Courthouse
Independence Mall West
601 Market Street
Philadelphia, PA 19106
215-597-7333

Puerto Rico

Federal Building, Room 170
Chardon Street
Hato Rey, Puerto Rico 00936
809-753-4280

Texas

Room 6 A21, Federal Building
1100 Commerce Street
Dallas, TX 75242
214-767-0514

700 East San Antonio
P.O. Box 9398
El Paso, TX 79984
915-543-6770

2102 Teege Avenue
Harlingen, TX 78550
512-425-7333

509 North Belt (Main Floor)
Houston, TX 77060
713-847-7900

United States Federal Building
727 East Durango, Suite A301
San Antonio, TX 78206
512-229-6350

Washington

815 Airport Way, South
Seattle, WA 98134
206-442-5959

INS Sub-Offices

The INS offices listed here can send you information and forms. You may also be able to file forms with some of them. Check with the local INS office.

Address all correspondence to: Immigration and Naturalization Service.

Alaska

P.O. Box 60208
Fairbanks, AK 99706
907-474-0307
(only accepts papers for filing)

Arizona

Federal Building
301 West Congress, Room 8-M
Tuscon, AZ 85701
602-629-6228

California

Federal Building
United States Courthouse
1130 O street
Room 1308
Fresno, CA 93721
209-487-5091

650 Capitol Mall
Sacramento, CA 95814
916-551-2785

280 South First Street
San Jose, CA 95113
408-291-7876

Connecticut

410 Ribicoff Federal Building
450 Main Street
Hartford, CT 06103
203-240-3171

Florida

Post Office Building
Room Z-18
400 West Bay Street
P.O. Box 35029
Jacksonville, FL 32210
904-791-2624

Federal Building
Room 113
5509 Gray Street
Tampa, FL 33609
813-228-2131

Guam

801 Pacific News Building
238 O'Hara Street
P.O. Box DX
Agana, Guam 96910
671-472-6411

Idaho

4620 Overland Road
Boise, ID 83705
208-334-1821

Indiana

46 East Ohio Street
Room 148
Indianapolis, IN 46204
317-269-6009

Kentucky

Room 601
United States Courthouse Building
600 Broadway (West 6th & Broadway)
Louisville, KY 40202
502-582-6375

Missouri

210 North Tucker Boulevard
Room 100
St. Louis, MO 63101
314-425-4532

Nevada

Federal Building
United States Courthouse
Room 104
300 Las Vegas Boulevard South
Las Vegas, NV 89101
702-388-6251

712 Mill Street
Reno, NV 89502
702-784-5427

New Mexico

517 Gold Southwest Avenue
Room 1114
Albuquerque, NM 87103
505-766-2378

New York

James T. Foley Courthouse
Room 227
445 Broadway
Albany, NY 12207
518-472-4621

410 Old Post Office Building
Rochester, NY 14614
716-263-6273

North Carolina

6 Woodlawn Green
Room 138
Charlotte, NC 28210
704-523-1704

Ohio

J.W. Peck Federal Building
550 Main Street
Room 8525
Cincinnati, OH 45202
513-684-3781

Oklahoma

215 Dean A. McGee Avenue
Oklahoma City, OK 73102
405-231-4121

Pennsylvania

2130 Federal Building
1000 Liberty Avenue
Pittsburgh, PA 15222
412-644-3356

Rhode Island

Federal Building
Room 203
Kennedy Plaza
Providence, RI 02903
401-528-5315

South Carolina

Federal Building
Room 110
334 Meeting Street
Charleston, SC 29403
803-724-4350

Tennessee

245 Wagner Place South
Room 250
Memphis, TN 38103
901-521-3301

Utah

230 West 400 South Street
Salt Lake City, UT 84101
801-524-5690

Vermont

Federal Building
P.O. Box 328
St. Albans, VT 05478
802-524-6743

Virginia

Norfolk Federal Building
200 Granby Mall, Room 439
Norfolk, VA 23510
804-441-3081

Virgin Islands

P.O. Box 1270
Kingshill
Christiansted, St. Croix, VI 00856
809-778-6559

Federal Building
P.O. Box 610
Charlotte Amalie, St. Thomas, VI 00856
809-774-1390

Washington

691 United States Courthouse Building
West 920 Riverside
Spokane, WA 99201
509-456-3824

Wisconsin

Federal Building
Room 186
517 East Wisconsin Avenue
Milwaukee, WI 53202
414-291-3565

INS Regional Processing Centers

Many routine petitions and applications are sent for adjudication to regional processing centers. The regional processing centers are listed on some forms. Check with the INS to find out which INS address will most quickly process your forms.

Eastern Regional Service Center

Immigration and Naturalization Service
Regional Service Center
1A Lemnah Drive
St. Albans, VT 05479-0001

Connecticut	New York
Delaware	Pennsylvania
District of Columbia	Puerto Rico
Maine	Rhode Island
Maryland	Vermont
Massachusetts	Virgin Islands
New Hampshire	Virginia
New Jersey	West Virginia

Southern Regional Service Center

Immigration and Naturalization Service
Regional Service Center
311 North Stemmons Freeway
Dallas, TX 75250

Alabama	Mississippi
Arkansas	New Mexico
Florida	North Carolina
Georgia	Oklahoma
Kentucky	South Carolina
Louisiana	Tennessee
	Texas

Northern Regional Service Center

Immigration and Naturalization Service
Regional Service Center
Federal Building and United States
  Courthouse
Room 393-100 Centennial Mall North
Lincoln, NE 68508

Alaska	Montana
Colorado	Nebraska
Idaho	North Dakota
Illinois	Ohio
Indiana	Oregon
Iowa	South Dakota
Kansas	Utah
Michigan	Washington
Minnesota	Wisconsin
Missouri	Wyoming

Western Regional Service Center

Immigration and Naturalization Service
Regional Service Center
801 East San Ysidro Boulevard
San Ysidro, CA 92073

Arizona	Guam
California	Hawaii
	Nevada

Translating Your Documents

The INS requires that any documents such as birth or marriage certificates that you submit in a foreign language be translated into English. You must find someone to translate your documents and swear that they translated the document accurately. You need not find a certified translator to translate your documents. Anyone competent in English and your native language can do the translation.

Have the translator complete a form like the one printed here. To be accepted by the INS, the form must be notarized by a certified notary public.

CERTIFICATE FOR ACCURACY OF TRANSLATION

STATE OF _____
COUNTY OF _____

_____ being duly sworn, deposes and says:

That I am familiar with the English and the _____ language(s) and am competent to translate from one language to another.

That I have made the attached translation from the annexed document in the _____ language and hereby certify that the same is a true and complete translation to the best of my knowledge, ability and belief.

_____

Sworn to before me this
_____ day of _____ 19____.

Other Forms You May Need

(Please tear off this sheet before submitting Affidavit)

U. S. Department of Justice
Immigration and Naturalization Service

Affidavit of Support

INSTRUCTIONS

I. EXECUTION OF AFFIDAVIT. A separate affidavit must be submitted for each person. You must sign the affidavit in your full, true and correct name and affirm or make it under oath. If you are **in the United States** the affidavit may be sworn or affirmed before an immigration officer without the payment of fee, or before a notary public or other officer authorized to administer oaths for general purposes, in which case the official seal or certificate of authority to administer oaths must be affixed. If you are **outside the United States** the affidavit must be sworn to or affirmed before a United States consular or immigration officer.

II. SUPPORTING EVIDENCE. The deponent must submit in duplicate evidence of income and resources, as appropriate:

A. Statement from an officer of the bank or other financial institution in which you have deposits giving the following details regarding your account:
1. Date account opened.
2. Total amount deposited for the past year.
3. Present balance.

B. Statement of your employer on business stationery, showing:
1. Date and nature of employment.
2. Salary paid.
3. Whether position is temporary or permanent.

C. If self-employed:
1. Copy of last income tax return filed or,
2. Report of commercial rating concern.

D. List containing serial numbers and denominations of bonds and name of record owner(s).

III. SPONSOR AND ALIEN LIABILITY. Effective October l, 1980, amendments to section 1614(f) of the Social Security Act and Part A of Title XVI of the Social Security Act establish certain requirements for determining the eligibility of aliens who apply for the first time for Supplemental Security Income (SSI) benefits. Effective October l, 1981, amendments to section 415 of the Social Security Act establish similar requirements for determining the eligibility of aliens who apply for the first time for Aid to Families with Dependent Children (AFDC) benefits. Effective December 22, 1981, amendments to the Food Stamp Act of 1977 affect the eligibility of alien participation in the Food Stamp Program. These amendments require that the income and resources of any person who, as the sponsor of an alien's entry into the United States, executes an affidavit of support or similar agreement on behalf of the alien, and the income and resources of the sponsor's spouse (*if living with the sponsor*) shall be deemed to be the income and resources of the alien under formulas for determining eligibility for SSI, AFDC, and Food Stamp benefits during the three years following the alien's entry into the United States.

An alien applying for SSI must make available to the Social Security Administration documentation concerning his or her income and resources and those of the sponsor including information which was provided in support of the application for an immigrant visa or adjustment of status. An alien applying for AFDC or Food Stamps must make similar information available to the State public assistance agency. The Secretary of Health and Human Services and the Secretary of Agriculture are authorized to obtain copies of any such documentation submitted to INS or the Department of State and to release such documentation to a State public assistance agency.

Sections 1621(e) and 415(d) of the Social Security Act and subsection 5(i) of the Food Stamp Act also provide that an alien and his or her sponsor shall be jointly and severably liable to repay any SSI, AFDC, or Food Stamp benefits which are incorrectly paid because of misinformation provided by a sponsor or because of a sponsor's failure to provide information. Incorrect payments which are not repaid will be withheld from any subsequent payments for which the alien or sponsor are otherwise eligible under the Social Security Act or Food Stamp Act, except that the sponsor was without fault or where good cause existed.

These provisions do not apply to the SSI, AFDC or Food Stamp eligibility of aliens admitted as refugees, granted political asylum by the Attorney General, or Cuban/Haitian entrants as defined in section 501(e) of P.L. 96-422 and of dependent children of the sponsor or sponsor's spouse. They also do not apply to the SSI or Food Stamp eligibility of an alien who becomes blind or disabled after admission into the United States for permanent residency.

IV. AUTHORITY/USE/PENALTIES. Authority for the collection of the information requested on this form is contained in 8 U.S.C. 1182(a)(15), 1184(a), and 1258. The information will be used principally by the Service, or by any consular officer to whom it may be furnished, to support an alien's application for benefits under the Immigration and Nationality Act and specifically the assertion that he or she has adequate means of financial support and will not become a public charge. Submission of the information is voluntary. It may also, as a matter of routine use, be disclosed to other federal, state, local and foreign law enforcement and regulatory agencies, including the Department of Health and Human Services, the Department of Agriculture, the Department of State, the Department of Defense and any component thereof (if the deponent has served or is serving in the armed forces of the United States), the Central Intelligence Agency, and individuals and organizations during the course of any investigation to elicit further information required to carry out Service functions. Failure to provide the information may result in the denial of the alien's application for a visa, or his or her exclusion from the United States.

Form I-134 (Rev. 12-1-84) Y

OMB No. 1115-0062

U. S. Department of Justice
Immigration and Naturalization Service

Affidavit of Support

(ANSWER ALL ITEMS: FILL IN WITH TYPEWRITER OR PRINT IN BLOCK LETTERS IN INK.)

I, _____, *residing at* _____
　　　　　　(Name)　　　　　　　　　　　　　　　　　(Street and Number)

_____
　(City)　　　　　　　(State)　　　　(ZIP Code if in U.S.)　　　(Country)

BEING DULY SWORN DEPOSE AND SAY:

1. I was born on_____at_____
　　　　　　　　(Date)　　　　　　(City)　　　　　　(Country)

　　If you are *not* a native born United States citizen, answer the following as appropriate:
　　a. If a United States citizen through naturalization, give certificate of naturalization number _____
　　b. If a United States citizen through parent(s) or marriage, give citizenship certificate number _____
　　c. If United States citizenship was derived by some other method, attach a statement of explanation.
　　d. If a lawfully admitted permanent resident of the United States, give "A" number _____

2. That I am_____years of age and have resided in the United States since (date) _____

3. That this affidavit is executed in behalf of the following person:

Name		Sex	Age
Citizen of--(Country)	Marital Status	Relationship to Deponent	
Presently resides at--(Street and Number)	(City)	(State)	(Country)

Name of spouse and children accompanying or following to join person:

Spouse	Sex	Age	Child	Sex	Age
Child	Sex	Age	Child	Sex	Age
Child	Sex	Age	Child	Sex	Age

4. That this affidavit is made by me for the purpose of assuring the United States Government that the person(s) named in item 3 will not become a public charge in the United States.

5. That I am willing and able to receive, maintain and support the person(s) named in item 3. That I am ready and willing to deposit a bond, if necessary, to guarantee that such person(s) will not become a public charge during his or her stay in the United States, or to guarantee that the above named will maintain his or her nonimmigrant status if admitted temporarily and will depart prior to the expiration of his or her authorized stay in the United States.

6. That I understand this affidavit will be binding upon me for a period of three (3) years after entry of the person(s) named in item 3 and that the information and documentation provided by me may be made available to the Secretary of Health and Human Services and the Secretary of Agriculture, who may make it available to a public assistance agency.

7. That I am employed as, or engaged in the business of _____with_____
　　　　　　　　　　　　　　　　　　　(Type of Business)　　　　　　(Name of concern)

at _____
　　(Street and Number)　　　　(City)　　　　(State)　　　(Zip Code)

I derive an annual income of *(if self-employed, I have attached a copy of my last income tax return or report of commercial rating concern which I certify to be true and correct to the best of my knowledge and belief. See instruction for nature of evidence of net worth to be submitted.)*　　　　$_____

I have on deposit in savings banks in the United States　　$_____

I have other personal property, the reasonable value of which is　$_____

Form I-134 (Rev. 12-1-84) Y　　　　　　　　　　　　　OVER

I have stocks and bonds with the following market value, as indicated on the attached list
which I certify to be true and correct to the best of my knowledge and belief. $ _____
I have life insurance in the sum of $ _____
With a cash surrender value of $ _____
I own real estate valued at $ _____
   With mortgages or other encumbrances thereon amounting to $ _____

   Which is located at_____
               (Street and Number)   (City)   (State)   (Zip Code)

8. That the following persons are dependent upon me for support: *(Place an "X" in the appropriate column to indicate whether the person named is **wholly** or **partially** dependent upon you for support.)*

Name of Person	Wholly Dependent	Partially Dependent	Age	Relationship to Me

9. That I have previously submitted affidavit(s) of support for the following person(s). If none, state *"None"*

Name   Date submitted
_____
_____

10. That I have submitted visa petition(s) to the Immigration and Naturalization Service on behalf of the following person(s). If none, state none.

Name   Relationship   Date submitted
_____
_____

11. *(Complete this block only if the person named in item 3 will be in the United States temporarily.)*
   That I ☐ do intend ☐ do not intend, to make specific contributions to the support of the person named in item 3. (*If you check "do intend", indicate the exact nature and duration of the contributions. For example, if you intend to furnish room and board, state for how long and, if money, state the amount in United States dollars and state whether it is to be given in a lump sum, weekly, or monthly, or for how long.)*

_____
_____
_____

OATH OR AFFIRMATION OF DEPONENT

I acknowledge at that I have read Part III of the Instructions, Sponsor and Alien Liability, and am aware of my responsibilities as an immigrant sponsor under the Social Security Act, as amended, and the Food Stamp Act, as amended.

I swear (affirm) that I know the contents of this affidavit signed by me and the statements are true and correct.

Signature of deponent _____

Subscribed and sworn to (affirmed) before me this _____*day of* _____ , 19_____

at _____ . *My commission expires on* _____

Signature of Officer Administering Oath _____ *Title* _____

If affidavit prepared by other than deponent, please complete the following: I declare that this document was prepared by me at the request of the deponent and is based on all information of which I have knowledge.

_____
(Signature)   *(Address)*   *(Date)*

OMB No. 1115-0038

U.S. Department of Justice
Immigration and Naturalization Service

PETITION TO CLASSIFY NONIMMIGRANT AS TEMPORARY WORKER OR TRAINEE

(PLEASE TEAR OFF THIS SHEET BEFORE SUBMITTING PETITION)
INSTRUCTIONS

READ INSTRUCTIONS CAREFULLY. FEE WILL NOT BE REFUNDED.
Failure to comply with instructions may make it necessary to reject your petition.

General

This petition must be filed in duplicate. (The alien spouse and minor children of the beneficiary of an approved petition are automatically entitled to the same nonimmigrant classification he/she has been accorded if accompanying him/her or following to join him/her. No petitions for them are required.)

All supporting documents must be submitted in original and one copy. If the return of the original is desired, submit two copies with the original and request that the original be returned to you after an immigration officer has compared it with the copies. Copies in duplicate unaccompanied by the original may be accepted if one of the copies bears a certification by an immigration or consular officer or an attorney that the copy was compared with the original and found to be identical.

Any document in a foreign language must be accompanied by a translation in English. The translator must certify that he/she is competent to translate and that the translation is accurate.

Fee

A fee of thirty-five dollars ($35) must be paid for filing this petition. It cannot be refunded regardless of the action taken on the petition. DO NOT MAIL CASH. ALL FEES MUST BE SUBMITTED IN THE EXACT AMOUNT. Payment by check or money order must be drawn on a bank or other institution located in the United States and be payable in United States currency. If petitioner resides in Guam, check or money order must be payable to the "Treasurer, Guam." If petitioner resides in the Virgin Islands, check or money order must be payable to the "Commissioner of Finance of the Virgin Islands." All other petitioners must make the check or money order payable to the "Immigration and Naturalization Service." When check is drawn on account of a person other than the petitioner, the name of the petitioner must be entered on the face of the check. If petition is submitted from outside the United States, remittance may be made by bank international money order or foreign draft drawn on a financial institution in the United States and payable to the "Immigration and Naturalization Service" in United States currency. Personal checks are accepted subject to collectibility. An uncollectible check will render the petition and any document issued pursuant thereto invalid. A charge of $5.00 will be imposed if a check in payment of a fee is not honored by the bank on which it is drawn.

Where to file petition

The petition must be filed with the office of the Immigration and Naturalization Service having jurisdiction over the area in which the services will be performed or the training received. Where the services will be performed or the training will be received in more than one area, the petition must be filed in an office of this Service having jurisdiction over at least one of those areas.

In the case of an L-1 blanket petition, the petition must be filed at the petitioner's main office.

More than one H beneficiary may be included in one petition where the beneficiaries will all be performing services in a single operation or receiving the same type of training and, if visas are required, will all be applying for their visas at the same American Consulate and will all be performing the services or receiving the training within the same immigration district. Separate petitions must be filed where the beneficiaries will be performing services in different operations or will not be receiving the same type of training or, if visas are required, will be applying for visas at different American Consulates or will perform the services or receive the training in different immigration districts.

A separate petition must be filed for each L-1 alien, except in the case of an L-1 blanket petition.

H-1 Petition for alien(s) of distinguished merit and ability to perform services of an exceptional nature (Also see special instructions for nurses and physicians)

If petition is for an alien or aliens of distinguished merit and ability, the following supplemental documents must be attached:

High education or technical training shall be supported by diplomas, school certificates, or equivalent documents or affidavits, attesting to such education or technical training and executed by the person in charge of the records of the educational or other institution, firm, or establishment wherein such education or training was acquired, improved, or perfected.

Specialized experience or exceptional ability shall be supported by affidavits attesting to and describing the degree and extent of the experience or ability, executed by the appropriate officer of the firm, organization, establishment, or other institution wherein the alien(s) acquired or perfected such experience or ability.

Copies of written contracts or summaries of oral contracts between petitioner and beneficiaries must be attached.

H-2 Petition for alien(s) to perform temporary service or labor

If petition is for an alien or aliens to perform temporary services or labor, the following supplemental documents must be attached:

Form I-129B (Rev 7-1-83)N

A certification from the Department of Labor indicating that qualified applicants in the United States are not available for referral to the employer and that employment of the alien(s) will not adversely affect wages and working conditions of workers in the United States similarly employed, or a notice from the Department of Labor that such certification cannot be made; also, a statement containing a full and complete and detailed description of the situations or conditions which make it necessary to bring the alien or aliens to the United States, whether the necessity is temporary, seasonal, or permanent and, if temporary or seasonal, whether it is expected to recur.

To apply for the certification, the petitioner must place a job order with the local office of the state Employment Service serving the area of proposed employment. In order that the Department of Labor may make a determination as to the availability of qualified applicants in the United States, the order must accurately report the occupational requirements of the job. If local and inter-area recruitment of qualified workers in the United States proves unsuccessful, copies of the certification are furnished to the petitioner through the local Employment Service office where the job order was filed.

If more than one certification is issued by the Department of Labor, a separate petition must be filed for the aliens covered by each certification.

Employers of agriculture workers may be requested to enter into a written agreement in lieu of posting a bond.

H-3   Petition for alien trainee(s) (Also see special instructions for nursing trainees)

If petition is for one or more alien trainees, there must be attached a statement describing the kind of training to be given the alien and setting out the proportion of time that will be devoted to productive employment, the number of hours that will be spent respectively in his classroom instruction, in on-the-job training, and in his/her performance without supervision; the position or duties for which this training will prepare him/her; the reason why such training cannot be obtained in the alien's country, and, if you answered "yes" to item 25A, why it is necessary for alien to take training in the United States.

If this petition is approved, the approval does not signify that the wages shown in item 8 of the petition meet the minimum wage requirements of any state or federal laws. Any questions regarding compliance with those requirements should be addressed to the appropriate state or federal labor authorities.

Physicians and nurses

In the case of an H-1 petition for a physician or nurse or an H-3 petition for a nurse, the additional documents are required:

1. Evidence that the beneficiary has obtained a full and unrestricted license to practice medicine or nursing in the country where he/she obtained medical or nursing education (Not required if evidence is submitted showing that the beneficiary's education was obtained in the United States or that he/she is a physician who passed the examination given by the Educational Council for Foreign Medical Graduates.) and

2. A statement from the petitioner if required by petitioner's answer to item 24 on Form I-129B.

3. In the case of an H-1 petition for a nurse, evidence that the beneficiary has a full and unrestricted license to practice professional nursing in the State where services are to be performed or a passing score on the examination administered by the Commission on Graduates of Foreign Nursing Schools.

L-1   Petition for intra-company transferee (Individual Petition)

If petition is for an L-1 alien, attach a statement describing the capacity in which he/she was employed abroad and the capacity in which he/she is to be employed in the U.S. If the alien's services involve specialized knowledge, describe briefly the nature of the specialized knowledge which makes his/her services here necessary. If the beneficiary is coming to be employed in an establishment being newly opened in the United States by his/her employer, or by the parent company, a subsidiary, or an affiliate of the employer, the statement shall include information concerning the new establishment such as its nature, relationship to the petitioning firm or corporation, its name and address, when it was or will be opened at that address, when and where it was incorporated (if it is a corporation), and the total number of employees who will be employed there. Evidence must also be submitted that physical premises for the new establishment have been acquired by purchase, lease, or rental and will be occupied by that establishment.

L-1   Petition for intra-company transferee (Blanket Petition)

Attach evidence that at least 5 managerial or executive beneficiaries have been transferred to the United States in the last 12 months. Evidence of corporate interrelationships of all foreign and domestic entities which the petitioner identifies in the petition. The petitioner must also list all positions to which its executive or managers may be assigned. If the organization will identify more than 10 positions the petitioner may furnish a description of its personnel structure and identify the level above which it will or may seek to transfer managers and executives. To amend an approved blanket petition a new I-129B is filed with evidence supporting only the change.

Extension of visa petition validity

This petition form shall be used as an application for an extension of the validity of a visa petition pursuant to the approval of a previous petition by the same petitioner. It may be filed concurrently with form I-539 for an extension of stay of an individual beneficiary. Supporting documents are not required if all relationships remain the same.

Penalties

Severe penalties are provided by law for knowingly and willfully falsifying or concealing a maternal fact or using any false document in the submission of this petition.

U.S. Department of Justice
Immigration and Naturalization Service

OMB No. 1115-0038

PETITION TO CLASSIFY NONIMMIGRANT
AS TEMPORARY WORKER OR TRAINEE

To be submitted in duplicate, with supplementary documents described in instructions, to the District Director having administrative jurisdiction over the place in the United States in which it is intended the alien(s) be employed or trained. L–1 blanket petition must be submitted to the District Director having jurisdiction over petitioner's main office.)

Date Filed	Fee Stamp

File No.

(THIS BLOCK NOT TO BE FILLED OUT BY PETITIONER)

The Secretary of State is hereby notified that the alien(s) for whom this petition was filed is (are) entitled to the nonimmigrant status checked below:

☐ H–1   ☐ H–3

☐ H–2   ☐ L–1

☐ L–1 (blanket petition)

This petition is valid to _____.
The admission of the alien(s) may be authorized to the above date.

REMARKS:

DATE OF ACTION DD

DISTRICT

☐ **NEW PETITION**   ☐ **PETITION EXTENSION**   ☐ **AMENDED BLANKET PETITION**

I hereby petition, pursuant to the provisions of section 214(c) on the immigration and Nationality Act, for the following: (Check one.)

H–1 ☐ Alien(s) of distinguished merit and ability to perform services of an exceptional nature requiring such merit and ability.

H–2 ☐ Alien(s) to perform temporary service or labor for which a bona fide need exists. (One who is to perform duties which are themselves temporary in nature.)

H–3 ☐ Alien trainee(s). (One who seeks to enter at the invitation of an individual, organization, firm, or other trainer for the purpose of receiving training in any field of endeavor. Incidental production necessary to the training is permitted provided a United States worker is not thereby displaced.)

L–1 ☐ Intra-company transferee. (One who has been employed abroad continuously for one year and who seeks to enter in order to continue to render services to the same employer or a subsidiary or affiliate thereof in a managerial or executive capacity or in a capacity which involves specialized knowledge.)

L–1 ☐ Intra-company transferee blanket petition. (A petitioner who had 5 executive or managerial L–1 petitions approved within the last year, and desires to bring into the United States employees who have been employed abroad continuously for one year who will continue to render services to the same employer or a subsidiary or affiliate thereof in a managerial or executive capacity.)

1. NAME OF PETITIONER	2. DATE BUSINESS ESTABLISHED
3. ADDRESS (NUMBER, STREET, CITY, STATE, ZIP CODE)	TELEPHONE NUMBER

4. DESCRIPTION OF PETITIONER'S BUSINESS, INCLUDING ITS NATURE, NUMBER OF EMPLOYEES, AND GROSS ANNUAL INCOME

5. LOCATION OF AMERICAN CONSULATE AT WHICH ALIEN(S) WILL APPLY FOR VISA(S): (Not required for L–1 blanket petition)	(City in Foreign Country)	(Foreign Country)

(If petition is for more than one H alien and application for visas will be made at more than one American Consulate, a separate petition must be submitted for each consulate at which H visa applications will be made. Separate petition must be filed for each L–1 alien.)

6. THE ALIEN(S) WILL PERFORM SERVICES OR LABOR FOR OR RECEIVE TRAINING FROM THE FOLLOWING ESTABLISHMENT IN THE U.S.: (Name of Establishment) (If L–1 blanket petition items 6-11 not applicable, show N/A)

(Street and Number)	(City or Town)	(State)	(Zip Code)

Attach list or itinerary if services will be performed at more than one location.

7. PERIOD REQUIRED TO COMPLETE SERVICES OR TRAINING			8. WAGES PER WEEK	8A. HOURS PER WEEK	9. OVERTIME RATE
From (date)	To (date)	No. of days or months			

10. OTHER COMPENSATION (Explain)	10A. VALUED AT $ WEEKLY	11. BY WHOM PAID?

Form I-129B (Rev 7-1-83)N

RECEIVED	TRANS. IN	RET'D-TRANS. OUT	COMPLETED

(Page 2)

QUESTIONS 12A THRU 32 NEED NOT BE COMPLETED TO FILE EXTENSION OF VISA PETITION VALIDITY WITH CONCURRENTLY FILED 1-539 APPLICA-TION FOR EXTENSION OF STAY.

ALL NEW PETITIONERS COMPLETE ITEMS 12A THROUGH 22, except L-1 blanket petitioners. If petition is for more than one H alien, give required information for each additional alien in space provided on page 3. If the identity of the H aliens is not known at present, you must furnish information conce.ning them as soon as that information be-comes known to you.

12A. ALIEN'S NAME (Family name in capital letters)   (First name)   (Middle name)

12B. OTHER NAMES (Show all other past and present names, including maiden name if married woman.)   **12C.** NUMBER OF ALIENS IN-CLUDED IN THIS PETITION

13. ADDRESS TO WHICH ALIEN WILL RETURN   (Street and Number)   (City)   (Province)   (Country)

14. PRESENT ADDRESS   **15.** PROPOSED PORT OF ENTRY

16. DATE OF BIRTH   **17.** PLACE OF BIRTH   **18.** PRESENT NATIONALITY OR CITIZENSHIP   **19.** PRESENT OCCUPATION

20. HAS AN IMMIGRANT VISA PETITION OR APPLICATION FOR PERMANENT LABOR CERTIFICATION EVER BEEN FILED ON THE ALIEN'S BEHALF? ☐ YES ☐ NO
If "Yes", where was it filed?

21. HAS THE ALIEN EVER APPLIED FOR AN IMMIGRANT VISA OR PERMANENT RESIDENCE IN THE U.S.?   ☐ YES   ☐ NO
If Yes", where did he apply?

22. TO YOUR KNOWLEDGE, HAS ANY VISA PETITION FILED BY YOU OR ANY OTHER PERSON OR ORGANIZATION FOR THE NAMED ALIEN(S) BEEN DENIED? ☐ YES ☐ NO
If you answered "yes", complete the following: Date of filing of each denied petition _____
Place of filing of each denied petition (city) _____
TO YOUR KNOWLEDGE, HAVE ANY OF THE NAMED ALIEN(S) EVER BEEN IN THE U.S.?   ☐ YES   ☐ NO (If "yes" identify each on Page 3)

23. NONTECHNICAL DESCRIPTION OF SERVICES TO BE PERFORMED BY OR TRAINING TO BE RECEIVED BY ALIEN(S) (THIS BLOCK NEED NOT BE COMPLETED IF PETITION IS FOR H-2 WORKERS)

24. IS THE BENEFICIARY FULLY QUALIFIED UNDER THE GOVERNING LAWS IN YOUR JURISDICTION TO PERFORM THE DESIRED SERVICES (OR TO RECEIVE THE DESIRED TRAINING) AND ARE YOU AUTHORIZED TO EMPLOY THE BENEFICIARY TO SUBSTANTIALLY PERFORM SUCH SERVICES? ☐ YES ☐ NO (If "NO" or if beneficiary will be restricted in performance of services, please explain in detail on separate statement.

25. (If you are petitioning for a trainee, complete this block)
A. IS SIMILAR TRAINING AVAILABLE IN ALIEN'S COUNTRY? ☐ YES ☐ NO
B. WOULD ALIEN'S TRAINING RESULT IN DISPLACEMENT OF UNITED STATES WORKER? ☐ YES ☐ NO
C. WILL YOU USE THE ALIENS TO OVERCOME A LABOR SHORTAGE? ☐ YES ☐ NO

26. (If you are petitioning for an L-1 alien, complete this block.) (Check appropriate boxes.) (Does not apply to L-1 blanket petition)
a. The alien has been employed in an   ☐ executive;   ☐ managerial capacity;   ☐ in a capacity which involves specialized knowledge

by _____ since _____
(name and address of employer)   (date)
b. The petitioner is ☐ the same employer ☐ subsidiary ☐ an affiliate of the employer abroad.

FILL IN ITEMS 27 THROUGH 31 INCLUSIVE ONLY IF PETITION IS FOR H-2 ALIEN(S)

27. DESCRIPTIVE JOB TITLE OF WORK TO BE PERFORMED BY ALIEN(S) (Enter title which was used by the Department of Labor in processing labor certification application.)

28. IS (ARE) ALIEN(S) SKILLED IN WORK TO BE PERFORMED? ☐YES ☐NO ☐UNKNOWN

29. IS ANY LABOR ORGANIZATION ACTIVE IN THE LABOR FIELD(S) SPECIFIED IN ITEM 27? ☐ YES ☐ NO
(If "yes", specify organization(s) and labor field(s).)

30. IS THE PETITIONER INVOLVED IN, OR ARE THERE THREATENED, ANY LABOR RELATIONS DIFFICULTIES, INCLUDING STRIKES OR LOCKOUTS? (Specify)

31. I HAVE NOT BEEN ABLE TO FIND IN THE UNITED STATES ANY UNEMPLOYED PERSON(S) CAPABLE OF PERFORMING THE DUTIES OF THE POSITION(S) TO BE FILLED. THE FOLLOWING EFFORTS HAVE BEEN MADE TO FIND SUCH PERSON(S). (Complete only if labor certification not attached.)

32. If petition is for extension the petitioner must certify that all data from the previously approved petition remains the same. ☐ YES ☐ NO

ALL PETITIONERS MUST FILL IN ITEMS 33 & 34B.

(Page 3)

33. THE DOCUMENTS SUBMITTED HEREWITH ARE HEREBY MADE A PART OF THIS PETITION.

I am willing (unwilling) to post any bond required as a condition to the approval of this petition.
I agree that as soon as known I shall furnish the District Director to whom this petition is being submitted with the names of those alien(s) not currently identified. (does not apply to L-1 blanket petition)
If the petition is for temporary worker(s), I certify that I have a bona fide need of such worker(s).
If the petition is for trainee(s), I certify he/she is coming to the United States to participate in a bona fide training program.
I certify that the statements and representations made in the petition are true and correct to the best of my knowledge and belief.

34A. SIGNATURE OF PETITIONER	DATE	34B. TITLE (Must be petitioner or authorized employee of petitioner)

SIGNATURE OF PERSON PREPARING FORM, IF OTHER THAN PETITIONER

35. I declare that this document was prepared by me at the request of the petitioner and is based on all information of which I have any knowledge.

(Signature)	(Address)	(Date)

If this petition is for more than one alien of distinguished merit and ability (H-1), or trainee (H-3) use spaces below to give required information. If additional space is needed, attach separate sheet executed in same general manner.

NAME	DATE OF BIRTH	PLACE OF BIRTH	NATIONALITY	OCCUPATION

PRESENT ADDRESS

ADDRESS TO WHICH ALIEN WILL RETURN

NONTECHNICAL DESCRIPTION OF SERVICES TO BE PERFORMED BY OR TRAINING TO BE RECEIVED BY ALIEN

NAME	DATE OF BIRTH	PLACE OF BIRTH	NATIONALITY	OCCUPATION

PRESENT ADDRESS

ADDRESS TO WHICH ALIEN WILL RETURN

NONTECHNICAL DESCRIPTION OF SERVICES TO BE PERFORMED BY OR TRAINING TO BE RECEIVED BY ALIEN

NAME	DATE OF BIRTH	PLACE OF BIRTH	NATIONALITY	OCCUPATION

PRESENT ADDRESS

ADDRESS TO WHICH ALIEN WILL RETURN

NONTECHNICAL DESCRIPTION OF SERVICES TO BE PERFORMED BY OR TRAINING TO BE RECEIVED BY ALIEN

If this petition is for more than one (H-2) alien to perform temporary service or labor, use spaces below to give required information. If additional space is needed, attach separate sheet executed in same general manner. Identify each alien who has been in the U.S., by placing an ''X'' in the last column.

NAME	NATIONALITY	DATE AND PLACE OF BIRTH	PRESENT ADDRESS	X

U. S. Department of Justice
Immigration and Naturalization Service

Application for Change
Of Nonimmigrant Status
(Please Tear Off This Sheet Before Submitting Application)

READ INSTRUCTIONS CAREFULLY, FEE WILL NOT BE REFUNDED
Failure to comply with instructions may make it necessary to reject your application

1. PENALTIES - Severe penalties are provided by law for knowingly and willfully falsifying or concealing a material fact or using any false document in the submission of this application. Also, a false representation may result in the denial of this application and any other application you may make for any benefit under the immigration laws of the United States. Any statement submitted with this application is considered part of the application.

2. PREPARATION - Use typewriter or print in block letters with ball-point pen. Be sure this application and attached Form I-506A are legible. Do not leave any question unanswered.

When appropriate, insert "None" or "not applicable." If you need more space to answer fully any question on this form, use a separate sheet of paper this size and identify each answer with the number of the corresponding question.

3. NON-ELIGIBILITY - The following classes of aliens are *NOT ELIGIBLE* to change their nonimmigrant status:

a. Any alien in immediate and continuous transit through the United States without a visa (TWOV).

b. Any alien classified as a nonimmigrant under section 101(a)(15)(C),(D) or (K) of the Act.

c. Any alien admitted as a nonimmigrant under section 101(a)(15) (J) of the Act, or who acquired that status after admission in order to receive graduate medical education or training.

d. Any alien classified as a nonimmigrant under section 101(a)(15) (J) of the Act *(other than an alien described in paragraph (c) above)* who is subject to the foreign residence requirement of section 212(e) of the Act is not eligible for a change of nonimmigrant classification other than for a change to classification under section 101(a)(15) (A) or (G).

e. Any nonimmigrant to status under section 101(a)(15) (K) of the Act.

f. Any alien classified as a nonimmigrant student under section 101(a)(15)(M) of the Act is not eligible for a change of classification to that of a nonimmigrant student under section 101(A)(15) (F).

4. SUBMISSION - This application must be submitted to the Immigration and Naturalization Service office having jurisdiction over your place of temporary residence in the United States. If you are applying for change of status under section 101(a)(15)(H) or (L), this application must be submitted with the nonimmigrant visa petition (Form I-129B) or with the notice of approval of that petition (Form I-171-C), to the office having jurisdiction over the Form I-129B.

A separate application and fee must be submitted by each person applying for a change of nonimmigrant classification, with the following *EXCEPTIONS*:

a. Neither an application nor fee is required to be filed by a spouse or unmarried minor child of a principal alien-applicant for reclassification under the same subparagraph of section 101(a)(15) as the principal alien-applicant.

b. Neither an application nor fee is required for reclassification from that of a visitor for pleasure (B-2) under section 101(a)(15)(B) to that of a visitor for business (B-1) under the same section.

c. Neither an application nor fee is required for a change of status under section 101(a)(15) (J) if the change is requested by an agency of the U.S. Government and accompanied by Form IAP-66.

d. Neither an application nor fee is required for a change to classification under section 101(a)(15) (A) or (G) of the Act.

e. Neither an application nor fee is required for a change from a classification as the prinicpal alien under section 101(a) (15) (F), (J), (L), or (M) to the accompanying spouse or unmarried minor child under that same section or vice versa.

f. Neither an application nor fee is required for a change from any classification within section 101(a) (15) (H) of the Act to any other classification within section 101(a) (15) (H) of the Act provided that the necessary Form I-129B has been filed and approved.

Form I-506 (Rev. 7-1-84) N

OVER

5. FEE - Except as indicated above, a fee of fifteen dollars ($15) must be paid for filing this application. It cannot be refunded regardless of the action taken on the application. DO NOT MAIL CASH. ALL FEES MUST BE SUBMITTED IN THE EXACT AMOUNT. Payment by check or money order must be drawn on a bank or other institution located in the United States and be payable in United States currency. If applicant resides in Guam, check or money order must be payable to the "Treasurer, Guam." If applicant resides in the Virgin Islands, check or money order must be payable to the "Commissioner of Finance of the Virgin Islands." All other applicants must make the check or money order payable to the "Immigration and Naturalization Service." When a check is drawn on an account of a person other than the applicant, the name of the applicant must be entered on the face of the check. Personal checks are accepted subject to collectibility. An uncollectible check will render the application and any document issued pursuant to it invalid. A charge of $5.00 will be imposed if a check in payment of a fee is not honored by the bank on which it is drawn.

6. DOCUMENTS/GENERAL -

The burden is upon you to establish your eligibility for the change of status you are seeking. If you fail to supply the information and documents required, your application will not be approved.

Your, your spouse's and children's Form(s) I-94 "Arrival-departure Record," must be submitted with this application. (*If you are an F-1 or M-1 seeking a change to a classification other than F-1 or M-1, you must also submit your Form I-20 ID copy.*) *DO NOT SUBMIT YOUR PASSPORT.*

Submit the following if you are applying for a:

CHANGE TO STUDENT -

(a) Form I-20 A-B or I-20 M-N,"Certificate of Eligibility" issued by the school you are attending or wish to attend

(b) A statement and evidence showing that sufficient funds will be available to you for your support and all costs of attending school, giving the source of your support and the amount received from each source. If you are not self-supporting, you must submit a Form I-134, "Affidavit of Support", executed by each person from whom you will receive support and with the evidence suggested on that form to support the affidavit.

(c) A Form I-20 ID copy with your name, date of birth, and country of citizenship filled out.

CHANGE FROM F-1 TO M-1 STUDENT-

(a) A Form I-20 M-N.

(b) Proof of financial ability as described in (b) of the previous section of item 6.

(c) Your Form I-20 ID copy *BUT NOT YOUR FORM I-94.*

CHANGE TO EXCHANGE ALIEN-

Form IAP-66,"Certificate of Eligibility for Exchange-Visitor-Status", from the sponsor of the exchange-visitor program you wish to participate in. You must complete the reverse of Form IAP-66.

CHANGE TO TEMPORARY WORKER/ TRAINEE/INTRA-COMPANY TRANSFEREE-

Form I-129B,"Petition to Classify Nonimmigrant as Temporary Worker or Trainee", completed by your prospective employer or trainer, *OR* the Form I-171C, "Notice of Approval of the Nonimmigrant Petition", Form I-129B.

CHANGE TO TREATY TRADER OR INVESTOR -

A completed Form I-126,"Report of Status by Treaty Trader or Investor."

U.S. Department of Justice
Immigration and Naturalization Service

**APPLICATION FOR
CHANGE OF
NONIMMIGRANT STATUS**
(Under Section 248 of the Immigration and Nationality Act)

**FOR OFFICIAL USE ONLY
MICROFILM INDEX NUMBER**

OMB No. 1115-0033

I hereby apply to have my status in the United States changed
to that of a nonimmigrant _____
(Student, visitor, etc.)

I wish to remain in the United States in that new status until

_____ (Your passport must be valid for 6 months beyond the date indicated unless you seek F-1 student status in which
(Month, Day, Year)
case your passport must be valid for at least 6 months at all times while in the United States.)

Fee Stamp

PRESS FIRMLY — LEGIBLE COPY REQUIRED. PRINT OR TYPE YOUR NAME EXACTLY AS IT APPEARS ON YOUR ARRIVAL — DEPARTURE RECORD FORM I-94. IF YOUR MAILING ADDRESS IN THE
U.S. IS WITH SOMEONE WHOSE FAMILY NAME IS DIFFERENT FROM YOURS, INSERT THAT PERSON'S NAME IN THE C/O BLOCK.

1 YOUR NAME	FAMILY NAME *(Capital Letters)*	GIVEN	MIDDLE	6. I AM IN POSSESSION OF PASSPORT
IN CARE OF	C/O			NUMBER: *
				ISSUED BY (Country)
2 MAILING ADDRESS IN US	NUMBER AND STREET *(Apt. No.)*			WHICH EXPIRES ON: (Month, Day, Year)
	CITY	STATE	ZIP CODE	

3 DATE OF BIRTH *(Month, Day, Year)* — COUNTRY OF BIRTH — COUNTRY OF CITIZENSHIP

7. MY I-94 AND OR FORM I-20 ID COPY IF F-1 OR M-1 STUDENT
IS ATTACHED ☐ YES ☐ NO
If "No", It was ☐ Lost ☐ Stolen ☐ Destroyed
☐ Other (Specify) _____

4 PRESENT NONIMMIGRANT CLASSIFICATION — DATE ON WHICH AUTHORIZED STAY EXPIRES

5 DATE AND PORT OF LAST ARRIVAL IN UNITED STATES — NAME OF VESSEL, AIRLINE, OR OTHER MEANS OF LAST ARRIVAL IN U.S.

8. I ENTERED WITH NONIMMIGRANT VISA NO.

9. MY NONIMMIGRANT STATUS IN THE UNITED
STATES ☐ HAS ☐ HAS NOT BEEN CHANGED
SINCE MY ENTRY (if changed, give details)

FOR GOVERNMENT USE ONLY

ADMISSION NUMBER

Reclassification to

☐ STAY GRANTED TO (Date)

☐ Application DENIED V.D. TO (Date)

DATE OF ACTION
DD OR OIC OFFICE

J,H,OR L PROGRAM OR PETITION NO.: OCCUPATION

CHECK IF BOND HAS BEEN POSTED: ☐ BOND CONTROL OFFICE:

ALIEN REGISTRATION NUMBER: TELEPHONE NUMBER

10. MY PERMANENT ADDRESS OUTSIDE THE UNITED STATES IS: (Street) (City or Town) (County, District, Province or State) (Country)

11. I RESIDED AT THE ADDRESS IN ITEM 10 FROM: (Month, Day, Year) — To: (Month, Day, Year)

12. SINCE MY ENTRY INTO THE UNITED STATES, I HAVE RESIDED AT THE FOLLOWING PLACES:

(Street and No.) (City or Town) (State)	FROM: (Month, Day, Year)	TO: (Month, Day, Year)
		Present Time

13. I DESIRE TO HAVE MY NONIMMIGRANT STATUS CHANGED FOR THE FOLLOWING REASONS:

14. I DID NOT APPLY TO THE AMERICAN CONSUL FOR A VISA IN THE NONIMMIGRANT STATUS WHICH I AM NOW SEEKING FOR THE FOLLOWING REASONS:

15. I SUBMIT THE FOLLOWING DOCUMENTARY EVIDENCE TO ESTABLISH THAT I WILL MAINTAIN THE NONIMMIGRANT CLASSIFICATION TO WHICH I WISH TO BE CHANGED:

ATTACH YOUR FORM I-94 AND/OR FORM I-20 ID COPY
***DO NOT SEND YOUR PASSPORT**

RECEIVED	TRANS. IN	RET'D. TRANS. OUT	COMPLETED

FORM I-506 (Rev. 7-1-84)N

MICROFILM INDEX NUMBER

16. COMPLETE THIS BLOCK ONLY IF YOU ARE APPLYING FOR CHANGE TO STUDENT STATUS.

THE COUNTRY IN WHICH I INTEND TO LIVE AND WORK AFTER I COMPLETE MY SCHOOLING IN THE UNITED STATES IS _____

(IF YOU ARE SEEKING TO ATTEND A VOCATIONAL OR BUSINESS SCHOOL, COMPLETE THE FOLLOWING ADDITIONAL STATEMENTS BY CHECKING THE APPROPRIATE BOXES.)

THE SCHOOLING I AM SEEKING ☐ IS   ☐ IS NOT AVAILABLE IN MY COUNTRY.

I ☐ INTEND   ☐ DO NOT INTEND TO WORK IN THE OCCUPATION FOR WHICH THIS SCHOOLING WILL PREPARE ME.

17. MY OCCUPATION IS:

18. SOCIAL SECURITY NO. (If none, state "none")

19. I ☐ HAVE ☐ HAVE NOT BEEN EMPLOYED OR ENGAGED IN BUSINESS SINCE ENTERING THE UNITED STATES. IF ANSWER IS HAVE BEEN, COMPLETE THE FOLLOWING:

NATURE OF OCCUPATION OR BUSINESS IN WHICH I ☐ AM ☐ WAS EMPLOYED:

NAME OF EMPLOYER OR BUSINESS FIRM | ADDRESS

MY EMPLOYMENT OR ENGAGEMENT IN BUSINESS BEGAN ON: (Month, Day, Year) | AND ENDED ON: (Month, Day, Year)

MY MONTHLY INCOME FROM EMPLOYMENT OR BUSINESS ☐ IS ☐ WAS: $

20. IF NOT EMPLOYED OR ENGAGED IN BUSINESS IN THE UNITED STATES, DESCRIBE FULLY THE SOURCE AND AMOUNT OF YOUR INCOME ABROAD AND HOW SUPPORTED WHILE IN THE UNITED STATES: (If applying for change to student status, see Instruction #6.)

21. I ☐ AM ☐ AM NOT MARRIED

Name of Spouse | Present Address of Spouse | Citizenship (Country) of Spouse

22. I HAVE _____ (Number) CHILDREN: (List children below)

Name	Age	Place of Birth	Present Address

23. I HAVE _____ (Number) RELATIVES IN THE UNITED STATES OTHER THAN MY SPOUSE AND/OR CHILDREN: (List relatives below)

Name	Relationship	Immigration Status	Present Address

24. HAS AN IMMIGRANT VISA PETITION EVERY BEEN FILED IN YOUR BEHALF?   ☐ YES   ☐ NO   (If "YES", WHERE WAS IT FILED?)

25. HAVE YOU EVER APPLIED FOR AN IMMIGRANT VISA OR PERMANENT RESIDENCE IN THE U.S.? ☐ YES   ☐ NO (If "YES", WHERE DID YOU APPLY?)

26. I ☐ HAVE ☐ HAVE NOT BEEN ARRESTED OR CONVICTED OF ANY CRIMINAL OFFENSE IN THE UNITED STATES OR IN ANY FOREIGN COUNTRY. IF ANSWER IS HAVE BEEN, GIVE DETAILS.

27. I certify that the above is true and correct to the best of my knowledge and belief. (If form prepared by other than applicant, that person must execute item 28.)

(Signature of Applicant) | (Date)

SIGNATURE OF PERSON PREPARING FORM, IF OTHER THAN APPLICANT

28. I declare that this document was prepared by me at the request of the applicant and is based on all information of which I have any knowledge.

(Signature) (Name — Printed or Typed) | (Address) | (Date)

(Please tear off this sheet before submitting application)

U.S. Department of Justice
Immigration and Naturalization Service

APPLICATION TO EXTEND TIME OF TEMPORARY STAY

INSTRUCTIONS: READ CAREFULLY, FEE WILL NOT BE REFUNDED
Failure to comply with instructions may make it necessary to reject your applications.

1. GENERAL. An alien admitted in transit (class C-1, C-2, C-3 or TWOV); or as a crewman (class D-1 or D-2); or as the fiance(e) of a United States citizen and his or her children (class K-1 or K-2) is ineligible for an extension of temporary stay.

A student (class F-1) must apply for extension of temporary stay on Form I-538. An exchange alien (class J-1) must apply for extension of temporary stay on Form IAP-66 executed by his/her sponsor. Spouses and children of students and exchange aliens may be included in their applications.

Any other nonimmigrant admitted for a temporary period of time may apply for an extension of temporary stay by completing this form.

A separate application must be completed by each applicant for an extension of temporary stay with the following exception:

A nonimmigrant who desires an extension of temporary stay for his/her spouse and unmarried children under age 21 who have the same nonimmigrant classification as the applicant should include the spouse and children in the application (Block 16). A spouse or child having a different nonimmigrant classification than the applicant must make a separate application. (See instruction under 4 for payment of fee.)

2. WHEN TO SUBMIT THIS APPLICATION. You should submit this application not less than fifteen nor more than sixty days before your authorized stay expires, except that you may submit this application at any time prior to the expiration of your authorized stay if you were issued a Form I-444 when you were admitted to the United States.

3. WHERE TO SUBMIT APPLICATION. Take or mail your completed application to the office of the Immigration and Naturalization Service having jurisdiction over the place where you are staying.

When you submit your application you must also send in your temporary entry permit. Form I-94 ARRIVAL-DEPARTURE RECORD or Form I-444. (If your temporary entry permit is attached to your passport, the permit should be removed for this purpose.) *DO NOT SEND IN YOUR PASSPORT.* However, you must be in possession of a passport valid for at least six (6) months beyond the expiration date of the extension requested. If this application includes your spouse or children their Forms I-94 must be submitted with the application. They, too, must be in possession of passports valid for at least six months beyond the expiration date of the extension requested.

4. FEE. A fee of thirty-five dollars ($35) must be paid for filing this application. It cannot be refunded regardless of the action taken on the application. DO NOT MAIL CASH. ALL FEES MUST BE SUBMITTED IN THE EXACT AMOUNT. Payments by check or money order must be drawn on a bank or other institution located in the United States and be payable in United States currency. If applicant resides in Guam, check or money order must be payable to the "Treasurer, Guam." If applicant resides in the Virgin Islands, check or money order must be payable to the "Commissioner of Finance of the Virgin Islands." All other applicants must make the check or money order payable to the "Immigration and Naturalization Service." When check is drawn on account of person other than the applicant, the name of the applicant must be entered on the face of the check. If application is submitted from outside the United States, remittance may be made by bank international money order or foreign draft drawn on a financial institution in the United States and payable to the Immigration and Naturalization Service in United States currency. Personal checks are accepted subject to collectibility. An uncollectible check will render the application and any documents issued pursuant thereto invalid. A charge of $5.00 will be imposed if a check in payment of a fee is not honored by the bank on which it is drawn.

However, no fee is required for A-3 employees of government officials and their immediate families, G-5 employees of representatives to an international organization and their immediate families, and the spouse and all unmarried children under age of 21 if they are properly included in one application.

5. NONIMMIGRANT CLASSIFICATION (BLOCK 4). Indicate in this block the classification symbol shown in the admission stamp on your Form I-94 immediately after the word "class", for example B-1, H-3, etc., or whatever it may be.

6. ATTENDANT, SERVANT, OR PERSONAL EMPLOYEE (INCLUDING MEMBERS OF HIS FAMILY) OF CERTAIN FOREIGN GOVERNMENT OFFICIALS (A-3 or G-5). If you are in the United States under an A-3 or G-5 nonimmigrant classification, you must submit with this application a statement from the employing official describing the current and intended employment of the attendant, servant or personal employee.

7. TREATY TRADER OR INVESTOR (E-1 or E-2). If you are in the United States under an E-1 or E-2 nonimmigrant classification, you must submit with this application a Form I-126 properly executed, with such additional documents as are required by that form.

8. REPRESENTATIVE OF FOREIGN PRESS, RADIO, FILM, OR OTHER INFORMATION MEDIUM ("I"). If you are in the United States under an "I" nonimmigrant classification, you must submit with this application a statement from your employer establishing that you are the representative of such medium in the United States and setting forth your current and intended activities and the reason for the extension.

9. ALIEN ADMITTED TO PERFORM TEMPORARY SERVICE OR LABOR, OR AS A TRAINEE OR INTRA-COMPANY TRANSFEREE (H-1, H-2, H-3, or L-1). If you are in the United States under an H-1, H-2, H-3 or L-1 nonimmigrant classification, you must submit with this application a statement from your employer or trainer describing your current and intended employment or training and the reason for the extension. In addition, if you are an H-2 applicant, you must submit a certification from the Department of Labor concerning availability of workers domestically and effect on wages and working conditions of persons similarly employed in the United States, unless the extension of time requested will not exceed the period of validity of the certification previously submitted by your employer. For a group extension of stay of H-1, H-2 or H-3 nonimmigrants. Form I-129B shall be used.

10. PENALTIES — Severe penalties are provided by law for knowingly and willfully falsifying or concealing a material fact or using any false document in the submission of this application. Also, a false representation may result in denial of this application and or any other application you may make for any benefit under the immigration laws of the United States. Any statement submitted with this application is considered part of the application.

For sale by the Superintendent of Documents, U.S. Government Printing Office
Washington, D.C. 20402 (per 100)

Form I-539 (Rev. 5-4-89)N

UNITED STATES DEPARTMENT OF JUSTICE
IMMIGRATION AND NATURALIZATION SERVICE

READ INSTRUCTIONS CAREFULLY
FEE WILL NOT BE REFUNDED

OMB No. 1115—0093
Expires 1-84

FEE STAMP

APPLICATION TO EXTEND
TIME OF TEMPORARY STAY

I HEREBY APPLY TO EXTEND MY
TEMPORARY STAY IN THE UNITED STATES

6. DATE TO WHICH EXTENSION IS REQUESTED

PRESS FIRMLY — LEGIBLE COPY REQUIRED. PRINT OR TYPE YOUR NAME EXACTLY AS IT APPEARS ON YOUR ARRIVAL—DEPARTURE RECORD FORM I-94. IF YOUR MAILING ADDRESS IN THE U.S. IS WITH SOMEONE WHOSE FAMILY NAME IS DIFFERENT FROM YOURS, INSERT THAT PERSON'S NAME IN THE C/O BLOCK.

7. REASON FOR REQUESTING EXTENSION

1. YOUR NAME — FAMILY NAME (CAPITAL LETTERS)   FIRST   MIDDLE

IN CARE OF   C/O

2. MAILING ADDRESS IN U.S. — NUMBER AND STREET (APT. NO.)   FILE NUMBER

CITY   STATE   ZIP CODE

3. DATE OF BIRTH (MO./DAY/YR.)   COUNTRY OF BIRTH   COUNTRY OF CITIZENSHIP

4. PRESENT NONIMMIGRANT CLASSIFICATION   DATE ON WHICH AUTHORIZED STAY EXPIRES   TELEPHONE NUMBER

5. DATE AND PORT OF LAST ARRIVAL IN U.S.   NAME OF VESSEL, AIRLINE, OR OTHER MEANS OF LAST ARRIVAL IN U.S.

8. REASON FOR COMING TO THE U.S.

THE ADMISSION NUMBER FROM MY I-94 IS: ▶

FOR GOVERNMENT USE ONLY

☐ EXTENSION GRANTED TO (DATE)   DATE OF ACTION

9. HAS AN IMMIGRANT VISA PETITION EVER BEEN FILED IN YOUR BEHALF?
☐ YES ☐ NO IF "YES", WHERE WAS IT FILED?

☐ EXTENSION DENIED V.D. TO (DATE)   DD OR OIC OFFICE

10. HAVE YOU EVER APPLIED FOR AN IMMIGRANT VISA OR PERMANENT RESIDENCE IN THE U.S.? ☐ YES ☐ NO IF "YES", WHERE DID YOU APPLY?

11. I INTEND TO DEPART FROM THE U.S. ON (DATE)   I AM IN POSSESSION OF A TRANSPORTATION TICKET FOR MY DEPARTURE ☐ YES ☐ NO

12. PASSPORT NO. *   EXPIRES ON (DATE)   ISSUED BY (COUNTRY)   13. NUMBER, STREET, CITY, PROVINCE (STATE) AND COUNTRY OF PERMANENT RESIDENCE

14. MY USUAL OCCUPATION IS: 15. SOCIAL SECURITY NO. (IF NONE, STATE "NONE")

16. I ☐ AM ☐ AM NOT MARRIED. IF YOU WISH TO APPLY FOR EXTENSION FOR YOUR SPOUSE AND CHILDREN, GIVE THE FOLLOWING: (SEE INSTRUCTIONS # 1)

NAME OF SPOUSE AND CHILDREN	DATE OF BIRTH	COUNTRY OF BIRTH	PASSPORT ISSUED BY (COUNTRY) AND EXPIRES ON (DATE)

NOTE — IF SPOUSE AND CHILDREN FOR WHOM YOU ARE SEEKING EXTENSION DO NOT RESIDE WITH YOU, GIVE THEIR COMPLETE ADDRESS ON A SEPARATE ATTACHMENT TO THIS APPLICATION.

17. I (INSERT "HAVE" OR "HAVE NOT") _____ BEEN EMPLOYED OR ENGAGED IN BUSINESS IN THE UNITED STATES. (IF YOU HAVE BEEN EMPLOYED OR ENGAGED IN BUSINESS IN THE UNITED STATES, COMPLETE THE REST OF THE BLOCK.)

NAME AND ADDRESS OF EMPLOYER OR BUSINESS   INCOME PER WEEK   DATES EMPLOYMENT OR BUSINESS BEGAN AND ENDED

I certify that the above is true and correct

SIGNATURE OF APPLICANT   DATE

SIGNATURE OF PERSON PREPARING FORM, IF OTHER THAN APPLICANT

I declare that this document was prepared by me at the request of the applicant and is based on all information on which I have any knowledge.

SIGNATURE   ADDRESS   DATE

ATTACH YOUR FORM I-94 OR I-144—*DO NOT SEND YOUR PASSPORT

RECEIVED	TRANS. IN	RET'D. TRANS. OUT	COMPLETED

Form I-539 (Rev. 5-4-89)N

U.S. Department of Justice
Immigration and Naturalization Service

Application by Nonimmigrant Student for Extension of Stay,
School Transfer, or Permission to Accept or Continue Employment

Instructions - Form I-538
Failure to comply with instructions may make it necessary to reject your application.

(Parts 1 through 3 and 8 through 11 apply to both F-1 and M-1 students. Parts 4
through 6 apply to F-1 students only and Part 8 applies to M-1 students only.)

1. **General.** Complete this application if you are an:

   A) F-1 or M-1 student and want an extension of authorized stay so that you may continue your studies.

   B) M-1 student and want to transfer to another school. (You may not transfer to another school after six months from the date you were first in M-1 classification unless you are unable to remain at the school to which you were initially admitted due to circumstances beyond your control.)

   C) F-1 or M-1 student and want permission to engage in practical training.

   D) F-1 student and want permission to engage in off-campus employment.

   Application may be made simultaneously on this form for more than one purpose, e.g., for extension of temporary stay and permission to accept employment or continue previously authorized employment.

   The application must be typewritten or printed legibly in ink. *If you need more space to answer fully any question on this form, use a separate sheet of paper and identify each answer with the number of the corresponding question.*

   If you are carrying less than a full load of classroom hours, attach a statement explaining why.

2. **Form I-20 ID Copy.** You must submit your Form I-20 ID copy with your application. Do not send in your passport or Form I-94 (Arrival-Departure Record). You must, however, be in possession of a valid passport.

3. **Application for extension of stay.** An F-1 or M-1 student who desires an extension of stay for his or her spouse and children as F-2 or M-2 nonimmigrants should include them in this application (Block C) and include their Forms I-94 with this application. They, too, must be in possession of valid passports.

   An F-1 student who has been in student status for eight consecutive academic years or has remained in one educational level for an extended period of time must request an extension of stay.

   A) *When to submit application.* Submit your application for extension of stay not less than 15, and no more than 60 days before your authorized stay expires.

   B) *Where to submit application.* Take or mail your application to the office of the Immigration and Naturalization Service which has jurisdiction over the school you were last authorized to attend.

4. **Application for permission to accept or continue off-campus employment because of economic necessity.**

   A) *Eligibility.* A nonimmigrant student is not permitted to work off campus for a wage or salary or to engage in business while in the United States unless permission to do so has first been granted by the Immigration and Naturalization Service. An F-1 student may not be granted permission to engage in employment during his or her first full year in the United States. The F-2 spouse or child of an F-1 student may not apply for or be granted permission to accept employment.

   B) *Economic Necessity.* If you are a nonimmigrant student requesting permission to accept or continue part-time employment off campus because of economic necessity you must:

   1) Establish that the necessity is due to unforeseen circumstances arising subsequent to entry or subsequent to change of your status to nonimmigrant student;

   2) Obtain certification, on page 2 of this application, of an authorized school official that part-time employment will not interfere with your ability to carry successfully a full course of study.

   When part-time employment is authorized, a student may work off campus not more than 20 hours per week while school is in session, and full-time during vacation or recess periods when school attendance is not required.

   C) *Termination of permission to accept or continue off-campus employment.* Permission to engage in off-campus employment is terminated when the student transfers from one school to another or when the need for the employment ceases.

5. **Application for permission to accept or continue practical training.**

   A) *Eligibility.* A student may apply for permission to accept or continue practical training:

   1) After completion of the course of study if the student intends to engage in only one course of study;

   2) After completion of at least one course of study if the student intends to engage in more than one course of study;

   3) After completion of all course requirements for the degree if the student is in a bachelor's, master's or doctoral degree program;

   4) Before completion of the course of study if the student is attending a college, university, seminary, or conservatory which requires practical training of all degree candidates in a specified professional field and student is a candidate for a degree in that field;

   5) Before completion of the course of study during the student's annual vacation if recommended by the designated school official as beneficial to the student's academic program.

   Students in a language training program are not eligible for practical training.

   B) *Certification of designated school officials.* Employment authorization for pre-graduation practical training and the first period post-graduation practical training may be granted by designated school officials. When authorizing employment for practical training, the DSO must certify on page 2 of a Form I-538 that comparable employment is not available in the country of the student's foreign residence and that it is directly related to the student's field of study. Certification by the DSO to this effect is required of all students seeking employment for practical training except for students attending a school which makes practical training a mandatory part of its curriculum and students applying for the second period practical training after completion of studies.

   C) *Duration of practical training.*

   1) Prior to completion of studies. A student may be granted practical training not to exceed twelve months in the aggregate.

   2) After completion of studies. A student may be granted practical training for up to twelve months.

For sale by the Superintendent of Documents, U.S. Government Printing Office
Washington, D.C. 20402

Instructions - Form I-538
Continued

D) *When and where to submit application.*

1) Prior to completion of studies. The application must be submitted to the designated school official of the school the student is authorized to attend.

2) Post Completion of studies.

a) First period practical training. The application must be submitted to the designated school official of the school the student is attending not more than sixty days prior to and not later than thirty days after completion of studies and graduation.

b) Second period practical training. An application to continue practical training should be submitted to the office of the Immigration and Naturalization Service having jurisdiction over the actual place of employment within 30 days after the student begins qualified employment.

An application to continue practical training must be accompanied by a letter from the employer stating the occupation, the exact date employment began and the date the employment will terminate, and describing in detail the duties of the occupation. Certification of designated school official is required for the second period of practical training. Designated school officials should review the letter of the student's employer before making the certification on Form I-538.

6. **Curricular practical training.** An F-1 student enrolled in a college, university, or seminary having a curricular practical training program as a part of its regular curriculum may participate in those courses after having been in status for nine months.

Such programs shall be treated similarly to practical training prior to completion of studies. Periods of actual off-campus employment in any such program which is full-time will be deducted from the total of twelve months of practical training time before graduation for which the student is eligible. Periods of actual off-campus employment in any such program in which coursework and employment take place at the same time will be deducted from the total of twelve months' practical training time at the rate of 50% (one month deducted for every two months of parallel coursework and practical training). A student who participates in a curricular practical training experience for which six months or more of the practical training time prior to graduation is deducted is not eligible for practical training after completion of studies.

7. **Application to accept practical training for M-1 student.**

A) An M-1 student must apply for permission to accept employment for practical training on this form accompanied by the student's Form I-20 ID copy prior to the expiration of the student's authorized period of stay and not more than sixty days before completion of the course of study and no more than thirty days after completion of the course of study.

B) An M-1 student may be granted only one period of practical training time equal to one month for each four months during which the student pursued a full course of study. An M-1 student may be granted up to a maximum of six months of training.

Practical training can be authorized for an M-1 student only after completion of the student's course of study.

C) Permission to accept employment may not be granted if the training applied for cannot be completed within the maximum period of time for which the applicant is eligible.

The M-2 spouse and children may not accept employment.

8. **Application for permission to transfer to another school.** An M-1 Student seeking a transfer to another school must file an application for school transfer on this form with a properly completed Form I-20 M-N, Certificate of Eligibility for Nonimmigrant (M-1) Student Status. Sixty days after having filed this application, you may transfer to the new school, subject to approval or denial of the application. If the application for transfer is approved, the approval of the transfer will be retroactive to the date of filing the application. Submit the application to the office of the Immigration and Naturalization Service having jurisdiction over the school you were last authorized to attend. Permission to transfer may be granted only to a bona fide nonimmigrant student who intends to take a full course of study. In addition, the applicant must be a full-time student at the school which he or she was last authorized to attend.

If the designated official at the school you were last authorized to attend refuses to execute the Certification of Designated School Official on a school transfer application within 30 days of the date that you requested the official to do so, you may explain this refusal to the Immigration and Naturalization Serivce office having jurisdiction over the school. In that case, the Immigration and Naturalization Service may, at the discretion of the district director, make a decision on your application without such a certification.

9. **Labor disputes.** Permission to engage in any employment is automatically suspended while a strike or other labor dispute involving a work stoppage is in progress. You must suspend employment immediately if such a situation arises.

10. **Fee.** A fee of thirty-five dollars ($35.00) is required when an applicaton is filed with the Immigration and Naturalization Service. This fee is not refundable regardless of the action taken on the application. Do not mail cash. All fees must be submitted in the exact amount. Payments by check or money order must be drawn on a bank or other institution located in the United States and be payable in United States currency.

The check or money order should be payable to the "Immigration and Naturalization Service." (If applicant resides in Guam, the check or money order must be payable to the "Treasurer, Guam." If applicant resides in the Virgin Islands, the check or money order must be payable to the "Commissioner of Finance of the Virgin Islands.")

When a check is drawn on the account of a person other than the applicant, the name of the applicant must be entered on the face of the check. If the application is submitted from outside the United Stees, remittance may be made by bank international money order or foreign draft drawn on a financial institution in the United States and payable to the Immigration and Naturalization Service in United States currency. Personal checks are accepted subject to collectability. An uncollectable check will render the application and any documents issued pursuant to it invalid. A charge of five dollars ($5.00) will be imposed if a check in payment of a fee is not honored by the bank on which it is drawn. The authority for collecting a fee is granted to Federal agencies by 31 U.S.C., Section 483a, and OMB Circular A-25.

11. **Penalties.** Severe penalties are provided by law (18 U.S.C., Section 1001) for knowingly and willfully falsifying or concealing a material fact or using any false document in the submission of this application. Also, a false representation may result in denial of this aplication and any other application you may make for any benefit under the immigration laws of the United States. Any statement submitted with this application is considered part of the application.

Form I-538 (05/04/89) N

U.S. Department of Justice
Immigration and Naturalization Service

Application by Nonimmigrant Student for Extension of Stay, School Transfer, or Permission to Accept or Continue Employment

OMB #1115-0060

I am an:	For Official Use Only	Date of Action
☐ F-1 Student	☐ Extension Granted	DD
☐ M-1 Student	☐ Extension Denied	or
I am applying for:	☐ Transfer Granted	OIC
☐ Extension of stay	☐ Transfer Denied	Office
☐ School transfer	☐ Employment Granted	
☐ Off-campus employment due to economic necessity	☐ Employment Denied	
☐ Practical training	☐ Practical Training Granted	
☐ Prior to completion of studies	☐ Practical Training Denied	
☐ Curricular or work/study	From To (or VD to)	
☐ Post completion of studies		

A. This Section to be completed by all applicants.

1. Name (Family in CAPS)   (First)   (Middle)

2. U.S. Address (Street number and name)   (Apt. number)

   (City)   (State)   (ZIP Code)

3. Telephone number (include area code)

4. Student admission number

5. Social Security number

6. Date of birth

7. Country of birth

8. Country of citizenship

9. Passport issued by (country)

10. Passport expires on (date)

11. Date of intended departure

12. Has an immigrant visa petition ever been filed on your behalf?

    ☐ No   ☐ Yes (If yes, where was it filed?)

13. Have you ever applied for an immigrant visa or permanent residence in the U.S.?

    ☐ No   ☐ Yes (If yes, where did you apply?)

14. Have you been arrested or convicted of any criminal offense since entry into the U.S.?

    ☐ No   ☐ Yes (If yes, explain.)

15. Have you engaged in unauthorized employment while in student status?

    ☐ No   ☐ Yes (If yes, explain.)

B. This Section to be completed only by applicants for extension of stay.

1. Current means and source of support.

2. Reason for requesting extension of stay

C. This Section to be completed only if applying for extension of stay for your F-2 or M-2 dependents.

Name of dependent	Relationship	Country of birth	Date of birth	Passport issued by (country)	Passport expires on (date)

Block below for INS use only.

Microfilm index number	Initial Receipt	Resubmitted	Relocated		Completed		
			Received	Sent	Approved	Denied	Returned

Form I-538 (05/04/89) N

C. This Section to be completed only if an M-1 student applying for school transfer.

1. Date first granted M-1 status
2. Date (s) of absence from the U.S. since granted M-1 status

3. Reason you are requesting a transfer

D. This Section to be completed only if applying for permission to accept off-campus employment.

1. Date first granted F-1 status
2. Date (s) of absence from the U.S. during first year in F-1 status

3. Explain the financial changes that make it necessary for you to seek off-campus employment.

E. This Section to be completed only if applying for permission to engage in practical training.

1. Describe the proposed employment, giving beginning and ending dates and number of hours per week.

2. List all periods of previously authorized employment for practical training.

A. Prior to completion of studies	B. Curricular or work/study	C. Post completion of studies

Signature of applicant
I certify, under penalty of perjury, that the information in this form is true and correct.

Signature   Date

Signature of person preparing form, if other than the applicant
I declare that this application was prepared by me at the request of the applicant and is based on all information of which I have any knowledge.

Signature   Date

Name (type or print)   Address

CERTIFICATION OF DESIGNATED SCHOOL OFFICIAL
(This section must be completed by the designated school official of the school the student is attending or was last authorized to attend.)

1. Name (Family in CAPS) (First) (Middle)   4. Level of education being sought

2. Student admission number   3. Date of birth   5. Student's major field of study

I hereby certify that:

- ☐ **A.** The student named above;
  - ☐ Is taking a full course of study at this school, and the expected date of completion is: _____
  - ☐ Is taking less than a full course of study at this school because: _____
  - ☐ Completed the course of study at this school on (date): _____
  - ☐ Did not complete the course of study. Terminated attendance on (date): _____
- ☐ **B.** The employment is for practical training in the student's field of study and, upon my information and belief, is not available in the country of the student's residence. The student has been in the educational program for at least 9 months and is eligible for the requested practical training in accordance with INS regulations at 8 CFR 214.2(f)(10).
- ☐ **C.** Employment off-campus is due to unforeseen circumstances arising after entry. Acceptance of employment will not interfere with the student's carrying a full course of study.

If application is for extension of stay or for permission to accept or continue off-campus employment, complete the following:

A. Student's cost for an academic term of
(number of months, not to exceed 12). _____

B. Student's means of support estimated
for the same period of time as in item A.

Tuition and fees $ _____	Personal funds of student $ _____
Living expenses $ _____	Family funds from abroad $ _____
Expenses of dependents $ _____	Funds from the school (specify type) $ _____
Other $ _____	Funds from other source (specify type) $ _____
TOTAL $ _____	Employment, if applicable $ _____
	TOTAL $ _____

Name and title of designated school official	*Signature*	Date	**For Official Use Only** Microfilm Index Number
Name of school	School file number (including suffix)	Telephone number	

Form I-538 (05/04/89) N

U.S. Department of Justice
Immigration and Naturalization Service

OMB No. 1115-0153

Data Sheet for Derivative Citizenship
(Please See Instructions on Reverse)

Office processing case _____
(for INS use only)

Applicant:

	Name (last, first, middle initial)	Alien Registration Number	Country of Nationality	ZIP Code of Residence	Month and Year Naturalized
Father		A-			
Mother		A-			

Please list your foreign-born children under age 18 below.

Examiner check off each derivative child below	Name (last, first, middle initial)	Alien Registration Number	Year of Birth	Country of Birth	Country of Nationality	Year of Entry as a Permanent Resident	Sex	ZIP Code of Residence	Month and Year of Derivation	Application Filed	For N-600 Applicants only: Reason for Derivation
1		A-					Male ☐ / Female ☐			N-400 ☐ (1) / N-600 ☐ (2)	Adoption ☐ (1) / Parents' Naturalization ☐ (2)
2		A-					Male ☐ / Female ☐			N-400 ☐ (1) / N-600 ☐ (2)	Adoption ☐ (1) / Parents' Naturalization ☐ (2)
3		A-					Male ☐ / Female ☐			N-400 ☐ (1) / N-600 ☐ (2)	Adoption ☐ (1) / Parents' Naturalization ☐ (2)
4		A-					Male ☐ / Female ☐			N-400 ☐ (1) / N-600 ☐ (2)	Adoption ☐ (1) / Parents' Naturalization ☐ (2)
5		A-					Male ☐ / Female ☐			N-400 ☐ (1) / N-600 ☐ (2)	Adoption ☐ (1) / Parents' Naturalization ☐ (2)
6		A-					Male ☐ / Female ☐			N-400 ☐ (1) / N-600 ☐ (2)	Adoption ☐ (1) / Parents' Naturalization ☐ (2)
7		A-					Male ☐ / Female ☐			N-400 ☐ (1) / N-600 ☐ (2)	Adoption ☐ (1) / Parents' Naturalization ☐ (2)
8		A-					Male ☐ / Female ☐			N-400 ☐ (1) / N-600 ☐ (2)	Adoption ☐ (1) / Parents' Naturalization ☐ (2)
9		A-					Male ☐ / Female ☐			N-400 ☐ (1) / N-600 ☐ (2)	Adoption ☐ (1) / Parents' Naturalization ☐ (2)
10		A-					Male ☐ / Female ☐			N-400 ☐ (1) / N-600 ☐ (2)	Adoption ☐ (1) / Parents' Naturalization ☐ (2)

INS Examiner—Please verify the information on this form for completeness and indicate in the appropriate box before each child's name those who will derive U.S. citizenship upon the naturalization of the parents. After the applicants have naturalized or the certificate of citizenship has been issued, complete the remaining sections of the form—date naturalized and/or date of derivation and the office processing the case. Submit completed forms to the Central Office: Statistical Analysis Branch, 425 Eye Street, N.W., Washington, DC 20536.

Form N-642 (04/14/88)

☆U.S. GOVERNMENT PRINTING OFFICE: 1989 231-633/99260

U.S. Department of Justice
Immigration and Naturalization Service

Data Sheet for Derivative Citizenship

INSTRUCTIONS:

Applicant—Please complete this form if you are in one of the following groups: (1) an applicant for naturalization who has foreign-born children under 18 (children born outside the United States and its territories), or (2) a U.S. citizen who has adopted a foreign-born child and is requesting that the child derive U.S. citizenship, or (3) a naturalized U.S. citizen who is requesting that a certificate of citizenship be issued to a foreign-born child who entered the U.S. as a lawful permanent resident after your naturalization. Complete one form for a family unit. Please type responses or print neatly.

(1) Applicants for naturalization —Complete all sections of the form except the date naturalized and date of derivation. If either you or your spouse already is a naturalized U.S. citizen, fill in the date naturalized for that person. Please submit this form to INS with your naturalization application.

(2) U.S. citizen applicants requesting that adopted children derive U.S. citizenship or (3) Naturalized U.S. citizens requesting certificates of citizenship for children who entered the U.S. as lawful permanent residents after your naturalization—Complete all sections of the form except the date of derivation for the child. Please submit this form to INS with the N-600 application.

Country of Nationality—This refers to your nationality prior to attaining U.S. citizenship. If you are a native-born U.S. citizen, then it is the United States.

For N-600 Applicants—Please identify in the block marked "Reason for Derivation" if the child deriving U.S. citizenship is doing so through (1) adoption by U.S. citizen parents, or (2) the naturalization of the child's parents.

Authority for Collecting this Information: The authority to prescribe this information is contained in Section 347 (8 U.S.C. 1458) of the Immigration and Nationality Act. This information is necessary for statistical purposes to determine the number of immigrant children who derive U.S. citizenship each year. Data will be published in aggregate form in the Statistical Yearbook of the Immigration and Naturalization Service. The information on the form may, as a matter of routine use, be furnished to federal, state, and local government agencies, as well as the general public, in statistical form with personal identifiers removed. Disclosure of this information is voluntary.

U.S. Department of Justice
Immigration and Naturalization Service

Application to File Petition for   OMB 1115-0010
Naturalization in Behalf of Child
Under Section 322 of the Immigration and Nationality Act

Take or Mail to:
Immigration and Naturalization Service

Child's Name and Alien Registration Number

Name _____

No. _____

I (We), the undersigned, desire that a petition for naturalization be filed in behalf of my (our) child.

1) My full, true, and correct name is   (Full, true name of citizen parent or citizen adoptive parent, without abbbreviations)

2) My present place of residence is   (Apt. No.)   (Number and street)   (City or town)   (Country)   (State)   (ZIP Code)

3) I am a citizen of the United States of America and was born on   (Month/Day/Year)   In   (City/State/Country)

(If not a native born citizen) I was naturalized on (Month/Day/Year)   At   (City and State)

Certificate No.   Or I became a citizen of the United States through

Is the child's other parent a citizen of the United States?
☐ Yes   ☐ No

Complete (1a) to (3a) only if second parent wishes to join in application.

1a) My full, true, and correct name is   (Full, true name of citizen parent or citizen adoptive parent, without abbbreviations)

2a) My present place of residence is   (Apt. No.)   (Number and street)   (City or town)   (Country)   (State)   (ZIP Code)

3a) I am a citizen of the United States of America and was born on   (Month/Day/Year)   In   (City/State/Country)

(If not a native born citizen) I was naturalized on (Month/Day/Year)   At   (City and State)

Certificate No.   Or, I became a citizen of the United States through

The following (4 to 19) must be answered by all applicants.

4) I am (we are) the parent(s) of (Full, true name of child, without abbreviations) in whose behalf this application for naturalization is filed.

5) The said child now resides with me (us) at   (Apt. No.)   (Number and street)   (City or town)   (Counry)   (State)   (ZIP Code)

6) The said child was born on (Month/Day/Year);   In (City/Country)

and is a citizen, subject, or national of (Country)   and is
☐ Single   ☐ Married

7) The said child was lawfully admitted to the United States for permanent residence on (Month/Day/Year)   At (City/State)

Under the name of;   and
☐ Does   ☐ Does not intend to reside permanently in the United States.

8) I (We) desire the naturalization court to change the name of the child to (Give full name desired, without abbreviations)

9) If application is in behalf of an adopted child: I (we) adopted said child on (Month/Day/Year)   At   (City) (State)

In the (Name of Court)   At   (City or town)   (State)   (Country)

The said child has resided continuously in the United States with me (us) in my (our) legal custody since (Month/Day/Year)

Form N-402 (10/31/89) N

10) Since such child's lawful admission to the United States for permanent residence, the child has not been absent from the United States at any time except as follows (If none, state "None")

Departed from the United States		Returned to the United States	
Port	Date (Month/Day/Year)	Port	Date (Month/Day/Year

11) Has such child ever been a patient in a mental institution, or ever been treated for a mental illness?
☐ Yes   ☐ No

12) The law provides that a person may not be regarded as qualified for naturalizaiton under certain conditions, if the person knowingly committed certain offenses or crimes, even though not arrested therefor. Has such child ever in or outside the United States:

a) Knowingly committed any crime for which he/she has not been arrested?
☐ Yes   ☐ No

b) Been arrested, charged with violation of any law or ordinance, summoned into court as a defendant, convicted, fined, imprisoned, or placed on probation or parole, or forfeited collateral for any act involving a crime, misdemeanor, or breach of any law or ordinancy?
☐ Yes   ☐ No

If the answer to a) or b) is "Yes." on a separate sheet, give the following information as to each incident: when and where occurred, offense involved, and outcome of case if any.

13) Are deportation proceedings pending against such child or has such child ever been deported or ordered deported, or has such child ever applied for suspension of deportation or for preexamination?
☐ Yes   ☐ No

14) List the child's membership in every organization, association, fund, foundation, party, club, society, or similar group in the United States and in any other place, during the past ten years, and his foreign military service. (If none, write "None.")
☐ Yes   ☐ No

15) Has such child ever served in the Armed Forces of the United States?
☐ Yes   ☐ No

16) (Answer only if the child is of an understanding age.) If the law requires it, is the child willing to bear arms or perform noncombatant service in the Armed Forces of the United States or perform work of national importance under civilian directon? If "No" explain fully on a separate sheet of paper.
☐ Yes   ☐ No

17) Since the child's lawful admission to the United States for permanent residence, my wife (husband) and I have been absent from the United States as follows (if no absences, state "None"):

18) My wife (husband) and I have been married as follows (give informaton as to each marriage): (Use extra sheet of papaer if necessary.)

Date Married	Date Marriage Ended	Name of Spouse	How Marriage Ended (Death or divorce)

19) A petition for naturalization:
☐ Has not   ☐ has been filed on behalf of said child (if one has been filed, complete all of item 19)

Filed on (Month/Day/Year)   At (City/County/State   In (Name of court)

The present status of the previously filed petition is:
☐ Denied   ☐ Unknown   ☐ Other (explain)

Form N-402 (10/31/89) N

_____ | _____
(Signature of 1st parent) | (Signature of 2nd parent)
_____ | _____
(Address of 1st parent) | (Address of 2nd parent)
_____ | _____
(Telephone No.)   (Date) | (Telephone No.)   (Date)

SIGNATURE OF PERSON PREPARING FORM, IF OTHER THAN APPLICANT(S)

I declare that this document was prepared by me at the request of the applicant(s) and is based on all information of which I have any knowledge.

_____
(Signature)   (Address)   (Date)

TO APPLICANTS: DO NOT WRITE BELOW THESE LINES

AFFIDAVIT

I do swear (affirm) that I know the contents of this application comprising pages 1 to 3, inclusive, subscribed by me; that the same are true to the best of my knowledge and belief; that correction(s) number(ed) ( ) to ( ) were made by me or at my request; and that this applicaton was signed by me with my full, true name.

Subscribed and sworn (affirmed) to before me at the preliminary investigation (examination) at

this _____ day of _____ , 19 ____

I certify that before verification the parent(s) stated in my presence that he (she/they) had read or heard the foregoing application and corrections therein and understood the contents thereof.

_____
(Complete and true signature of 1st parent)

_____
(Complete and true signature of 2nd parent)

_____
(Naturalization Examiner)

Nonfiled _____

(Date, Reasons) _____

*U.S. Government Printing Office: 1990-262-210/08849

Form N-402 (10/31/89) N

U.S. DEPARTMENT OF JUSTICE
IMMIGRATION AND NATURALIZATION SERVICE

APPLICATION FOR CERTIFICATE OF CITIZENSHIP

OMB No. 1115–0018

FEE STAMP

Take or mail this application to:
IMMIGRATION AND NATURALIZATION SERVICE

Date ....

(Print or type) .... nee ....
       (Full, True Name, without Abbreviations)   (Maiden name, if any)

....
(Apartment number, Street address, and, if appropriate, "in care of")

ALIEN REGISTRATION
No. ....

....
(City)   (County)   (State)   (ZIP Code)

....
(Telephone Number)

(SEE INSTRUCTIONS. BE SURE YOU UNDERSTAND EACH QUESTION BEFORE YOU ANSWER IT.)

    I hereby apply to the Commissioner of Immigration and Naturalization for a certificate showing that I am a citizen of the United States of America.

(1) I was born in .... on ....
                (City)   (State or country)   (Month) (Day) (Year)

(2) My personal description is: Sex ....; complexion ....; color of eyes ....; color of hair ....;
height .... feet .... inches; weight .... pounds; visible distinctive marks ....
.... Marital status: ☐ Single;   ☐ Married;   ☐ Divorced;   ☐ Widow(er).

(3) I arrived in the United States at .... on ....
                        (City and State)   (Month) (Day) (Year)
under the name .... by means of ....
                                 (Name of ship or other means of arrival)

☐ on U.S. Passport No. .... issued to me at .... on ....;
                                        (Month) (Day) (Year)
☐ on an Immigrant Visa.   ☐ Other (specify)

(4) FILL IN THIS BLOCK ONLY IF YOU ARRIVED IN THE UNITED STATES BEFORE JULY 1, 1924.
    (a) My last permanent foreign residence was ....
                                    (City)   (Country)
    (b) I took the ship or other conveyance to the United States at ....
                                    (City)   (Country)
    (c) I was coming to .... at ....
             (Name of person in the United States)   (City and State where this person was living)
    (d) I traveled to the United States with ....
             (Names of passengers or relatives with whom you traveled, and their relationship to you, if any)

(5) Have you been out of the United States since you first arrived? ☐ Yes ☐ No. If "Yes" fill in the following information for every absence.

DATE DEPARTED	DATE RETURNED	NAME OF AIRLINE, OR OTHER MEANS USED TO RETURN TO THE UNITED STATES	PORT OF RETURN TO THE UNITED STATES

(6) I _____ filed a petition for naturalization.
    (have) (have not)
(If "have", attach full explanation.)
TO THE APPLICANT.—Do not write between the double lines below. Continue on next page.

ARRIVAL RECORDS EXAMINED	ARRIVAL RECORD FOUND
Card index	Place .... Date ....
Index books	Name ....
Manifests	
....	Manner ....
....	Marital status .... Age ....
	....
	(Signature of person making search)

Form N–600 (Rev. 5–5–83)N   (1)

(CONTINUE HERE)

(7) I claim United States citizenship through my (check whichever applicable) ☐ **father;** ☐ **mother;** ☐ **both parents;**

☐ **adoptive parent(s)** ☐ **husband**

(8) **My father's name is** ....; he was born on ....
                                                                                          (Month)   (Day)   (Year)

at ....; and resides at ....
         (City)   (State or country)   (Street address, city, and State or country. If dead, write

.... He became a citizen of the United States by ☐ birth; ☐ naturalization on ....
"dead" and date of death.)   (Month)   (Day)   (Year)

in the .... Certificate of Naturalization No. ....;
                      (Name of court, city, and State)

☐ through his parent(s), and .... issued Certificate of Citizenship No. A or AA ....
                                        (was)   (was not)

(If known) His former Alien Registration No. was ....

He .... lost United States citizenship. (If citizenship lost, attach full explanation.)
      (has) (has not)

He resided in the United States from .... to ....; from .... to ....; from .... to ....
                                              (Year)   (Year)   (Year)   (Year)   (Year)   (Year)

from .... to ....; from .... to ....; I am the child of his .... marriage.
        (Year)   (Year)   (Year)   (Year)   (1st, 2d, 3d, etc.)

(9) **My mother's present name is** ....; her maiden name was ....;

she was born on ....; at ....; ....; she resides
                      (Month)   (Day)   (Year)   (City)   (State or country)

at .... She became a citizen of the United States
         (Street address, city, and State or country. If dead, write "dead" and date of death.)

by ☐ birth; ☐ naturalization under the name of ....

on .... in the ....
      (Month)   (Day)   (Year)   (Name of court, city, and State)

Certificate of Naturalization No. ....; ☐ through her parent(s), and .... issued Certificate
                                                                                                          (was)   (was not)

of Citizenship No. A or AA .... (If known) Her former Alien Registration No. was ....

She .... lost United States citizenship. (If citizenship lost, attach full explanation.)
      (has) (has not)

She resided in the United States from .... to ....; from .... to ....; from .... to ....; from ....
                                              (Year)   (Year)   (Year)   (Year)   (Year)   (Year)   (Year)

to ....; from .... to ....; I am the child of her .... marriage.
      (Year)   (Year)   (Year)   (1st, 2d, 3d, etc.)

(10) My mother and my father were married to each other on .... at ....
                                                                                    (Month) (Day) (Year)   (City)   (State or country)

(11) If claim is through adoptive parent(s):

I was adopted on .... in the ....
                        (Month)   (Day)   (Year)   (Name of Court)

at .... by my ....
         (City or town)   (State)   (Country)   (mother, father, parents)

who were not United States citizens at that time.

(12) My .... served in the Armed Forces of the United States from ....
            (father)   (mother)   (Date)

to .... and .... honorably discharged.
      (Date)   (was)   (was not)

(13) I .... lost my United States citizenship. (If citizenship lost, attach full explanation.)
          (have) (have not)

(14) I submit the following documents with this application:

Nature of Document   *Names of Persons Concerned*

---------------------------------------   ---------------------------------------

---------------------------------------   ---------------------------------------

---------------------------------------   ---------------------------------------

---------------------------------------   ---------------------------------------

---------------------------------------   ---------------------------------------

(15) Fill in this block if your brother, sister, mother or father ever applied to the Immigration Service for a certificate of citizenship.

Name of Relative	Relationship	Date of Birth	When Application Submitted	Certificate No. and File No., If Known, and Location of Office

(16) Fill in this block only if you are now or ever have been a married woman. I have been married .... time(s), as *(1, 2, 3, etc.)* follows:

Date Married	Name of Husband	Citizenship of Husband	If Marriage Has Been Terminated:	
			Date Marriage Ended	How Marriage Ended *(Death or divorce)*

(17) Fill in this block only if you claim citizenship through a husband. *(Marriage must have occurred prior to September 22, 1922.)*
Name of citizen husband .... *(Give full and complete name)* ....; he was born on .... *(Month) (Day) (Year)*
at .... *(City)* .... *(State or country)*; and resides at .... *(Street address, city, and State or country. If dead, write "dead" and date of death.)*
He became a citizen of the United States by ☐ birth; ☐ naturalization on .... *(Month) (Day) (Year)*
in the .... *(Name of court, city, and State)* .... Certificate of Naturalization No. ....;
☐ through his parent(s), and .... *(was) (was not)* issued Certificate of Citizenship No. A or AA ....
He .... *(has) (has not)* since lost United States citizenship. *(If citizenship lost, attach full explanation.)*
I am of the .... race. Before my marriage to him, he was married .... *(1, 2, 3, etc.)* time(s), as follows:

Date Married	Name of Wife	If Marriage Has Been Terminated:	
		Date Marriage Ended	How Marriage Ended *(Death or divorce)*

(18) Fill in this block only if you claim citizenship through your stepfather. *(Applicable only if mother married U.S. Citizen prior to September 22, 1922.)*
The full name of my stepfather is ....; he was born on .... *(Month) (Day) (Year)*
at .... *(City)* .... *(State or country)*; and resides at .... *(Street address, city, and State or country. If dead, write "dead" and date of death.)*
He became a citizen of the United States by ☐ birth; ☐ naturalization on .... *(Month) (Day) (Year)*
in the .... *(Name of court, city, and State)* .... Certificate of Naturalization No. ....;
☐ through his parent(s), and .... *(was) (was not)* issued Certificate of Citizenship No. A or AA ....
He .... *(has) (has not)* since lost United States citizenship. *(If citizenship lost, attach full explanation.)*
He and my mother were married to each other on .... *(Month) (Day) (Year)* at .... *(City and State or country)*
My mother is of the .... race. She .... *(was) (was not)* issued Certificate of Citizenship No. A ....
Before marrying my mother, my stepfather was married .... *(1, 2, 3, etc.)* time(s), as follows:

Date Married	Name of Wife	If Marriage Has Been Terminated:	
		Date Marriage Ended	How Marriage Ended *(Death or divorce)*

(19) I _____ *(have) (have not)* previously applied for a certificate of citizenship on _____ *(Date)*, at _____ *(Office)*

(20) Signature of person preparing form, if other than applicant. I declare that this document was prepared by me at the request of the applicant and is based on all information of which I have any knowledge.

SIGNATURE:

ADDRESS: _____ DATE: _____

(SIGN HERE) ....
(Signature of applicant or parent or guardian)

(3)

APPLICANT.—Do not fill in or sign anything on this page

AFFIDAVIT

I, the ...., do swear
(Applicant, parent, guardian)
that I know and understand the contents of this application,
signed by me, and of attached supplementary pages numbered (   ) to (   ), inclusive; that the same are true to the
best of my knowledge and belief; and that corrections numbered (   ) to (   ) were made by me or at my request.

Subscribed and sworn to before me upon examination of the
applicant (parent, guardian) at ....
........................, this .... day of ...., 19......
and continued solely for:

....
(Signature of applicant, parent, guardian)

....
(Officer's Signature and Title)

REPORT AND RECOMMENDATION ON APPLICATION

On the basis of the documents, records, and persons examined, and the identification upon personal appearance of the underage
beneficiary, I find that all the facts and conclusions set forth under oath in this application are .... true and correct; that the
applicant did .... derive or acquire United States citizenship on ...., through
(Month)   (Day)   (Year)

and that (s)he .... been expatriated since that time. I recommend that this application be .... and that
(has) (has not)
.... Certificate of citizenship be .... issued in the name of ....
(A)   (AA)
(granted) (denied)

In addition to the documents listed in Item 14, the following documents and records have been examined:

Person Examined	Address	Relationship to Applicant	Date Testimony Heard
....	....	....	....
....	....	....	....
....	....	....	....

Supplementary Report(s) No.(s) .... Attached.

Date ...., 19......

....
(Officer's Signature and Title)

I do .... concur in the recommendation.

Date ...., 19......

....
(Signature of District Director or Officer in Charge)

(4)

INDEX TO FORMS

* Form can be obtained from the United States Department of Labor, not the INS.

DATE DUE

FOLLETT